PATRICK DUNN

The Practical Art of DIVINE MAGIC

Contemporary & Ancient Techniques of Theurgy

Llewellyn Worldwide
Woodbury, Minnesota

First Edition
Fifth Printing, 2023

Book design by Bob Gaul
Cover art: iStockphoto.com/3223936/©azndc
Shutterstock/55666789/©Oxa
Cover design by Kevin R. Brown
Editing by Laura Graves
Interior art by Llewellyn Art Department

Library of Congress Cataloging-in-Publication Data
Dunn, Patrick, 1975–
The practical art of divine magic: contemporary & ancient techniques of theurgy/ Patrick Dunn.—First Edition.
pages cm
Includes bibliographical references and index.
ISBN 978-0-7387-4528-2
1. Theurgy. I. Title.
BF1623.T56D86 2015
133.4'3—dc23
2015012049

Llewellyn Publications
A Division of Llewellyn Worldwide Ltd.
2143 Wooddale Drive
Woodbury, MN 55125-2989
www.llewellyn.com

Printed in the United States of America

Contents

About the Author

Patrick Dunn (Chicago, IL) is a poet, linguist, Pagan, and university English professor with a PhD in modern literature and language. His understanding of semiotics and the study of symbols arise from his training in linguistics and literary theory. He has practiced magic since childhood. Visit him online at Pomomagic.nfshost.com.

To Write to the Author

If you wish to contact the author or would like more information about this book, please write to the author in care of Llewellyn Worldwide, and we will forward your request. Both the author and the publisher appreciate hearing from you and learning of your enjoyment of this book and how it has helped you. Llewellyn Worldwide cannot guarantee that every letter written to the author can be answered, but all will be forwarded. Please write to:

Patrick Dunn
℅ Llewellyn Worldwide
2143 Wooddale Drive
Woodbury, MN 55125-2989

Please enclose a self-addressed stamped envelope for reply, or $1.00 to cover costs. If outside the USA, enclose an international postal reply coupon.

Many of Llewellyn's authors have websites with additional information and resources. For more information, please visit us at: www.llewellyn.com.

Acknowledgments

I am extremely grateful to the people in my life who make it possible for me to live my dreams. These includes my family, my friends, and my students. I want to thank some of them by name: Richard, who regularly makes my life ridiculously wonderful (and wonderfully ridiculous); my mother, Joyce, who taught me more than I can possibly enumerate and always encouraged my dreams; Chris, Ryan, Pete, Eric, who argued, discussed, debated, listened, and talked me through graduate school. I also want to thank my teachers, both those who taught me mundane things and those who taught me magical things (as if there's a difference). Some I had as a teacher for one day, some for years: Jason, John, Karen, Betty, Gustav, and many others.

I also want to thank John Michael Greer, whose workshop on sacred geometry gave me the oomph to finish this book. I must, in addition, thank Lon Milo DuQuette, who several years ago said a single sentence that totally blew my mind and changed my view of magic forever.

It's also fitting that I thank my editor, Elysia, for her extremely helpful suggestions. She has a tremendous eye for detail, and has prevented me from embarrassing myself in print more times than I care to count.

And, finally, those heroes and intellectual ancestors, who generously left us their words to guide us, not knowing or guessing what sorts of people we might be: Aristocles, Socrates, Plotinus, Iamblichus, Proclus, and countless others.

A Note on Sources and Translations

For the most part, I have selected sources for classical texts that are online and in the public domain for the reader's convenience. In some cases I could not find an online translation or edition acceptable to me and have therefore cited print versions of these books. In other cases, such as that of the Chaldean Oracles, these print versions are academic editions, which tend to be expensive. If you wish to consult those editions, I would encourage using your local library, where you can request to borrow those books from libraries that have them in their possession.

In some places I have done my own translations of some Greek texts. I sometimes chose to do so to make a particular distinction from the original text clearer than it is made in some other translations. Sometimes I chose to do my own translations so they would fit better in ritual (a precise academic translation does not always trip nicely off the tongue during a ceremony). Sometimes I chose to do it for the practice and sheer fun of it—and to show off a little. I most assuredly did not do it because I quibble with the commonly available academic translations of these works, which are always excellent.

Introduction

This book attempts to explore and revitalize the spiritual techniques of diverse times and places all under the loose heading of "theurgy." Theurgy is a collection of spiritual practices ranging from antiquity to modern times by people of many different religious and philosophical backgrounds. In its heyday, in Late Antiquity, it competed with Christianity and other religious and philosophical movements. In fact, ideas from theurgy planted themselves in Christian, Muslim, and Jewish practices and remain there even today.

This book does not attempt to reconstruct the religious practices of Late Antiquity or ancient Pagan religions. Any attempt to revitalize an ancient way of life that ignores the cultural differences between now and antiquity cannot, in my opinion, succeed. We do not live in ancient Greece or ancient Rome. We don't even live in places *like* ancient Greece or Rome. Ancient Greece would be, to modern American minds—or modern European minds, for that matter—an alien culture, with institutions we would not recognize and practices like slavery we could not support. We can admire their accomplishments, learn from their teachings, even revitalize some of their practices, but we must ultimately understand, as L. P. Hartley said, that the past is a different country.

Nor do I throw ideas and concepts together willy-nilly, because this kind of irresponsible eclecticism doesn't work either. It also ignores the cultural context, and leads to muddied thinking and contradiction. The ancients were themselves a bit eclectic, worshiping Isis alongside Zeus, but I prefer to approach this kind of eclecticism with care.

The attitude with which I approach this book, then, is neither eclectic nor reconstructionist. It is postmodern. I am an unusual breed of postmodernist in that I think there is an ultimate truth that is not culturally constructed. But at the same time, the paths we cut to this truth are indeed made by our hands. In other words, the terrain exists but we know it only by our maps, which we have made. When I pray to Iuppiter, I am praying to a god who exists, I believe, independently of any culture. At the same time, I'm taking a Roman name and image and method of prayer, applying it to the reflection of the god I have constructed in my mind, and using those as a way back to that ultimate ideal deity. Someone wise (and I don't remember who) once put it this way to me: The gods give the world its being; we give gods their forms.

That's why at some points in this book I delve into original sources and put on the hat of a scholar, while at other points I gleefully make something up that works. My promise to you is that I will cite my scholarship and identify those things I have made up to fill the gaps. When I guess at what an ancient source meant, I'll give my reasoning for that guess and other possibilities. When I make a claim, I will try to back it up or explain why I cannot.

I am no authority. The only authority is your own experience with the gods: not your wishes and fantasies, but your genuine experiences. I hope that by engaging with the exercises in this book, you will have enough experience of the divine that you can edit and modify and add to these practices as needed in order to continue your theurgy. Always, throughout this book, my watchword is practicality: how can this be used, now, today, by us?

We naturally begin with this question: How was it used then?

Historical Context

The practice of theurgy—a word that comes from Greek roots meaning, literally, "godwork"—probably began when humans looked up at the stars for the first time. But the Greco-Roman tradition that we'll be examining and that we'll trace up to modern times began in Greece with a group of philosophers called the Pre-Socratics. The most important of these for our purposes is Pythagoras. He laid the foundation for later philosophers in suggesting that reality was not as multifarious and divided as it appeared, that instead a single principle may underlay the whole thing. For him, this principle was mathematical. He discovered the fundamental harmonies of music and various principles of geometry that were suggestive of a reality outside of mere matter. After all, if we can predict the harmony of strings by their length, those laws of harmony must exist separate from the strings themselves. Since those ratios are nonmaterial, they must exist outside of the world of matter in a world somehow inhabited by mathematical abstraction.

It's significant that we call philosophers like Pythagoras "Pre-*Socratic*." Socrates was such an important figure to the history of Western thought that he split philosophy in two: pre- and post-. Living from 469 to 399 BCE, around the same time as the historical Buddha (who died circa 480), he took Pythagoras's idea of mathematical reality and developed it. He suggested that the world of Ideas might be inhabited by more than just mathematical abstractions; it might contain a prototype of "goodness," for example. His student Plato developed these ideas further—or according to some, came up with them himself. The notion that our physical reality is a reflection of archetypal and perfect images in a world of Ideas is therefore called Platonism.

Plato's student Aristotle broke with Plato, suggesting that while these prototypes exist, they do not exist in a separate nonmaterial world. Instead, we build them in our minds as we experience the material world. This is more consistent with the modern and postmodern ideas of what reality consists of, but it's not universally accepted even today. In our postmodern era, there are those—like me—who remain unconvinced that these archetypes do not exist separate from matter.

Plenty of people at the time also remained unconvinced, and these came to be called "middle Platonists" by later scholars (although they no doubt just called themselves "Platonists," not having anything to be in the middle of yet). They continued teaching and developing Plato's doctrines. The turn toward Platonism in the late empire—a period of time that historians call "Late Antiquity"—would later be named "Neoplatonism." The Neoplatonism of these late philosophers was more mystical and simultaneously more practical than the pure philosophy of Middle Platonism. It was more mystical because it aimed toward a particular spiritual goal: *henosis*, a sense of unity with the divine. It was more practical because the Neoplatonists offered specific techniques for achieving that henosis.

Two schools of Neoplatonism offered techniques for henosis: the contemplative and the ceremonial. The contemplative school, typified by Plotinus, emphasized purely mental exercises: meditations and contemplations. The ceremonial school, typified by Iamblichus, offered a ritual technique, in which religio-magical practices united the worshiper upward to the One. Individual practitioners probably did not maintain hard and fast lines between the approaches.

Hermeticism also influenced theurgic practices. Hermeticism consisted of a loose conglomeration of vaguely Platonic mystical and religious writing. These writings are less philosophically unified than the Platonic tradition and less rigorous in terms of method of reasoning, which is one reason they are mostly ignored by contemporary philosophers. They do have value, however, as an example of how these philosophical ideas worked their way out in different populations of worshipers and practitioners.

The rise of Christianity did not kill theurgy; in fact, in many ways it invigorated it. Theurgic practices adapted well to the theology of Christianity and were sometimes incorporated wholesale. The gods became angels, the One became God, and the *logos* became Jesus. When the gospel of John begins "In the beginning was the Word, and the Word was with God, and the Word was God,"[1] the Greek for "word" is *logos*. We could do a Neoplatonic translation of this just as easily, without having to modify the original Koine text at all: "In the beginning was the rational basis of the universe, and the rational basis of the universe was with the One, and it was also the One." Late Christian Neoplatonists such as John Dee, Henry Agrippa, and so forth all contributed their philosophies to the practice of magic.

Each of these phases illustrates an important point: the theurgic practices of antiquity developed, changed, and adapted to the changing context of the time. This is why I am leery of a strict reconstructionist approach to these practices. The fetishization of research and the past is counterproductive to a living tradition, and if theurgy is to be anything it needs to be alive.

The Renaissance, one of the high points of practical theurgy, had such a well-developed Neoplatonic view of the world that it was almost an assumption about reality, as obvious to the thinkers of that time as gravity is to us. Of course, there's a danger in that, too: what is obvious is what goes unquestioned, and what goes unquestioned is what is often misunderstood. Hence when the scientific revolution started, many thinkers regarded the empirical method as a refutation of Platonism. It was not really such a refutation, not if one understands the philosophies behind those movements. But the cursory and unquestioned assumption of Platonism fell before the new vivid empiricism. Empiricism, in destroying Platonism, destroyed a straw man—but few realized that something beyond that straw man existed. Only a few thinkers, mostly poets like William Blake and (to the great discomfort of many contemporary historians of science) Isaac Newton, recognized that a real, vibrant, and living Platonism lived behind the unquestioned assumptions. Sadly, it was too little to preserve the tradition, and instead of the new empirical science offering its insights alongside the mystical and practical theurgy of Platonism, we abandoned one and embraced the other.

---

1 John 1:1

So where does that put us? Where we find ourselves now is a strange stage in the history of ideas, because we have taken empiricism so far it has begun to show some cracks. We recognize that as powerful and wonderful as science is, there are questions it cannot approach, and many people are looking back at mysticism for the answers. The problem is, a lot of those old—and very effective!—methods are lost, so what we have on things like theurgy is whatever a few people in the early twentieth century were able to gather and cobble together with their limited materials. Now, granted, people like S. L. Macgregor Mathers, Aleister Crowley, and Israel Regardie were fair to middlin' good scholars, but they had few sources and fewer resources. We have a great advantage over them—access to not just our local research library but to any library in the world. Moreover, we have found some lost sources, and scholars have found new reason to look again at old texts. And a few magicians trained in the traditions of good scholarship are looking at Renaissance stuff and even materials from Late Antiquity as well. Sure, much is lost and must be wired together out of the scraps whether we like it or not if we're to make a practical go at it. But much remains, and we're in the unique position of caring and being able to do something about it, perhaps for the first time in an age. It's an exciting time to be a Pagan, a magician, and a mystic.

So that's the purpose of this book: take what remains, find what can be found, and build a working system out of it. I don't pretend that I've reconstructed the theurgy of Late Antiquity since I feel quite free borrowing from Renaissance Christian sources as much as the old Pagans. And as I said before, from time to time I'm willing to invent and experiment and figure out a new path through some thicket of lost knowledge that otherwise we'd have to detour around forever. At the same time, I'm keeping the star of scholarship in my sights and aiming toward it as I travel. I may not always hit it; errors have a tendency to pop up like mushrooms in work like this. But I'll certainly try.

Early chapters of this book will explore the divine technology of theurgy, offering some methods and exercises and techniques we can use to start experiencing the results of godwork in a practical sense. They'll also lay down the theory, so that we know why we're doing what we're doing. We'll investigate what we mean by "god" and what kind of "work" is involved. In chapter 4 we'll start looking at ritual, and in chapter 5 we'll discuss the most theurgic of magical works—divination. We'll turn to the much confused issue of daimones in chapter 6. In chapter 7, we'll ground our study of theurgy in thaumaturgy, the art of practical magic. The final chapter will explore the concept of spiritual development from a theurgic perspective.

It is my hope that this book will revitalize the practice of theurgy in magic and inform those strains of it already present. Theurgy is the engine of magic and the component that makes magic itself a spiritual path of great value.

CHAPTER 1

A Divine Technology

Imagine, we are told by Plato, that there are a group of people living in a cave.

Stop me if you've heard this one before.

This group of people—Plato never gives them a name, but let's call them Chthonians—are born into strange circumstances. At birth, they are taken and bound to face a wall. They can eat and drink, but never turn their heads. They must always watch the wall.

Meanwhile, their wardens walk behind them, carrying an assortment of objects in front of a fire, so that the shadows of those objects display on the wall. So one of the wardens—again, Plato does not name them, but let's call them Aions—is carrying a vase, which casts a vase-shaped shadow on the wall. One of the Chthonians says, "Look, a vase." Another Aion carries by a sword, which casts a shadow that the Chthonians call "sword." And so on.

In fact, since the objects the Aions carry before the fire are cast on the wall only as two-dimensional shadows, very complex objects might end up having many different names, depending on from which vantage point the shadow is cast, which angle the light falls on the object. So perhaps an Aion might carry a book in front of the fire. If carried flat, it projects a wide rectangle; if carried lengthwise, a slender rectangle; and if open, a V shape, all of which the Chthonians call by different names and do not recognize that each of those shapes is the same object—although perhaps they notice, if they are really astute, that one such object might turn into another, under mysterious circumstances.

Now imagine a Chthonian gets free. She struggles past the stunned Aions, blinded by a glimpse of the great fire, and with the green afterimage of the flame over her vision she scrabbles on hands and knees over the hard, steep ascent of the cave. Finally she bursts into the light, which dazzles her to absolute blindness. She cowers in terror at first but finally her vision begins to clear and she sees things for which she has no name. For the first time, she sees three dimensions, color, texture, and she watches objects change their shapes as she walks around them. She understands finally that all she saw before were shadows of these real, vibrant, beautiful objects. And when she looks up at the sun, she knows it for what it is: a god.

So now she makes a life outside the cave, but she has friends back there, and finally she screws up her courage to its sticking place and goes back, armed this time with the truth. The Aions let her pass, and she sits again among her old friends. "Listen," she says. "I've discovered something amazing. This light, these shadows, are just pale reflections of the real reality."

"What do you mean?"

"Objects have multiple dimensions. See that book there? That's the shadow of an object—"

"That's not a book," another friends says. "It's a Slender Rectangle."

"Yes, Slender Rectangles are really Books. See, when you—"

"Slender Rectangles can turn into Books sometimes. Is that what you mean?"

"No, they don't turn into anything. They already are Books," she says, getting a little frustrated.

Her friends whistle and laugh. "She's gone a bit batty," they say.

"No, listen—"

But they won't.

In frustration, she tries to turn a few heads physically, but that causes terror and panic, and they impose their strongest punishment on her, and threaten to put her to death. She flees the cave, back into the world above.

But a few quiet people had heard what she said and wondered if she really was so crazy. One of them begins to reason: If there are objects being moved before the fire, then perhaps something moves them. He starts, when no one else notices, talking aloud to the Aions, not sure if anyone can hear him.

But the Aions have heard too, and some of them are sympathetic. One in particular comes closer and closer to the young acolyte. He listens, silently, until one day he leans close enough to whisper.

"I'm here."

The boy, taken aback by having his prayers answered, nevertheless rallies quickly. "What is your name?"

"I am called Poimander," the Aion says.

"Is what she said true? Is there a world different from these shadows?"

"Yes," Poimander tells him.

"I'll give you anything to free me."

"All you have are shadows. What could you give me?"

The boy thinks for a long time, and finally says, "I have reason and words. I will give you speech offerings. I will sing you songs, make you poems."

That is very little, but Poimander really just wants an excuse anyway. Compassion is already in him. So he unlocks the boy and quietly leads him out of the cave into the light of day.

I have embellished this story quite a lot from Plato's version. In his version, we have no specific account of how people escape, and no names for those who move the objects before the fire. But at its root, the moral is the same.

We are the Chthonians—or Earthlings—locked in a cave of perception, and our everyday experiences are shadows on a wall. The fire is the light that gives us vision but outside is a greater light and greater forms than we can perceive with our senses. When we do achieve perception of them even for a moment, we are blinded by their splendor and cannot think of words to describe them because we only have words for shadows.

You live in a cave. But you don't have to. There are ways out, and theurgy is one of them.

When the boy began to whisper to Poimander, he was engaging in theurgy. He had a technology to make contact and gain divine help for his release.

Theurgy comes from two Greek words: *theos*, meaning "god"; and *ergon*, meaning "work." It's a way of appealing to the divine using our reason, intuition, and aesthetic powers, in order to gain a greater perspective on reality and ultimately achieve the highest perspective, that of henosis: oneness with the ground of existence itself. This henosis is a complex topic I'll explore more later, but it shares some resemblances—and some significant differences—with nirvana in Buddhism or moksha in Hinduism. It is a kind of universal liberation, an experience of perfect understanding.

What does theurgy look like in practice? On the surface it might be indistinguishable from an ordinary act of worship, and you'd be hard-pressed to identify a theurgist from actions alone. Yet theurgy isn't worship in the traditional sense of the word. Your German shepherd might worship you: jump up and smile a doggy smile when you come home, run in circles when it's time to play, bark playfully and do a little shuffling dance during walks. But if you train your dog to do some service, to act to a purpose, all those acts of worship take second fiddle to doing its duty. Just look at a service dog some time and watch it work. They kind of remind me of soldiers or police officers with their single-minded attention, no-nonsense attitudes, and direct focus. Theurgy is similar. For a theurgist, an offering and a prayer is a kind of work, an act with a purpose.

Don't misunderstand: theurgy isn't some mercenary bribery of divine forces. There's plenty of ridiculous prosperity gospel books about that blasphemous attitude; I'm not going to add to the stack. It's also not abasement or grim grit-teethed willpower. It's not work on a god, or even work for a god—it's work *with* a god. In theurgy, you are not serving god, nor are you bribing god to serve you. Instead, you are collaborating together to achieve a joint goal: henosis.

I've used that word several times already, and only barely defined it. Henosis is union of perspective with the highest reality in the universe, the one thing from which everything else proceeds. It's hard for us to understand what that oneness might mean. Attempts to describe it fall short, because language is inherently dualistic. For example, people might ask, "Does the personality dissolve in henosis? Do I remain who I once was, or do I cease to exist?" As unsatisfying as it might seem, there's no good answer to that. If I say, "your personality ceases to exist," then that's not henosis: that's not oneness, but noneness: that's just deleting yourself out of the equation of you and the one. If I say, "your personality remains; you remain who you are," that's not henosis: that's duality. There's still you and the one. I suppose I could try to say something like "the personality you are, who you are, becomes the exact same thing as the one," but that's almost ridiculous. Could you imagine if I were the one from which the entire universe proceeds? I'm a weird little man with strange hobbies and a fondness for fine food. I couldn't imagine what universe would proceed from that: one with lots of artisanal cheeses and a lot of dead languages with plenty of good study materials, I suppose.

So I can't construct a good definition of henosis. But let me put it this way. Henosis will, perhaps only temporarily at first but later with more and more reliability, solve your problems. Sometimes those solutions will be miraculous, and sometimes you'll just see your problems from a perspective that makes them irrelevant. It won't necessarily cure your obesity—but it might help dissolve the boundaries that prevent you from exercising. It might not balance your checkbook—but it might help you see money differently. And it might not find you one true love—but it can help you learn how to love and be loved. Henosis isn't a magic bullet, but it is magic. Henosis—even just chasing henosis—will make you a better person, more competent at life, and probably happier.

Is This a Religion?

It's surprisingly difficult to find a definition of "religion" that satisfies everyone's intuition. We could take the simple dictionary definition, and say that religion is a system of beliefs and rituals that center on the belief in a supernatural being or beings, especially a God or gods. But it's not hard to find examples that don't fit under that umbrella. Not all forms of Buddhism require the belief in supernatural beings at all, for example, and there are aboriginal religions that center on ancestors or the power inherent in certain places and objects. To try to roll all the world's religions up in this same blanket makes for an odd bundle indeed.

In fact, this definition may just be the result of a Judeo-Christian history. If you ask a person from a typical Judeo-Christian culture how many religions they have, they will probably either say "none" or "one." It is impossible (for such a person) to have multiple religions, because the models for this definition of religion are inherently exclusionary. One cannot take communion as a Christian while simultaneously being a Jew, and one cannot be Jewish and Muslim at the same time. But in areas not dominated by a Judeo-Christian history, another model of religion dominates. A typical Chinese person might hold Taoist, Buddhist, and Confucian beliefs all at the same time, and if asked "how many religions do you have" say "none." While there are certainly exclusionary religions in the East (and inclusionary religions in the West, like Baha'i), the general pattern holds: in those cultures where exclusionary—monotheistic, orthodox, and often proselytizing—religions are dominant, it's hard to imagine having multiple religions.

But it's not so easy to draw this line and say "these religions are splendid for being inclusionary, while these others are icky for being exclusionary" because each of those exclusionary religions has a branch that is much more inclusionary. In its public rituals, dogmata, and doctrines, a religion may be exclusionary and clear-cut. I call this popular and public face of a religion its exoteric face. But every Western monotheistic religion has another face: a private face with flexible rituals, a greater emphasis on pragma (practical activities) than dogma, and contemplation rather than doctrine. This is its esoteric face.

We need only look at the three dominant monotheistic religions of the West to see this play out. The esoteric face of Islam, of course, is Sufi. An esoteric face of Judaism is Kabbalah, while an esoteric face of Christianity is contemplative Christianity. Each of these offers something the exoteric face does not.

Where the exoteric face offers dogma—a line of belief that adherents must internalize—the esoteric face offers pragma—a set of practices that the adherent may use for specific purposes. For example, while exoteric Islam requires adherence to a particular set of beliefs (often summarized as the five pillars), the esoteric branch of Sufi gives a set of spiritual exercises aiming at union with Allah. Similarly, the required beliefs of Christianity are supplemented by the practices of contemplative Christianity.

Where the exoteric face offers ritual and ceremony, the esoteric face often has its own rituals, again for specific aims. Some kinds of Sufi are famous for spinning, for example, while others elevate the *dhikr*, a simple prayer asserting the unity of God, to a central place in their ritual. Often these rituals are inward-turning, such as the practice of contemplative prayer or the meditations on the letters of Hebrew Kabbalah. There is also more room, often, to create or borrow new rituals and interweave them into private practice, because the esoteric practice of a religion is often done alone rather than communally.

Finally, the teachings of a religion can be divided into their exoteric teachings and their esoteric teachings. Western Christianity teaches that human sins were forgiven by the sacrifice of Jesus. But some kinds of esoteric Christianity go further, suggesting that this forgiving of sins wasn't simply a negative act but a positive one, not just wiping the slate clean but elevating man, potentially, to the position of Christ. Similarly, where the *dhikr*—"There is no god but God, and Muhammed is his prophet"—is central to Islam, to the Sufi it takes on additional meaning. "There is no god but God" can be interpreted "there is no reality but God." In other words, everything is divine.

Obviously, the esoteric faces of religions with their innovative rituals and controversial doctrines sometimes skirt heresy. And sometimes, when their teachings, practices, or beliefs run too far away from the dominant stream, the orthodox cracks down on the esoteric branches of the faith. Historical examples of this tendency are not difficult to find.

Neoplatonic and Hermetic Esotericism

In the third century CE, the indigenous pagan religions of Rome—which included a complex network of traditional practices, foreign religions, and religious innovations—were faltering before the popular mystery religion of Christianity. As the exoteric practices of these ancient religions began to wane, as sacrifices went unperformed and temples began to empty out, the esoteric practices began to rise to the fore. These practices began with the allegory of the cave above, and from it and the other writings of Plato, philosophers created a system of philosophy and practice that promised a technology for salvation rather than a mystery religion.

Sadly, we do not have all the practices anymore, as they are at best hinted at in the writings of the primary proponents of what came to be called Neoplatonism. Yet we do have their philosophies. The philosophers of this new movement often disagreed with each other, even about fundamental issues, but this is a result of the movement's origin in philosophy, where disagreement and dialogue are signs of robust reasoning, not failure. Perhaps this complexity of opinions is one reason Neoplatonism faded away in favor of Christianity, whose doctrines were much more simple. Of course as any theologian can tell you, the doctrines of Christianity are anything but simple, but much of that complexity is a result of wrestling with the same complex questions as Neoplatonism (and sometimes, importing answers wholesale).

The central problem Neoplatonism addresses in all its various forms and with all its various complex cosmologies is a simple one: What exists?

That might seem like a simple question. Since there's such a venerable tradition of dialogues in Platonic philosophy, let's imagine how it might play out in a conversation between two people, a philosopher named Philanike and her student Euthymios.

Philanike: So, what exists?

Euthymios: Matter exists. This table, for example, is real.

Ph: What is matter?

Eu: Well, this coffee mug is matter, isn't it?

Ph: So is matter solid or liquid?

Eu: I suppose it can be either.

Ph: The mug is brown; is matter brown?

Eu: It can be.

Ph: Can it be red?

Eu: Yes, that too.

Ph: Is matter heavy or light?

Eu: It can be either, I suppose. This mug is heavier than a feather, and gases are material too, and very light.

Ph: So it seems matter can be anything I describe it to be. If I say "what is an animal?" you could answer that by listing every kind of animal, although that would not be the most efficient way to do so. But with matter, you cannot even define it by listing everything it can be, because it seems it can be everything.

Eu: My thoughts are not material.

Ph: Oh, good! Then it can't be everything.
What differentiates your thoughts from matter?

Eu: They are not extended in space.

Ph: So matter is that which occupies space.

Eu: It would seem so.

Ph: Then what is space?

Eu: Einstein tells us that space and time are the same thing.

Ph: I thought we were ancient Greeks. How do we know about relativity, if we're ancient Greeks?

Eu: No, I think we just have really unusual names.

Ph: That's a relief. I'm such a fan of air conditioning and antibiotics. But we're off topic. What is space-time?

Eu: If I said "the thing which material objects occupy," would that cut it?

Ph: You know it wouldn't. If we cannot define a thing by listing it, we can define it by cutting it free from other things, by saying what it is not. So—what is not space-time? What is outside it?

Eu: My thoughts. Ideas about things.

Ph: Such as?

Eu: $E = mc^2$. It's an equation that describes the equivalence of mass and energy, that defines matter, but doesn't exist in space-time. I can write it in matter, but that's not the equation: the equation is the nonmaterial reality these letters describe, whether marks of chalk or graphite or ink or sketched in sand.

Ph: And if Einstein hadn't figured it out, would it still be true?

Eu: Yes, I suppose so. It'd be true even if no one ever figured it out. So it exists outside of time, as well as outside of space.

Ph: Go back to the mug. You said it was brown, which means it reflects light in certain wavelengths we can describe in the same sorts of immaterial ideas.
So: is "brown" an idea outside of time and space?

Eu: I guess so. If we exist in a universe with the sort of light that we have, then those wavelengths exist whether or not we call them brown or dun or whatever, and even if no one existed to perceive them, those wavelengths would exist and behave according to the laws that give rise, in us, to the perception we label "brown."

Ph: So reality exists in the form of ideas, which we can think of crudely as equations describing eternal or timeless laws, although that may lead us astray a bit later and we'll find it more complicated than that. But for now, let's say that: what, then, is matter?

Eu: It seems matter is that which can instantiate these ideas in the realm of space-time. Matter brings down immaterial and eternal ideas and plants them in space-time.

Ph: So is matter real?

Eu: Well, not as real as the ideas it instantiates.

The process by which matter does this—receive the impressions of these eternal ideas—is an issue of very fine wrangling among the Neoplatonists; those with an interest in the philosophers of Late Antiquity can dig up writings and dive into it. They're wonderful examples of pure reason applied to complex problems, argued and negotiated across hundreds of years. We do not live in Late Antiquity, however. Rather than learning all these complex and ancient cosmologies, we're going to reason out a position of our own, understanding as only we postmoderns can, that we are building a model that must not be confused with the thing it models, a map that is not the territory. There may be gaps, areas where we could spill gallons of ink on forests of paper to tease out an answer, and that may be a worthwhile exercise for someone at some time. But this is a book about practical theurgy, so what do we need to know right now to get started on the road to henosis?

Try to imagine matter without any qualities: an object with no adjectives to describe it, no nouns to classify it. What you end up with is a concept the philosophers sometimes called *hyle*, a Greek word meaning "forest" or "timber." We might say "clay." Consider this clay of no qualities. If I impose a quality on it, it becomes a thing: if I color it and shape it, it becomes a mug, a knife, a stapler. If I attenuate it and give it certain chemical properties, it becomes water vapor, nitrogen, xenon. Ultimately, with my scientific understanding, I can break it down and say I am making it into collections of electrons, protons, and so forth. Or go further and say I'm making my clay into bosons and quarks. Even then I'm merely imposing qualities, ideas, on the matter itself.

Now, for this creation of matter to work, I need to move from ideas which have no form or temporal or spatial existence into matter situated in space-time. How do I do this? First, I have to give it a start point: anything that exists materially must exist in time. Second, I have to give it a location: it must exist somewhere. Therefore, I must postulate two things that come between the world of Ideas and the world of matter: space and time, which we postmoderns understand to be related to each other as space-time. Let's start drawing a diagram:

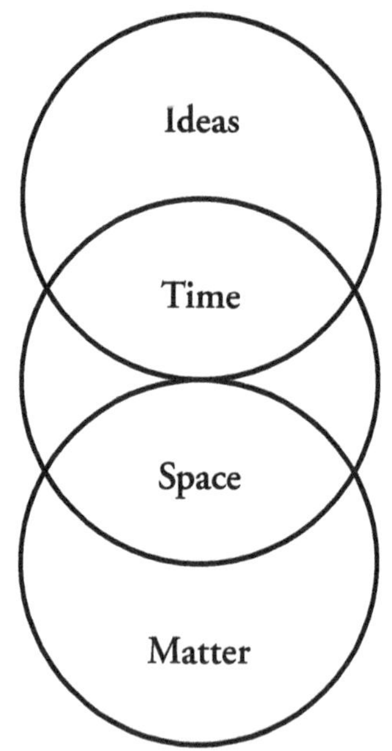

Fig. 1: Ideas, Matter, and Space-Time

We can logically work out a chain of what exists prior to what so matter may arise, but before we do so it's important to define "prior." If time is one of those things that exists before matter does, then some of these things will exist before time does, so "prior" cannot mean "prior in time." Instead, think of it as a structure: the whole building stands at once, but the girders are prior to the walls, the walls prior to the roof. If we take off the roof, the wall doesn't fall; if we take off the walls, the roof collapses. We could, rather than speaking of one thing being prior to another, speak of one emanation depending on another, hanging on it like the links of a chain.

Once we have time and space, we can begin talking about things having qualities: they can be red, shiny, big, or sweet. We can also begin talking about them having quantity: three, four, five, six, and so on. We never see number or quality separate from matter: we never see "red," without something being red, even if it's just a ray of light. And we never see three without three of something. But we can abstract away the idea of red and the idea of three from stuff, which means that it must exist prior to that stuff: redness or threeness doesn't spread through the world like a virus. These ideas exist, and the world reflects them.

So time and space and quality and quantity—the ideas about things—must exist prior to matter; matter depends on them. Remove time, space, quality, or quantity, and matter cannot exist as we experience it. Time, space, quality, and quantity are ideas, and ideas—in our experience—exist only in a consciousness. But our experience of consciousness is material: it is something we experience in time, so there must be a kind of consciousness outside of time and prior to it, where ideas outside of time can exist. This other consciousness is called Nous by Neoplatonists, and the part of it where the ideas of time, space, and quality dwell—sometimes called the lower Nous—is called the Psyche. Let's amend our diagram with some labels:

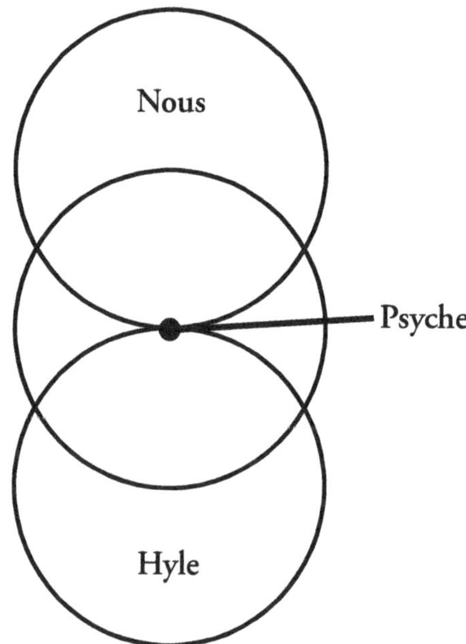

Fig. 2: Nous, Psyche, and Hyle

Now, various Neoplatonists provide competing cosmologies, and I could go into all the details of Iamblichus's cosmology compared to that of Plotinus and so on, but those differences have been treated well enough elsewhere. I could also go into all the philosophical debates against this particular model of reality, but that would make this a very different book. Instead, let's stick with this simplified scheme for now, recognizing that centuries of reasoned debate have refined it but that we can get by for our practical purposes with the simplification. In fact, since we are postmoderns seeing this not as a perfect map of reality but as a model of how we may conceive reality in order for us to accomplish certain things, many of those later arguments are irrelevant to us anyway. How convenient.

What relationship do I—or you—have to this model? We say there is an idea in the Nous—$E = mc^2$, let's say—and that idea exists whether a human mind holds it or not. But human minds do hold it. We do not merely receive perceptions of the universe and act on them as automata.

We think, and we think timeless thoughts. We can recognize the timeless truth of these thoughts, without ourselves being fully timeless. How to explain that?

Hermeticism, a later esoteric movement, explained it with often contradictory and obscure arguments, but ultimately what it comes down to is that we are the universe. As above, so below; so below, as above. Our mind, our consciousness, reflects the reality of the universe. We can modify our diagram one more time:

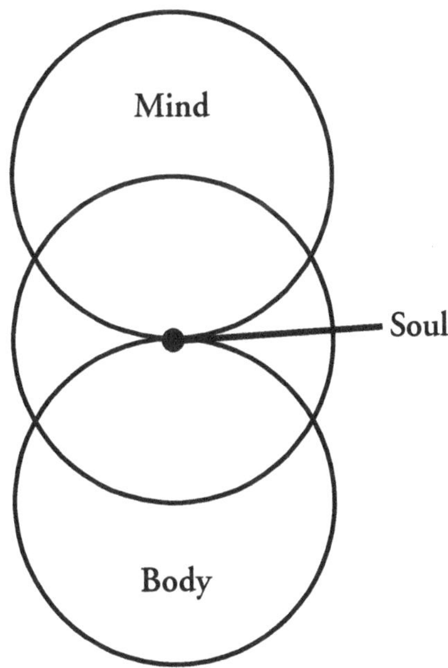

Fig. 3: As Above, So Below

Our Psyche is the Soul, receiving the perceptions of the body in two ways: through sensory perception and through phantasms, some of which arise from the memory and some through the Nous. Phantasms are images that arise in our mind, sensory impressions without senses. If I ask you to visualize a cat, the cat you "see" is a phantasm. Of course, sight is not our only sense, so if I ask you to imagine the smell of lilacs or the sound of seagulls, those sensory imaginings are also phantasms. Some of our phantasms come from memories of other things, others are cut from whole cloth, and some come from the Nous. In fact, we are constructing a phantasm whenever we see, hear, smell, taste, and feel something. We never really taste matter or see matter: we experience only the phantasm we build in our mind around that sensory experience. This is why memories can emotionally move us: they are as real as the phantasms created from our direct sensory experiences.

Phantasms can also come from the Nous. Our Nous is the Mind, not the little to-do-list scribbling mind of our morning errands, but the mind that can think eternal thoughts. Let me show you how. Visualize a point. Move that point any distance in one direction, tracing out a line. Now move that line 90 degrees to itself, perpendicular, so it traces out a plane. You now have a square. Now move that square perpendicular to the direction of the plane, so it forms a cube. Now take that cube, and move it perpendicular to itself, 90 degrees away from itself: this object is a hypercube, an object that does not exist in our world. Yet with enough practice, we can visualize it. It may not be easy at first, but I assure you that it's possible with enough practice to visualize a hypercube. This image does not exist in physical matter, but it exists in the Nous as an idea, and we have access to it through our minds, and then can build phantasms of it.

So how does this model and similar models help us understand the nature of the divine or rise up to henosis? For that matter, why rise up to henosis at all? Is there something wrong with the lives we live, something wrong with matter? Again, opinions of the Neoplatonists are diverse and opinions of the Hermetic philosophers even more diverse. Plotinus regards matter as evil, at least at some points in his Enneads. And the Hermetica argue both that matter is evil and insist that it's not. I find no reason to condemn matter, since the ancients couldn't agree on the issue anyway.

I like to think of it this way: We are physical beings, true, but that's not all we are. We're capable of being, of doing more. And if we are capable, isn't it worth striving for those goals? Any physical goals we have, as valuable as they are, need to be valuable for something. A pile of money is worthless on a deserted island. So what good are career success, love, family—granted, all very nice things—unless they help us reach up to something greater?

Exercise 1.1: Contemplation of Matter

This exercise will, at its most basic level, give you a familiarity with the concept of hyle and an experience of it. If continued, you will also begin to understand the means by which spiritual forces affect matter. I doubt that it'll give you telekinetic powers, but you may gain an experiential understanding of the oneness of matter which will aid you in later exercises such as enlivening a statue and working with symbols.

Step 1: Begin by finding a small object. It literally does not matter what it is, and you don't need to strive for the mystical and poetic. An empty soda can will work as well as a seashell. As you repeat this exercise, you can choose different objects and objects of greater size and complexity, but for now aim for something you can hold in your hand.

Step 2: Analyze out from that object all of its qualities. These are descriptors, usually either adjectives or nouns, that you might use to describe the object to someone else. List them out, a word or a phrase at a time, on a piece of paper. The first few times you do this exercise, it's important to do this in writing so you can keep track. As you get better at it, you can forego the writing and hold these qualities in your mind. You can categorize those qualities by the kinds of phantasms they invoke: for example, visual, tactile, and so on.

Example: Let's imagine my object is an ink pen. I list qualities: "oblong, black, clicks, plastic, clear, solid, liquid ink, smooth, black rubber grip." Of these, the shape, state of matter, and texture are tactile. The colors are visible. The click is audible.

STEP 3: Put down the object. While looking over your list, call up a phantasm of the object in your mind. Now, begin removing qualities from the object. It's often easier to begin with smell, taste, and color before going on to form.

EXAMPLE: Holding the pen in my mind, I remove some of its incidental qualities. I take away its click mechanism, the rubber grip, the ink.

STEP 4: When you remove the incidental qualities, begin removing the essential qualities. Now it's very important not to cheat. When you remove color from the object, do not simply imagine it clear or white: imagine that it has no color, that color as a quality does not impinge on it at all. It's not clear, it's literally colorless. So don't replace one quality with another: taking away the quality "smooth" doesn't mean making the thing rough in your mind: it means abolishing texture as a category entirely.

EXAMPLE: Taking away the concept of color and texture, material phase (solid or liquid), and finally shape itself, I'm left with...

STEP 5: It's easy to say at this point that you're left with nothing, but do not succumb to that notion. Try to hold the pen in your mind without having any concept of its qualities for as long as you can. Perhaps you'll feel a curious mental blankness or fog. You will almost certainly experience the pen trying to take shape again, but whenever it does gently deny it qualities so it returns back to the formless chaos to which you have reduced it. You will not be able to articulate your experience of what remains, because to do so will be to apply qualities to it, but what remains is pure *hyle*, without any impression from the Nous at all: it's matter, receptive and malleable. It's substance, sub-stance, that which stands underneath.

If you do this exercise you may well have a sense that something remains—something tenuous, barely existent, but there. Notice that all the things we regard as existing are phantasms we create in regard to the object. Kicking a stone doesn't prove that the stone is hard: it creates a phantasm of the stone's hardness. The stone, we might say, is liable to create phantasms of hardness, but the stone itself is not hard outside of conceptions of its hardness.

Exercise 1.2: Experiencing the One

This exercise is the complement of the previous exercise. Where in the previous exercise we explored the nature of matter through our imagination and found that apart from our senses it is at best a tenuous fog of possibility, in this exercise we will strive for an experience of the One. This isn't an exercise you will succeed at immediately or find easy, and in many ways it is a constant practice you can and should undertake regularly, both to give yourself perspective and to continually strive for henosis. It is possible for us to experience the One as well as matter because we exist in every level of existence: we are bodies, minds, souls, and as such partake of the One itself. As Pauliina Remes puts it, "The fact that the human soul extends to as many, or almost as many, levels as the metaphysical hierarchy ensures that it has the cognitive and other powers suitable for the penetration of all these levels."[2] The more work with theurgy you do, the easier a taste of the One will become.

I take this exercise from the Hermetica, where it is described like this:

> Enlarge yourself to an unmeasurable size, leaping out from the whole body, and, having transcended time, become Eternity, and you will know the divine. Think that nothing is impossible to you; consider yourself to be immortal and able to understand

---

2 Pauliina Remes. *Neoplatonism.* (Berkeley, CA: Unversity of California Press, 2008), 166. For more elaborate and historically detailed accounts of the various Neoplatonic cosmologies, I highly recommend this book.

> everything: all arts, all sciences, all the ways of life; become the highest of the heights, and the lowest of the depths. Gather together all the sense perceptions of objects in yourself, of fire and water, dry and wet, and in the same way, be everywhere—in earth, in sea, and in the heavens. Be not yet existing. Be in the womb, newborn, old, dead, and that which is after death. And understanding all such things the same—time, place, events, qualities, quantities—then you will be able to know the divine.[3]

STEP 1: When first beginning this exercise, it helps to get as comfortable as you can. As you become familiar with it, you can do it while doing other things (although I wouldn't recommend doing it while driving!).

STEP 2: Focus on your breath. Aim for a four-fold breath, where you inhale for a count of four, hold for a count of four, exhale for a count of four, and hold for a count of four. If you're sitting still, with some practice you should be able to do this, but if you're moving about you may find it easier to aim for a count of two rather than four or otherwise modify the time.

STEP 3: Imagine yourself from outside yourself, as if you have a floating-eye perspective of the scene. It is as if you are watching yourself sitting or lying there, like in a movie. You may close your eyes if you want.

---

3 Corpus Hermeticum XI:20. My translation. My source for the Greek Hermetica is A. D. Nock and A.-J. Festugière, trans. *Corpus Hermeticum.* (Collection des Universités de France. Paris, 1945). A very readable English translation also exists: Brian Copenhaver, trans. *Hermetica: The Greek Corpus Hermeticum and the Latin Asclepius in a New English Translation with Notes and Introduction.* (Cambridge: Cambridge University Press, 1992).

Step 4: Build up this image of yourself as accurately as you can. Then slowly begin to lift your perspective upward, taking in the room, then the building (assuming, of course, that you're inside), then the city. With each breath, take in a bit more, and don't be afraid to go slow. If you begin to lose focus, rest on that level of perspective for a while.

Step 5: Eventually, you will take in the whole world, then the solar system, then the galaxy, then the whole universe as a whole. If you don't manage this the first few times, don't worry. You are gaining benefit just by seeing the big picture as high as you can.

Step 6: When you can hold the universe in your imagination, contemplate the totality of it without focusing in or catching on any one thing for a few breaths.

Step 7: Now, holding it all in your mind at once, let the boundaries between all its parts dissolve: the galaxy is the same as the people, and all perspectives collapse. If you can do this, you may glimpse a moment of unity.

Step 8: If you can achieve step 7, which may take some time, try now to abolish even the boundary around the universe. The experience of this is hard to describe, but you will probably find your discursive, binary mind stopping in a sudden awareness of unity. This is a glimpse of henosis.

Step 9: Whether you got to step 7 or not, after holding the image of the entire universe, or the oneness behind it, for a while start to move back inwards to the galaxy, solar system, planet, continent, and location. This helps ground the experience; in theurgy the return is as important as the journey.

Structure of the Soul

The ancients were masters of introspection, and they could look within their own souls with a clarity and precision we can't match with scientific instruments. As can be expected with something so subjective, though, the lines and borders of the parts of the soul differ from formulation to formulation. That's not a sign of a flaw in the system or the unreality of the soul. On the contrary, it's a sign that we are looking at the complexity of people's experience of themselves as ensouled beings. And by studying the differences in these systems as well as the similarities, we can begin to see some of the richness of the soul itself and perhaps begin to identify our own personal psychology.

That the soul is a single thing, indivisible, comes from Aristotle, and this notion was a new one. Aristotle defined the soul as that first cause of thing, its purpose of being. The soul of a clock is to tell time. The soul of a dog is to be a dog. But thc soul, for Aristotle, was merely the cause of the body; without the body, there was no soul, or need for one. Aristotle was responding to Platonism, which argues that not only is there a soul, it is the intermediary between the human consciousness and the world of Ideas, or Nous. The soul, in Neoplatonic doctrine, is a marvelous thing: "Unlike the rest of the universe, the human soul is not a prisoner of any one form or way of looking at the world."[4] Our souls are the things that can lead us out of the cave.

Plato describes the soul as having three parts. In the Phaedrus, he says that the soul is like a chariot with two horses. I'm going to steal and modify his allegory a bit. Imagine you're driving a chariot. You know where you're going; you have the route planned out, and you also are sitting up on the chariot and can see where you're going. You can see the road is clear here, bumpy there, obstructed over there. You've got the traffic report from LOGO FM, the radio station of rationality. But your chariot is bound to two horses. The first horse, whom you've named Thymos, is a spirited and clever mare. She sometimes is spooked by shadows on the road, and sometimes she's intrigued by a strange smell or sight and wants to run after it and find out what it is. Sometimes she's just gloomy and stubborn and doesn't want to move. Her partner, however, is a powerful stallion you've named Eros. He knows what he wants and he gets it, which is usually anything in heat. But he's also got a huge appetite, and

---

4 Pauliina Remes. *Neoplatonism.* (Berkeley, CA: University of California Press, 2008), 120.

will veer off the road at the sight of anything green, good for him or not. He's strong, so he often pulls Thymos along with him. But sometimes Thymos balks, pulls back, or goes along or a while and then seems to change her mind and fights against him. Overall, you've got your hands full controlling these two horses so you can get that chariot up Henosis Hill!

The logos or driver is the part of our soul that is rational. It is the reflection of the capital-n Nous in our own being: it's where reason and logic and understanding live. In some formulations, it's the highest part of the soul. In a well-regulated soul, it directs the other two parts, thymos and eros. The thymos of our soul is our spiritedness, our emotional drive. This can be all the higher emotions of compassion and aspiration, or it can be the emotions of anger, jealousy, and fear. It's interesting that this word, which meant among other things "aspiration" in ancient Greek, now means just "anger" in modern Greek. It's easy for thymos to run away. The eros—which shouldn't be confused with the god of the same name—is the part of our soul that wants stuff. It's the appetite, be it for sex or food or pleasure. Well regulated, we can let it go and enjoy a nice big plate of crab and some lentil stew, perhaps even a glass of wine, or a recreational romp in the sheets. Poorly regulated, we are haunting nightclub bathrooms looking for a fix, eating ourselves to death with greasy burgers at a fast food joint we don't even really like, or drinking our liver into stone.

Most of us do all right most of the time in controlling these two wild horses. Why not just cut them loose, though, for all the trouble they cause us? We could surrender our emotions, like the character Spock in the old Star Trek shows. In fact, that's what a lot of people think the point of the Stoic philosophy was, although that's not at all the truth. The Stoics were a philosophical school that argued that we are happiest when we are not trying to control things outside of our control. Since the only things within the scope of our control are our emotions and reactions to events, Stoics taught that the way to happiness was to achieve control of those things, but that doesn't mean to abolish emotion. In fact, the Stoics tell us that emotion serves a powerful and valuable purpose. Without it, life isn't worth living—but we also need to know that we don't have to be miserable. In fact, the Stoic says, you can be happy right now, regardless of your circumstances. You're under no obligation to be miserable. That's a hefty expectation, and not even the Stoics all lived up to it all the time (some of Marcus Aurelius's meditations read like they were written on the edge of despair). But it's a thought: well regulated, our emotions can lead us upward through joy and compassion, without which we are no longer sentient—the word *sentient* literally means "feeling"—beings.

But surely we can cut off appetite? Many great mystics have tried, but a chariot with one horse doesn't get too far. That's why I have borrowed this image. It's a wonderful argument against excessive asceticism such as that of Plotinus, whom his biographer describes as "embarrassed to be in a body."[5] As big as a fan I am of Plotinus, and as big a fan as I am of Neoplatonism, the ascetic turn of Late Antiquity never sat terribly well with me as a means of learning self-control.

I've always preferred the Stoic approach: Instead of the logos getting off the chariot and kicking eros until it stops moving, which seems to be the ascetic method, in Stoicism logos learns to steer the chariot. You control a horse by putting up fences. And when you train a horse, you can train it to learn its limits so that instead of tying it, all you need to do is loop the bridle over a branch. The horse will not even try to pull away, because it knows its limits and no longer needs to be tied. Such is the Stoic approach to eros or desire.

You give desire its reins when it is safe to do so, but the logos is in control. The logos sets the limits of the fences. The eros demands a night of chocolate cake and pornography? The logos offers a slice of cake after a nutritious meal and a French film. The eros demands extravagant expenditures, and the logos consults the budget and decides yea or nay. All impulsive desires are watched

5 Mark Edwards, trans. *Neoplatonic Saints: The Lives of Plotinus and Proclus by their Students.* (Liverpool: Liverpool University Press, 2000), 1.

and controlled, and periodically you practice poverty, by going without for a set time, just to find the limits.

One way to do this is to recognize the desire consciously and sit with it rather than pushing it away. Those who diet know the sensation of overwhelming desire for some specific treat; a donut can expand into a universe of cream cheese frosting. The initial desire for a donut turns into a desire for cake, and the logos, the reins slipping, gives in again and again, cake after cake, until it would have been better just to eat the initial donut. Of course, the problem with eating the donut is wanting another afterwards, so the logos sits mindfully with the experience of that donut, makes it a production, and savors every bite.

The eros never really wants an object in the physical world. The eros is driven toward or away from *phantasms* of things, coming either from our senses or our memories. If we have a memory of a tasty treat and we desire it, we don't desire the treat—we desire the phantasm. Those who eat—or fulfill any other erotic drive—unconsciously are enjoying the phantasm of memory rather than the phantasm of the senses that might satisfy the eros. And the eros can be trained to be satisfied with the phantasm itself, at least some of the time.

The drives of the eros play a large role in magic. When we want something and choose to do magic for it, we often want other things as well. The horse is spooked on all sides by phantasms of desire and aversion and so magic becomes impossible because the chariot cannot move forward. We need to train the eros by addressing each phantasm one by one and fulfilling those desires in some way consistent with the magical goal. The logos can do this: integration and synthesis are its talents.

If eros represents the desires that drive us, the thymos represents emotional needs. Whereas the eros accesses a phantasm from the senses or from memory and moves toward that phantasm with desire, the thymos responds not to phantasms but to thoughts about those phantasms. We are not made happy or sad by the things that happen to us, but by what we think about those things. This might seem counterintuitive. After all, if I win a prize, I am happy. If I lose something, I am sad. But it's obvious that I am not happy or sad about those things until I realize it. If I win a prize and don't hear about it for a couple months, I am not happy unaccountably and only later realize why. I am happy when I learn of having won the prize, because that's when I can begin thinking about it and responding to those thoughts.

Many of the thoughts that make us unhappy or angry or afraid are irrational thoughts, which the logos would never approve if it could see them. But they can speed by so quickly that the logos doesn't have time to stamp them with its approval or rejection. The trick to controlling this horse is to learn to see the thoughts that drive it rather than the horse itself. In other words, we don't look at the emotion but at the thoughts that provoke it, just as we don't look at the steering wheel but the road.

One way to do that is to write them down as they occur, but that's sometimes impractical. A more practical method is to write down the thoughts that spark particular emotions later from memory. For example, if I find myself annoyed at the store, I might sit down later and remember that feeling of annoyance and ask, why was I annoyed? Because the woman in front of me was slow and rude. But that's the phantasm: what thoughts about that phantasm led to annoyance? That she should be faster, that she should be politer, and that she should get out of my way. Once we do this, we can start to see the patterns of irrationality. For example, the word "should" is absurd in those thoughts: why *should* she be faster? By natural law? No, surely not, or she would have been. By moral law? What kind of ridiculous moral law would state that a person shouldn't take their time at the checkout? And even if it did, how can I expect every single person to follow every single moral rule or rule of politeness that exists? They wouldn't be rules if people just naturally followed them. A more rational thought to replace it with would be "I'd prefer that she speed up." That is true, rational, and not tremendously emotional.

Psychologists, particularly cognitive behavioral psychologists, have written extensively about this approach to controlling the thymos. The methods they derive are closely related to Stoic methods invented in Late Antiquity, as some psychologists are now recognizing.[6] Psychology, after all, is just a branch of philosophy, at least from the perspectives of the great philosophers of Greece and the late Roman empire.

What the therapists and even Stoics fail to mention is that it's also worthwhile to keep track of our happy thoughts. For example, perhaps we have a good day at work and we write "I was happy today." Why? "Because I was very well-prepared and my plan was quite successful." That's just the phantasm, though, and didn't cause the emotion of happiness. So what did I think about that phantasm that created happiness? "I helped people understand something complex today, and am a competent and skilled person." Now, we can begin to apply the searchlight of the logos on this thought: is it rational to be happy when you help someone? Yes, because we are social creatures and it is divine for us to aid each other. Is it rational to be happy when one is skilled? Perhaps, but it's important to recognize that a skilled person might act unskilled on some days. If we're only happy when we apply certain labels to ourselves, we must expend a lot of useless energy upholding those labels. Instead of selecting my happiness from that thought, I chose to focus on the first, more rational reason to be happy. While you may very well be skilled and competent at your work, someday you may goof up, and you don't want to be crushed when that happens.

If we start to dig into Egyptian, Hermetic, Neoplatonic, Qabalistic, and other psychologies we'll discover slightly different lists of parts of the soul arranged slightly differently. But they all have in common the Platonic realization that we are not a single, undifferentiated force of consciousness. We know this through mere observation, so why the concept of a unitary soul persists in our culture is beyond my comprehension. We all know we are thinking beings, whatever else we might be, as Descartes so succinctly puts it: *cogito ergo sum*, he writes, "I think, therefore I am," or less literally, "I know

6 Donald Robertson. *The Philosophy of Cognitive-Behavioural Therapy: Stoic Philosophy as Rational and Cognitive Psychotherapy.* (London: Karnac, 2010).

that I am thinking these thoughts, and therefore I know that I must exist to think them." But we also know that sometimes we think one thing and do another. Sometimes we want what we know will hurt us or feel emotions we don't want to feel. If you've ever had a crush on an unsuitable or unavailable person, you know quite well that our emotions and desires do not always match our thoughts.

What Plato recognized is that we are not a thing but a system. The logos reasons, the eros wants, and the thymos feels. And each communicates with the other. But he also recognized that we're not a democracy in our heads. Like a ship at sea, we're ruled by the captain, our logos—at least, unless there's a mutiny. Plato understood that many of us are just that: ships in mutiny, colliding into each other because the navigator is powerless, no matter how loudly he shouts, to bring the sailors back under control. Of course, he used the metaphor of a chariot because in a chariot race a horse going astray can lead to a spectacular wreck—which was probably half the reason people went to chariot races in the first place, just as we go to hockey games hoping to see a fight. It's less fun to watch when it's us, of course, and even the most skilled charioteer could have a bad race, just as even the most skilled theurgist can have a bad day, week, or month.

EXERCISE 1.3: CONTEMPLATING THE PARTS OF THE SOUL

This is a useful contemplation whenever you are feeling overwhelmed or conflicted about a course of action. I like to do it before I do any magic or undertake a big project to make sure that all the parts of my soul are pulling in the same direction and rein them in if they're not.

STEP 1: Begin by relaxing as you do when you are going to do a contemplation.

STEP 2: Imagine yourself in a room or temple. You are alone and looking out of your own eyes at a relatively empty and featureless room. Let this phantasm of yourself in such a place become as strong and vivid as you can.

Step 3: Feel whatever desires you are currently experiencing. These may be small—a desire to shift to a more comfortable position or eat something—or they may be much larger. Perhaps your eros is calm and satisfied right now or a raging storm of lust. Either way, feel it where it is in your body without responding to it.

Step 4: When you have a strong sense of that desire, let it take form in front of you. Perhaps it will look like a child, an animal, a double of yourself—it doesn't matter. Just let it take form and hold the visualization of it in this mental space.

Step 5: Now, determine which emotions you are feeling. What are your physiological responses to events, and how are you interpreting them? Are you feeling sad, happy, content, nervous—or some combination? Don't worry about listing the emotions by name: just feel them.

Step 6: Once you have a strong sense of those emotions, again, let them take form outside of you in that mental space.

Step 7: You've now got your eros and your thymos separated from you, and what remains is the logos. Now you can communicate with them directly, asking them questions and listening to their responses, as well as the reactions of your body. For example, if you wish to overeat, you could ask your thymos why your appetite exists from its perspective, what emotional needs it fulfills. Then you could turn to your eros and ask why it desires this, and would it settle for some other desire instead?

Eventually, you can begin to negotiate. Ask if your eros will be satisfied with something smaller than a whole tub of ice cream? You can even make bargains—"I tell you what. You can have one bowl of ice cream, but if you start demanding another bowl, I'm going to just dump the rest of the tub down the sink." You'll be surprised how far fair and rational bargaining will get you with your eros and thymos.

Wisdom and Virtue

In the occult community, we speak quite a lot about wisdom, but rarely do I see much practice of it. The question is, how would we know it when we see it? Some people seem to think wisdom is a particular bearing of the body; a mild smile and a soft, platitudinous way of speaking. Some think it's a haughty superiority, as if condescending to children. And some think it's portentous pronouncements. I suspect all these attempts to "look wise" might say more about how people's parents acted or what kind of novels they like to read than about true wisdom.

Fortunately, the ancients have a very good definition of wisdom that is hard to miss and a clear program for how to develop it. Wisdom, they said, was the perception of the good. If you know what is good and know how to achieve it, you have wisdom. This definition is quite practical: we can judge, moment to moment, whether we act wisely or unwisely by whether or not we have chosen the good. Food is good: if I forgo it and starve myself deliberately, I am being unwise. Even alcohol is good if taken in moderation, although I may be wise to forgo that entirely if I know myself inclined to a weakness toward it. If I eat a whole pizza in one sitting and drink a whole bottle of wine, I have exceeded the good: I have acted unwisely. In every instance, then, wisdom consists of finding the balance between extremes, the golden mean. Four particular golden means are enumerated by the ancients as virtues, or strengths, that a wise person would develop: temperance, prudence, courage, and justice.

The Neoplatonists seemed to think that developing virtue was a necessary first step for the practice of theurgy. A lot of life's problems are simply the result of a lack of wisdom and can be solved merely by rearranging one's thinking. Once solved, those problems no longer interfere with the quest for henosis. Moreover, if we are to call the gods to us, it stands to reason that we should be pleasing to them. What is pleasing to humans? Beauty and the goodness it reflects. So it stands to reason that the gods, too, will admire beauty. But whereas humans, dwelling in the world of matter, might be attracted to physical beauty, the gods will be attracted to beauty of the soul: virtue.

Temperance, or *sōphrosynē*, can be summed up in four words: "Know what is enough." We Americans live in a culture that does not encourage much temperance, sad to say. Americans have always had a weird relationship with the idea, from the Temperance movement of the early twentieth century (which reinterpreted temperance to mean absolute abstinence) to our current culture of 2,000-calorie sandwiches and coffee drinks with several days' worth of fat. This virtue, therefore, is one of the harder ones to develop for those who live in such a culture.

One way to develop temperance is to deliberately do without for a set time. How long can you go without eating fast food? At first you may think, not long. But eventually you'll realize you could go your whole life and never eat another bite of fast food. Knowing it's possible helps you see what is enough. Of course, temperance isn't absolute abstinence of all joy: on the contrary, it's knowing how much you can take in and enjoy and how much you can't. Another way to develop temperance is to take something you enjoy—video games, cookies, or anything else—and give yourself only a quarter of what you normally would of that thing. If you typically play video games for two hours, set a timer and play only for thirty minutes. If you normally eat a whole cookie, break it into quarters and eat only one—give the rest away if you can't resist it at first. You might still, from time to time, eat a whole cookie or spend a whole weekend playing games, but you'll do so consciously, knowing that you have exceeded what is enough by choice, rather than compulsion.

Another way to explore temperance as a virtue is, paradoxically, to develop new pleasures. Try sushi, go out dancing, go bowling, try learning a musical instrument or a new language. You might find you take joy in these activities that you didn't think you would. This also teaches you what is enough. Going out dancing every weekend might be a lot of fun, but you may learn that staying at home and reading a novel is also enough for you to enjoy your weekend.

Temperance also is that part of wisdom that sees what we have. Make a list of all the things that bring you gratitude and awe, and add to it frequently. Spend some time each morning giving thanks, perhaps just in general, perhaps to a deity, for what you have, even if it's meager. Even if you are scraping by, ill, unhappy, or unfortunate: you have something that you can be grateful for. I'm not saying that your suffering isn't real and serious, but that even in the darkest moments, we can find something precious, even if it's only the fact that we exist and *can* suffer.

The second virtue, *phronēsis*, usually translated "prudence," isn't like what we mean by that word now: saving our money and being cautious. It can be that, of course, because forethought is an important part of prudence, but a person with this virtue might not be cautious at all if caution is not called for. A better translation might be "practical wisdom" or "situational understanding." It starts in the awareness that an action that is right in one place and time may be uncalled for in another. For a trivial example, you wouldn't eat with the same manners at a fancy restaurant as you do in a backyard cookout. As a less trivial example, if someone needs your help, do you offer it? In some situations, perhaps even most, the right thing to do is to offer help; but in others, help may be counterproductive. I've often watched students work through a problem, and I've had to bite my tongue not to offer premature help before they had a chance to figure out where they went wrong themselves. It's easy to see how this gets translated as "prudence," but the meaning of that English word doesn't cover nearly as wide a range of care and awareness as *phronēsis*. Perhaps a better way to describe it is discernment, which is identifying and separating good from bad, true from false, and right from wrong.

Another way to think of it is that this is a virtue of perception: can you see things as they really are, or are you blinded by your preconceptions and language? This virtue is useful in analyzing our own right and wrong. If we look to our own souls, we might find things we don't like: a tendency to lie, let's say. Are we therefore liars? If you say, "yes, I am a liar," you have abandoned the possibility of change and self-forgiveness. If you say, "I have lied. I will be careful not to do that again," then you've opened yourself up for change and self-improvement. Similarly, when we look at ourselves, we're sometimes blind to our strengths and the good within us. We cannot succeed in theurgy if we cannot recognize the good when we see it. It is prudent, therefore, to listen to the compliments of friends as well as their criticisms to learn who we are.

The third virtue, *andreia*, or courage, is also a difficult one to understand, as we often call courage those things which are not actually virtuous or good. Ultimately, courage is the virtue of acting with contempt for the inconsequential. Our prudence will teach us that our physical body is not as important as our soul and that we are free to choose our actions even if that freedom is constrained. It is courage that makes a stand, even if it means losing a job or one's life, because courage recognizes that our values are more precious than our jobs or even lives. But courage isn't always a life-or-death matter. Courage is also how you deal with the daily difficulties and pains of life: do you suffer under them or do you face them with equanimity?

Courage is a good example of the golden mean. We should not be foolhardy, certainly, rushing into every dangerous situation without regard for our welfare. By the same token, we shouldn't be cowards, huddling in our homes with the doors locked. But how do we find a balance? We can't just be fools half the time and cowards the other half, because that'd be insane. No, we must look at each situation, judge it with prudence, and decide whether it is wiser to be safer or to take a risk. Finding this golden mean requires practice and an awareness of what you value and why.

The final virtue, *dikaiosynē*, is the virtue of "justice," which we might more accurately translate "fairness" or even "charity." Justice is the mean between unthinking retribution and absolute clemency, but it is closer to the pole of clemency than it is to revenge. But justice is also the scale on which we weigh our values. Is it better to save a hundred dollars or buy a new piece of jewelry? We tell ourselves, sometimes, that justice is involved: we deserve the treat. But what do we truly value? Moreover, what if the choice is saving a hundred dollars versus telling a lie?

Imagine after shopping and arriving at home, you discover that a distracted checker gave you a twenty-dollar bill instead of a one-dollar bill in change. Do you drive back to the store? We might rationalize that we should not, that it is out of the way, that it is not our problem. But what does real justice demand when we step back and look at the situation with prudence? I have not earned this money, the checker will have to pay for it or get fired, and so—what is just? As someone who has more than once returned to the store to pay for a single item that didn't ring up properly, it's obvious where my opinion falls. But you must let your own reason guide you.

The golden mean, mentioned earlier, is the teaching that each virtue is a mean between two extremes. That is, it's a golden mean because it shifts and changes due to circumstances: this is not a list of commandments but ethics built on reaction to the world as it is. So for each of the virtues there are two vices, which might seem an unduly harsh way to run a universe, but so it goes.

For prudence, we have foolishness on one extreme, and haughtiness on the other. The fool is the person who does not know nor cares to know. This is the person who covers his or her ears and eyes and yells "LA LA LA" when confronted with unpleasant truths. The haughty person is the know-it-all who offers an opinion on every occasion, always pointing out that others in the conversation are wrong. Where the fool might also do this, the haughty person has the advantage of usually being right. But it doesn't improve the experience for those involved that he or she is; if anything, it makes the listeners less likely to take that person's advice.

Temperance has two opposite poles, both denials of temperance. One is overindulgence. This might be drunkenness or eating too much, but it could even be reading too much, playing too many video games, and so on. Of course, "too much" is subjective, which is why temperance is a mean between the two extremes. If I want to spend Saturday reading a fun novel, that's not necessarily overindulgence; but if I neglect other work or my loved ones for the exciting book, that's another matter. The opposite, self-denial, is strangely just as common. People in America, at least, seem to swing back and forth wildly. One day, we might be eating huge hamburgers with thousands of calories; the next, we're on a cabbage soup diet. Of course, again, this is a matter of finding the mean. An alcoholic may indeed wisely decide never, ever to indulge in alcohol again without failing at achieving temperance. We don't need to have just a little bit of heroin in order to show that we have found a golden mean! But people have not really achieved temperance if they hurt themselves by starving, by refusing themselves time to relax and rest, or by living in unnecessary austerity they secretly hate.

Justice's two poles may seem familiar to many occultists: severity and excessive mercy. If you are severe, you are a person who has standards so high that no one can live up to them—probably not even yourself. In my experience, few people are as unjust to others as they are to themselves. If you beat yourself up because you are not perfect, you are being unjust. No one is perfect. And if you are disappointed with the effects of a ritual and think, "I suck at magic," you might want to withhold judgment. For one thing, one never knows until all forces have played out. But for another, no one is perfect all the time at any skill, even adepts at those skills. The polar extreme of severity is excessive mercy, which I must admit I see less often. When we do see this in our society, it's in the form of a person who never says no, even though he or she really wants to. But you also see it in the overindulgent parent or the boss or teacher who accepts excuse after excuse, rather than face the confrontation that is needful.

Of course, that might be a failure of courage as well, specifically cowardice. Cowardice isn't feeling fear; feeling fear is normal. Cowardice is giving in to that fear. We all have probably exhibited a bit of cowardice from time to time. Choosing not to go to the party because you don't want to meet people you might not like could be cowardice (or it might be prudence if you're doing it because you know you need to do other things at home—this can become sticky to tease out, as you see). Phobias and anxieties are medical conditions, of course, and not an indication that you lack virtue—although prudence would entail getting treatment, since they both usually respond well and quickly to it. The opposite of courage is foolhardiness, a word I've always loved, because it reminds me of Hardy of Laurel and Hardy, who is also a good icon of it. It's doing stupid things without thinking about the consequences, and even intelligent people can fall for it. It might mean having unprotected sex, gossiping about a colleague for a cheap laugh, or even drinking a milkshake even though you know you're lactose intolerant. Obviously, it can also mean rushing into danger, getting in fights, and so on. Now, if you're a stuntman or a professional racecar driver, you're not necessarily foolhardy. The way you can tell is that you take safety precautions: you behave prudently in the facc of the danger.

In fact, all these virtues can be reduced to prudence, which itself is a kind of wisdom. Ultimately, that's what virtue tries to inculcate in us: wisdom. And wisdom is a divine force in the universe, so by becoming virtuous we begin to build a mind that looks more and more like the mind of the divine.

EXERCISE 1.4: INVENTORY OF VIRTUES

You can do this exercise on three different levels. Start with the first level, the general assessment, then begin to practice the retrospective contemplation and the prospective contemplation. This exercise has the goal of giving you a firmer sense of who you are: your values and strengths as a person. It may not seem flashy or impressive for those who want to cut to the circumambulations and chanting, but it's extremely valuable to lay foundations for that kind of more overtly magical work later. It's not meant to be an excuse to beat your breast for your weaknesses, and if you begin to do that, stop the exercise for a while and work on developing self-compassion.

STEP 1: The general assessment. Get a small book or open a computer file in which you make four lists, headed: Temperance, Prudence, Courage, and Justice. Under each list, write down the qualities, experiences, and ideas you have about them. Some questions to get you started:

Temperance

- Where are you inclined to do too much? This can be food, drink, work, anger, or anything else that is best in moderation.
- What do you keep a close rein on that could run away from you? Perhaps it is a whim or desire you control, a fondness for a particular thing, or anything else.
- What do you deprive yourself of that you don't have to? Perhaps you tell yourself every year you'll go on vacation next year but never really do. Or perhaps you want a new computer and really need one but keep putting it off.

Prudence

- What are you blind to? Perhaps you have prejudices about a particular group of people (not necessarily a race or ethnicity; you might be prejudiced about Lexus drivers), or maybe you discount information on a particular topic you don't like.
- What are you particularly wise about? What do you know how to do well, and what kind of problems can you solve without much difficulty?
- What sorts of things do you overthink to the point of anxiety or paralysis?

Courage

- What are you afraid of to the point of not wanting to act? Perhaps you've put off a dental appointment for two years, or you don't want to fly because of fear.

- What are you brave about? You might still feel fear, of course, but where do you act in spite of that fear?
- When are you foolhardy, rushing in even though you know it's unduly dangerous? Perhaps you engage in risky behavior in one or more areas of your life.

Justice

- What do you have negative biases against? These might seem to be trivial things, like particular brands of computers or political parties, but it's worth putting down everything you can think of.
- Where in your life do you exhibit fairness and honesty?
- Where are you excessively lenient? Do particular types of people get away with more just because of who they are? Do you treat some people differently than others for no logical reason other than their power over you or their attractiveness, physical or otherwise?

You can add to this list over time. Be kind (exhibit justice, in other words) with yourself, but also be honest. You are not as bad as you might imagine, and you are not as great as you might hope. You're human and as we'll learn, the gospel of theurgy is that being human, flawed as we might be, is a wonderful thing to be.

STEP 2: The daily assessment: retroactive contemplation. For this step, you will do a similar activity but rather than write it down you'll run through it in your head. I like to do it before bed, but some people prefer to do it a bit before to give them time to unwind. Begin by imagining waking up the morning previous. Remember what you did at each step of the day, and for each significant decision, identify it as arising from a virtue, vice, or neutral trait. For example, I got up and went to work, where I met with clients. That action required prudence, because I had to identify their needs and react to them. It also required justice, because I had to react appropriately. Then, driving home, I got mad at someone in traffic. That was a failure of prudence, because it put me in danger and surrendered my equanimity to another, and it was also an absence of temperance, because I indulged unnecessarily in anger. Run through the whole day, taking mental note of what you did well and what you did badly. If you do this every day, you'll find yourself doing it during the day, thinking "how will this stand up to my assessment later?" Of course, what you don't want to do is worry or dwell. Once you identify something as a vice, simply let it go, knowing that identifying it is all you need to do for this step.

Step 3: Prospective contemplation. In the morning, before beginning your day (perhaps in the shower) take a few moments to think about what you might face. For example, if you have a project that needs to be done, ask yourself "what will be a prudent action to take? What would be the courageous, temperate, just course of action?" Do this for each of your day's planned activities, and you will find quickly that you have developed a habit of virtue that kicks in even when unexpected events surprise you.

How Is Theurgy Practical?

You might have gotten the impression from the last section that theurgy is just a tarted-up excuse for moral posturing and preaching. If so, I'd like you to understand me differently. The goal of achieving virtues is not to be "good," although you will be. The purpose of achieving virtue is to be strong enough to deal with the gods themselves. *Virtue* means, literally, "strength."

The entire path of theurgy is a path of practicality, rather than airy-fairy imaginings, despite historical impressions to the contrary. Some proponents of practical magic (although certainly not all) might say "if magic doesn't achieve an observable effect in the world, you can't know if it worked or not." This is an interesting statement because it seems reasonable and rational but encodes some assumptions about the world that are strangely contrary to most magical systems. For one thing, it assumes that the world is material, and the material world and our experiences of it are what is real. That's hardly accepted in most magical systems (except perhaps chaos magic). Also, the statement assumes that changing oneself isn't a change in the real world, but of course whatever the real world is, we exist in it, whether as bodies or as minds.

Theurgy achieves three fundamental and practical effects that are real and measurable and even affect the physical world. Theurgy makes the practitioner a good person, which isn't some vague moralistic smiling church-social happy-clappy space-cadet concept of "good" but a practical, real kind of good that can be observed objectively. Theurgy also makes the practitioner a better magician; in fact, I've come to believe that theurgy is the foundation of all other practical magic. If you want magic to be a tool to get you rich, laid, and powerful, that's fine. Theurgy can actually help with that, although perhaps not the way you might imagine. Finally, theurgy offers a goal and an aim for life and magic, something sorely missing in much postmodern magic—and for that matter, much religion.

From a theurgic perspective, being a good person isn't the same as being a "nice" person. A good knife is good for cutting; a good antibiotic is good for curing infections. A good person from this perspective is good for something. It isn't enough to be nice (in fact, niceness is often a way to avoid the requirements of justice and courage), and it isn't enough to be charitable alone. And yet even being good for something isn't enough: a knife can also be good for stabbing, an antibiotic can be too good at its job and weaken the immune system, and a person might be quite good at cheating and stealing. A good person must be good for something good.

But what is good?

Good is love.

But what is love?

I remember when my partner first said, "I love you." I answered back, "I love you too, but now we need to define 'love' to each other"—the perils of loving a philosopher. But the answer is pretty simple: love is when your growth and health and happiness and welfare are as valuable to me as my own. Notice that's not "more valuable"; justice demands that we be equal partners, and while self-sacrifice might be a noble thing in the right situation, it cannot be a way of life. Logic forbids it: if your growth is as important as mine and I sacrifice myself needlessly for your own growth, I have cut down one healthy tree in favor of another healthy tree. Of course, some situations may demand such a choice, but they are contrived and unlikely. By all means, care for the sick...but do not make yourself sick in the process.

Yet there is love and there is love. Loving someone else is one thing, loving the world is another. Can you live such that the growth and welfare of the world is as important to you as your own? Eventually you can or at least move toward that goal. I'm not talking about being a saint walking on water and curing lepers although if that's your aim in life, good for you. I'm talking about living in the world in such a way that the world is better off for your having lived in it. You don't need to be a plaster saint for that. In fact, it helps if you're not, if actually you're a person with a normal life who has an extraordinary effect on the world.

It's easy to get tangled up in specific actions. Is this action good or bad? That's why I advocate, as did the writers of Late Antiquity, a virtue ethic that sweeps aside questions of specific action in favor of particular dispositions that will serve us in any activity. If you develop courage, temperance, justice, and prudence, you will grow in wisdom. If you grow in wisdom, you will act out of love.

And, as you do this and as you work with the divine forces described in this book, you will begin to experience a sound and rational reason for love. You will learn that you *are* the world in which you live. There is no difference. I don't mean in the solipsistic sense that the world doesn't exist, but in the sense that if you didn't exist, we'd have a different world. You depend on the world and it depends on you, because you're part of the same thing.

Of course that's easy to write and it sounds a bit like a 1970s folk song, but the experience cannot be explained.

Most of my readers want to be good, as well, at magic. If you're already a practitioner of a magical path, you may have achieved some considerable skill in that field. Theurgy will help you achieve more. In fact, limits to your magic begin to melt away when you plug into the forces underneath reality. If you pick up some of the traditional magical texts from the Renaissance, you'll see this theme returned to again and again. In *Abramelin*, you must achieve knowledge and conversation of an angel before you begin. The majority of the *Arbatel* consists of moral aphorisms designed to make the magician pleasing to God. Even the *Key of Solomon* exhorts the reader to engage in constant prayer and piety: "Solomon, the Son of David, King of Israel, hath said that the beginning of our Key is to fear God, to adore Him, to honour Him with contrition of heart, to invoke Him in all matters which we wish to undertake, and to operate with very great devotion, for thus God will lead us in the right way."[7]

Perhaps these suggestions are merely pious dodging to throw off the scent of unfriendly critics, but I don't think so: I think these magicians knew that you had to reach up in order to reach down, like the magician in the Rider Waite Smith tarot. The social element of magic has been long overlooked in contemporary Western magical practices. Instead of considering whom we can cultivate as allies and friends in the invisible world, we concern ourselves with "magical energy" and other such models. But throughout most of human history, magic has been a social act, a way of interacting, positively or negatively, with people. Some of those people were material, some immaterial, but the relationship was paramount. Building this relationship is what theurgy is about, because as you work with the gods you begin to work with their daimones, their deputies, and in time you gain a familiar friendship with the underlying forces of the universe itself.

---

7 S. Liddell MacGregor Mathers, trans. *The Key of Solomon the King.* (York Beach, ME: Samuel Weiser, 1974), 10.

Of course, your goals going into theurgy might very well change as you practice. I sometimes think the practice of magic is a benign trap. Yes, you can be powerful, wealthy, sexually alluring, and so on—but by the time you've got all that, you won't want it anymore. You'll have better goals. But if what it takes to get you started is the promise of money and sex, then by all means, start with that. And who knows? Perhaps for you that is the purpose of your life, and when you reach up to the gods they'll say, "Hey, glad to get in touch with you. Here's a new sports car and a swimsuit model of your preferred gender/sex combination."

It might seem grand to say it, but this is a book about contacting gods, so why not be grand: I know the purpose of human life. It's the same for everyone. Sure, it looks different for different people: For some, it might just look like having lots of adventurous sex in exotic locales while lighting cigars with hundred-dollar bills. For others, it might look like founding a charitable foundation. For others, it's writing books, making art, cooking delicious food, sweeping streets, dancing beautifully, singing, gymnastics, football, astronomy, or gathering the world's largest ball of twine. From the perspective of a theurgist, ultimately the purpose of human life boils down to this (yes, I will now tell you the meaning of life—you've got your money's worth for this book; never say you didn't): *The purpose of human life is to join the gods in the great work of creation.*

Your skills, talents, dispositions, and even your vices all determine how you'll go about that. For me, it's teaching and writing. For others, it's making a room beautiful and functional by rearranging the furniture. For others, it might be playing tennis. But you'll know you've found this purpose because the gods will stand behind you as you work, and you will look up—even if you've felt like a slacker or a failure—and realize that you've accomplished a lot without ever being aware of it.

Theurgy can help you find the way you achieve this purpose, what Aleister Crowley called your "true will."

Nothing is more practical than that.

CHAPTER 2

What Is a God?

As I explained in the last chapter, monotheistic and exclusionary religions often have an orthodoxy, a set of beliefs to which every worshiper must adhere. Sometimes, these appear in a statement called a credo or a catechism. Pagans, as you might imagine, never had such a credo, and so they were often a bit more accepting of new ideas. Of course, they were not always the earth-loving and diversity-accepting people we wish to imagine them to be—after all, one of the (clearly false) accusations that got Socrates killed was that he introduced new gods. But at most times throughout antiquity in the West, different theories and idea of the gods coexist more or less peacefully. The ancients called these ideas "schools," although we now think of them as philosophies.

We can divide these schools into a couple groups, not just for the sake of classification but because we're likely to see ourselves in them. It's handy to have a label to attach to our introspective activities, although it's also worthwhile to keep in mind that any given individual, while identifying with one or another label, might study under several schools.

Ultimately, the theology of the schools hinged on two simple questions:

- What is the ground of being? What is really real?

- Is the divine immanent, transcendent, or both? In other words, are the gods in the world, out of the world, or both in and out of the world?

On the ground-of-being question were usually two different answers: matter and spirit. Among the materialists were such influential schools as the Stoics and the Epicureans, who also offered useful moral teachings and practical wisdom (in fact, even though not a materialist, I regard my philosophy as heavily influenced by the Stoics and have even called myself a Stoic). On the side of spirit were other, more esoteric philosophies sometimes called "mysteries." Among these were the religious mysteries, in Late Antiquity, of the Great Mother, Dionysos, and Isis. We will explore these mysteries more fully later. Often, modern philosophers discount the mystery schools as not really being philosophies, but Algis Uždavinys has argued that far from not being philosophies, they are actually foundational practical philosophies from which our modern ideas of philosophy derive.[8]

On the question of the nature of the divine, opinions ranged from the view that the gods exist but are so separate from the world that they have no effect on it at all, to purely pantheistic views that the gods are in fact not just *in* the world but *are* the world.

These questions gave rise in the fourth century to a system of philosophy—actually, a cluster of different systems of philosophy—that tried to reason its way out of manifold conundrums and objections. We now call this system Neoplatonism, but of course they just called themselves Platonist. The practice of theurgy in Late Antiquity was in part a response to the arguments of the Neoplatonists, so it's worth understanding those arguments even if our views of the divine differ.

In brief, the Neoplatonists answered the question of the ground of being by saying that what was really real were not things but the Ideas those things

---

8 Algis Uždavinys. *Philosophy and Theurgy in Late Antiquity.* (San Rafael, CA: Sophia Perennis, 2010).

reflect. The Neoplatonists were not solipsists; they did not believe that objects only existed in your head. The Ideas they were talking about did not exist in any head, but in the Nous itself. The universe, in other words, was a consciousness, and matter merely the reflection of its thoughts. This idea is actually consistent with some contemporary philosophies and speculations about cosmology, among them panpsychism.

For the Neoplatonic philosophers, matter wasn't evil or degraded, only vaguely existent. The exercise you did in the last chapter gave you a sense of why they thought that; separated out from every concept, matter only remains a *something* that takes on impressions. Matter is only evil insofar as it distracts us from the really real, at least for most Neoplatonists.

They answered the question about the nature of the divine with a bit more complexity. Recognizing that humans had a mortal part and an eternal part, they also recognized that the gods did as well. The gods were in the world as they impressed themselves as Ideas on matter. They were also transcendent of space and time because they did not change or die. So how was it possible that the gods were both in the world and out of it? This is a question I wish to explore, because I think it's one of the central theological questions of contemporary Paganism and has important practical implications for the work of theurgy, whether or not you approach theurgy from the position of a Neoplatonist.

Transcendent and Immanent Deity: Gods and Daimones

Let's eavesdrop again on the philosopher Philanike and Euthymios, once again in Philanike's kitchen, where she is sharing freshly baked cookies with her disciple.

Philanike: So, are the cookies good?

Euthymios: They certainly are. I love it when the chocolate is all gooey.

Ph: Are those things that you love good?

Eu: Some of them. But that really belongs in the previous chapter, don't you think, with all that virtue talk?

Ph: You're right. This chapter's about the gods. So—what's a god?

Eu: You tell me.

Ph: Cheater. Am I a god?

Eu: Keep the cookies coming, and I'll deify you all right… Fine, fine, no need to give me that look. No, you are not a god.

Ph: How do you know?

Eu: You're mortal, and we call the gods "*athanatoi*," the undying ones, because they are not subject to death.

Ph: So now we're Greek again? How inconsistent. Fine: they're undying. What in the world of matter is undying?

Eu: Nothing. Everything changes and is subject to death.

Ph: So the gods are not material? What are they, then?

Eu: They must be mental—ideas, in other words, in the cosmic sense, not in the day-to-day sense of "ooh, I've got an idea! These cookies would be even better with some milk!"

Ph: Fine, I'll get you a glass. But while I do that, tell me this: if the gods are not mortal because they are outside of matter, outside therefore of time and space, then can the gods change?

Eu: I suppose not, since change implies time. And if the gods, as you say, are ideas in the cosmic sense, they are prior to time and space. Hence, they are not extended in space nor are they existent in time. So no change.

Ph: Then why bother praying? Here's your milk.

Eu: I suppose there's no purpose. Should I become an atheist, then?

Ph: If you like. There's something to be said for atheism. But consider the sun.

Eu: If I'm quiet, it's because I'm considering the sun, not because my mouth is filled with gooey cookies and milk.

Ph: So much for temperance. Does the sun get brighter or darker?

Eu: Yes, but not so quickly that we'd ever notice it.

Ph: So when we say "the sun rose today," what we mean is—?

Eu: The earth turned to face the sun.

Ph: And when we say "the sun is bright today," what we mean is—?

Eu: There are no clouds or mist between us and the sun.

Ph: So when we say "The god Helios favors me" what we mean is—?

Eu: I've turned toward Helios. I've put my mind, in the personal sense, in harmony with the cosmic idea of Helios.

Ph: So Helios never needs to change: we change, and in that change, become aware of the god.

Eu: Neat. But what about miracles?

Ph: Such as?

Eu: Prophesy. Or just garden variety religious experiences.

Ph: The gods must work in the world of matter then, after all, yes?

Eu: How can that be, since they do not die and thus are not extended in matter?

Ph: How can it be that you are mortal, yet can think immortal thoughts?

Eu: Some part of me must extend beyond space and time.

Ph: So some part of the gods must extend into space-time, or at least be able to influence it, even if not material.

Eu: So the gods, like me, have bodies?

Ph: What's the sun, if not the body of Helios? But of course, Helios has lots of bodies. He's in the sun, in gold, in lions, in all sorts of things.

Eu: That sounds like a topic for another chapter, maybe chapter 3.

The late Neoplatonic philosopher Sallustius was an interesting figure. He was one of the leading Pagan thinkers under the reign of the last Pagan emperor of Rome, Julian the Philosopher (sometimes called Julian the Apostate by those with a different set of tools to grind). Sallustius struggled with this notion, that the gods were perfect and unchanging yet affected the world and were affected by our prayers and offerings. If you accept perfect, unchanging deities, there's no point to prayer or theurgy at all. (Of course, you could reject perfect, unchanging deities, but Sallustius didn't want to do that, because he felt it would compromise logic: after all, a thing can only change to become better, in which case it was not perfect before, or to become worse, in which case it stops being perfect. But he refuses to establish why the gods are perfect, insisting that it's an axiom that they must be.) He writes in his "On the Gods and the World":

> It is impious to suppose that the Divine is affected for good or ill by human things. The Gods are always good and always do good and never harm, being always in the same state and like themselves. The truth simply is that, when we are good, we are joined to the Gods by our likeness to them; when bad, we are separated from them by our unlikeness. And when we live according to virtue we cling to the gods, and when we become evil we make the gods our enemies—not because they are angered against us, but because our sins prevent the light of the gods from shining upon us, and put us in communion with spirits of punishment. And if by prayers and sacrifices we find forgiveness of

> sins, we do not appease or change the gods, but by what we do and by our turning towards the Divine we heal our own badness and so enjoy again the goodness of the gods. To say that God turns away from the evil is like saying that the sun hides himself from the blind.[9]

So it is the act of worship that draws the worshiper to the gods, not the gods to the worshiper. Theurgy, therefore, isn't like thaumaturgy, in which I ask a spirit to act upon the world. It's changing oneself to be the sort of person who achieves the relevant desires. For example, if I do a love spell, I might make someone love me. But if I perform relevant theurgy, I become a person who is loved. The difference is subtle but transformative.

Yet we live in a world of time and space, so how can the gods act at all in such a world even just to help us change ourselves if they are always outside of it? The same question puzzled thinkers like Sallustius, but the answer is clear when we consider ourselves: we, too, exist in the world of time and space, and also at the same time we exist outside of it. We have an eternal part and a temporal part and so do the gods. The gods have—or rather, are—daimones which act upon the world.

The Greek word *daimon* is the word from which we get our "demon," but it has a long history of referring not to evil demons but to spirits, some good, some bad, that interact with reality. The gods themselves are called daimones by ancient writers, and the line between daimones and deities is a fuzzy one. Plutarch went so far as to imagine that Apollo, for example, was an office, and mortal spirits filled that office in turn.

Of course, this isn't the only ancient view of deity. We modern Pagans might be more comfortable with the Roman view, which held that the gods were *numina* (sing. *numen*). A numen was the underlying reality, the force beneath any phenomenon. Here, rather than having to wrangle with the

9 Gilbert Murray. *The Five Stages of Greek Religion.* (Boston: Beacon Press, 1955), 218. Accessed 10 May 2013, http://www.gutenberg.org/files/30250/30250-h/30250-h.htm#Page_218

sticky issue of time and space (a fun thing to wrangle with, but with only some practical effects on our practice) we can conceive of the gods as animistic forces existent in our world of daily experience. But this view, too, smacks of Platonism. After all, how do these forces interact with matter? We can't measure, taste, hear, or smell the gods. Yet as Seneca the Younger writes, we feel the awe of the gods in the presence of nature:

> If you have ever come upon a grove that is thick with ancient trees which rise far above their usual height and block the view of the sky with their cover of intertwining branches, then the loftiness of the forest and the seclusion of the spot and your wonder at the unbroken shade in the mist of open space will create in you a feeling of the divine.[10]

How is this possible? The gods can be said to animate matter, and the word "animate" comes from from *anima*, "soul." The gods are the souls of matter.

In the Neoplatonic system, each god can be seen as threefold. First is the god as an idea in the Nous, pure and changeless as an equation, and beyond time and space. Let's take a deity like Apollo. In the world of Ideas, what does Apollo look like? In computer science, we now have intelligent algorithms not quite conscious but capable of doing complex decision making that looks a lot like intelligence. They are not even computer programs so much as mathematical expressions. Imagine Apollo as an algorithm—hardly the inspiring religious figure we might pray to! But consider how complex such an algorithm must be in the world of Ideas. It must contain all the laws of harmony, the behavior of light, beauty, standards of truth—all those things under the domain of Apollo.

Of course, I don't mean to imply that the Apollo of the world of Ideas is an equation or an algorithm in the literal sense. I wish only to create an

10 Valerie M. Warrior. *Roman Religion: A Sourcebook.* (Newburyport, MA: Focus, 2002). 2.

example of how a changeless thing—an algorithm in this case—can be said to exhibit the ability to "think." It's not thinking as we imagine it with our minds locked in time. But it isn't a contradiction to say that the gods exist in the world of Ideas outside of time yet still remain conscious beings rather than mere laws of the universe.

When these deities interact with matter, we have the part of the gods that are in relation to the world of psyche. Here we have the deities that ensoul matter, the daimones of the gods. From Apollo come daimones that govern music: Harmonia, for example, who is both a goddess and a part of Apollo. These are the personal gods, with names and images, and the worship of these gods is quite a bit easier than those abstract deity-concepts in the world of Ideas. And, in fact, there are daimones who simply take the name of Apollo, because they are clear reflections of that deity in the world of the psyche.

Finally, in the world of matter, in hyle, the gods manifest by imposing shape upon things. A piece of beautifully played music, here, can embody Apollo, as can a shaft of light. We will explore these manifestations of deity in a later chapter in greater depth, as such manifestations are useful tools for contacting the divine.

These levels of reality are not dimensions, but we can imagine an analogy in geometry. Take a cube and imagine that you slice across it in a plane. If you could live within that plane, you would see one of the two-dimensional shapes created by slicing a cube: a square, a tetrahedron, a number of other possibilities. Much like the shadows in the cave, the cube itself remains the same but we can turn our plane through it to give the impression of change and multiplicity. The daimones are like slices across the multidimensional forms of the gods.

While there are transcendent gods who exist outside the world of time and space, there are also gods—the "same" gods—that reach into our world of matter. Just like us, they have an eternal part and a physical part. To say that the daimones are mortal is to say that they, like the universe, change: when the universe suffers heat-death, they will fade away, but the eternal gods will remain because in their perspective, the universe has suffered, will suffer, is suffering its end, and its beginning.

I would contend that what slices across the unchanging forms of the gods to give the daimones form is the human mind. It is we who give the gods forms. The syncretic reflex of ancient people, who went to the north of Europe, for example, and met the god Odhinn and called him "the Germanic Mercury," is actually a valid one. As modern scholars, we sometimes sneer at it. After all, we say, the cultural forces that shaped Odhinn are very different from those that shaped Mercury, and if we look at the mythology and functions of those different gods, we find myriad differences, and so on. But perhaps that urge to syncretism wasn't so much an imperial leveling-out of religion but a recognition of a central truth: that Odhinn is a slice across the same vast divine Idea that Mercurius is.

Let me address a very popular theological idea in Pagan circles: the idea that we create the gods. Partially, I think this idea resonates with Pagans because it conforms to "enlightened" ideas about science and cultural studies. I also partially suspect it is appealing for the power it gives the worshiper, and partially, because perhaps it has some small part of truth. I think we do give the daimones their forms and names, just as we give our friends names by which we call them. But just like our friends, the daimones and the gods behind them exist before we do. Logic demands it. Something that creates something else is prior than that thing: a child comes after her parents, a computer program comes after the programmer, and so on. Yet the gods are prior to us: they have power and spiritual force well in excess of ours and existed before us. So how could we create them? Moreover, the gods are the divine ideas behind objects in the world. Helios (or Sunna or Sol) is the divine force behind the sun. Did we create the sun? Certainly not. So we did not create the gods, nor do they live on our prayers (this idea is easy to trace back to certain fantasy novels, hardly great sources of theology).

In conclusion, then, what we work with in theurgy are these culturally defined deities: entities to which we give names and forms. But we do not create them. They arise from divine figures external to space-time, Ideas in the world of Ideas. What we imagine as gods, as beings who move, think, and act in space-time are daimones of the unchanging gods in the world of Ideas. Through these temporal daimones, we can begin to approach the abstract and changeless gods. In practice, this can look quite a lot like Pagan worship as it has always been done: personal prayers to personal deities. But behind it is a deeper significance.

Pantheons

Every culture takes a census of their gods, which is one way they give them shape and form. These censuses are called pantheons, from Greek roots meaning "all the gods." In practice, rarely does a pantheon list all the gods except in rigidly controlled cultures, examples of which I cannot easily call to mind. Gods are always coming into a culture or going out, depending on the needs of the people and the ways in which they perceive the reflections of the gods in their souls. In fact, for cultures that spanned a long period of time such as Greek culture, it's hard to pin down one particular pantheon (and in fact it's kind of ridiculous to write "Greek culture," since that refers to cultures as different as Athens and Sparta, or Hellenic Alexandria and Bronze Age Achaeans). So any attempt to discuss the pantheons of particular religious groups will result in a more or less clumsy leveling. I want to make it clear how clumsy this leveling is because otherwise we might forget that we're leaving gods out of our lists. And because this isn't an exhaustive encyclopedia of ancient religious practices, I am limiting myself to some subpantheons in each larger pantheon.

I want to talk about two different pantheons, which for the sake of convenience I'll call the Egyptian pantheon and the Greco-Roman pantheon. These terms alone are a good example of the clumsiness of such a project. And let me hedge one final time: I am approaching these pantheons from a theurgic perspective. The practices I describe in this book are not an attempt to reconstruct the ancient religion of Egypt or the late Roman Empire. I am not even trying to reconstruct the theurgic practices of Late Antiquity, since I have no problem including modern ideas about theology and spirituality.

The reason I address these two pantheons is that they were the central pantheons of the theurgy of Late Antiquity. Yet we have certain advantages over our ancient friends. For example, we understand some of the cultural and historical reality of Egypt better than Egyptians of the fifth century did because unlike them, we can read hieroglyphic writing. The secret of hieroglyphic writing was lost in about the fourth century, when most Egyptian was written in a derived but very different script called Demotic. The ability to read the monuments of ancient Egypt was only restored in the late nineteenth century. So we may have an understanding of ancient Egyptian religion that perhaps the Egyptians of Late Antiquity no longer did.

The Ennead of Heliopolis

Heliopolis, a city on the Nile delta, thrived throughout the Old and Middle Kingdom periods of ancient Egypt, from about 2700 BCE to about 1700 BCE. Heliopolis is its Greek name; the Egyptians called it something like *Iwnw.* The religious beliefs of Egypt were not uniform across the country, and every city had its own cosmology, patron gods, and so forth. The religious practices of Heliopolis were highly developed and carefully thought out, so the gods of this city ended up having an important place throughout Egypt as well as a large influence on the larger Greco-Roman world. The nine gods worshiped at Heliopolis were called the Ennead, a Greek word meaning "collection of nine." They were far from the only pantheon, however, as different places had different arrangements, replacing Atum with Ptah for example, or adding Re to the mix. Don't get the impression that this is a monolithic, formulaic pantheon, or self-contained in any way. It's a snapshot of the religious beliefs of a very old and longstanding culture at one particular time.[11]

---

11 John Baines, Leonard H. Lesko, and David P. Silverman. *Religion in Ancient Egypt: Gods, Myths, and Personal Practice,* ed. Byron E. Shafer. (Ithaca, NY: Cornell University Press, 1991).

The chief of these gods is Atum, who is often depicted in art as a human wearing a red and white crown. Atum rose from the chaos of Nun to bring light to the world. Later, he became associated with Re, a solar god, hence giving Heliopolis its Greek name: "City of the Sun." Atum is self-created. This is the god of creation and order, symbolized by light. According to mythology, Atum masturbated and from his semen created two new gods, Tefnut and Shu.[12]

Tefnut is the goddess of moisture. She is associated with another goddess, Maat, the goddess of rightness and balance. The king's role in Egyptian politics and religions was to uphold Maat, or justice, and everyone whose heart is weighed at death is weighed in the scale of Maat, against a feather. Tefnut is also associated with Atum's eye, or the eye of Re. Since the hieroglyph for "to do" is also the symbol of the eye, this links her to Atum's action and efficacy in the world. With her brother Shu, she is also associated with time and eternity.[13]

Shu is a god of air and wind. Shu is also a kind of creator god, in that he makes existence possible by separating Nut and Geb, as explained below. Shu is often depicted with a feather on his head, just as Maat is, which links him and his sister Tefnut to the concept of primal rightness that Maat represents.

Shu and Tefnut together gave birth to two additional gods: Geb and Nut. Geb is the god of the earth, and Nut is the goddess of the sky. Geb is usually depicted as a reclining man with an erection pointed at the sky. Nut is usually depicted as a woman arched over the sky, the stars and sun and moon on her body, with her fingers and toes touching the earth at the farthest reaches of the cardinal points. According to the mythology of Heliopolis, when she and Geb were born, they copulated so fiercely and

---

12 Geraldine Pinch. *Egyptian Mythology: A Guide to the Gods, Goddesses, and Traditions of Ancient Egypt.* (Oxford: Oxford University Press, 2002), 111–112.

13 Pinch. *Egyptian Mythology*, 197.

continuously that Shu separated them, pulling her up into the sky. Nut and Geb then gave birth to four gods: Seth, Osiris, Isis, and Nephthys.[14]

Seth is sometimes regarded as an evil god, but there are instances of his worship and even a few kings who took his name. Seth's domain is destruction such as the destructive forces of weather in the desert, and he serves good by defending the sun from demonic attack. He's the god of the desert itself, and in that role can be invoked for protection from its dangers.[15] Seth is sometimes depicted as a creature that looks a bit like a greyhound with triangular ears, wider at the top than the bottom. Of course no such creature exists in Egypt, but it's possible that his image represents an extinct animal or cryptid.[16] The *was* scepter, a symbol of power, has Seth's head on it.

Nephthys, of these four, is the least well understood. Her name in Egyptian is Nebt-Het, which is sometimes written on her headdress in hieroglyphs. Her name means "Lady of the House" or "Lady of the Temple," and she is at least nominally Seth's wife, although she does not support his violence toward Osiris. She joined her sister Isis in mourning Osiris's death after Seth murdered him.[17]

Osiris began, apparently, as a deity of vegetation. Later, he became associated with embalming and rebirth. He is usually depicted as a mummy wearing a crown and holding the crook and flail.[18] His skin is often black—a color of fertility and growth in Egypt, which in the original language of the country was called *Kemt* or *Kemet*, "the black land." Sometimes, his skin is the green of new vegetation. Overall, Osiris is a god of life and the cycles of life. His cult is one of the most important in ancient Egyptian religion, although outside of Egypt two other gods, his wife and his son, take on greater importance.

---

14 Pinch. *Egyptian Mythology,* 174.

15 Pinch. *Egyptian Mythology,* 191.

16 Richard H. Wilkinson. *The Complete Gods and Goddesses of Ancient Egypt.* (Cairo: American University in Cairo Press, 2003), 198–199.

17 Wilkinson. *The Complete Gods and Goddesses of Ancient Egypt,* 159–160.

18 Wilkinson. *The Complete Gods and Goddesses of Ancient Egypt,* 119.

I have saved his sister-wife Isis for last in my list because of her great importance in later Roman mystery cults. To the Egyptians she was a mother goddess and a goddess of magic and resurrection. She resurrected Osiris from the dead using the name of power she tricked from Atum-Ra, so she has the power of *heka*, or magical speech. She is also the mother of Horus, a sun-deity who in later mythologies avenges his father Osiris upon Seth.[19] But her main popularity came in the Roman Empire when her cult became a Roman mystery religion, well after the heyday of Heliopolis.

This popular mystery religion offered salvation through initiation. Apuleius's *The Golden Ass*, a comedic novel written in the second century, is partially a tract for the Isis cult. In it, a young man named Lucius desires to experience magic. He gets his hands on a magical ointment and upon using it accidentally turns himself into an ass. He can transform back, he learns, if he simply eats a rose; but a series of unlikely coincidences continuously prevents him from ingesting the magical remedy. Ultimately he is saved through the divine intervention of Isis, and he joins her mystery religion.[20] While this book is obviously a comedy, the religious and didactic elements are hard to deny, and Apuleius implies that we can be transformed from our bestial state by the intervention of the goddess.

Horus, too, gains a certain popularity outside of Egypt as a solar deity. Within Egypt, he is worshiped as a god of the sky, of the sun, and of kingship. He seems to be a possible amalgam of several falcon-deities.[21] Outside of Egypt, he is most often depicted as the child of Isis, and becomes almost a symbol of her motherhood and nurturance. He also appears in a number of other forms, such Horus the Child (Harpocrates), who is depicted as a naked child representing the renewal of the universe. He is called upon in a

---

19 Pinch. *Egyptian Mythology*, 150.

20 Apuleius. *The Golden Ass*. trans. Robert Graves. (New York: Farrer, Straus, Giroux, 2009).

21 Wilkinson. *The Complete Gods and Goddesses of Ancient Egypt*, 202–203.

number of spells to cure the bite of poisonous animals.[22] Horus is not considered part of the Ennead, but as child of Isis and Osiris and enemy of his uncle Seth, he is often depicted along with images of the Ennead.

But let's return to the Ennead, looking at it as a whole. What does this particular company of gods tell us about the nature of the divine, not just from the Egyptian perspective but from our own, later understanding? First, we see that the gods are arranged in a geometrical order:

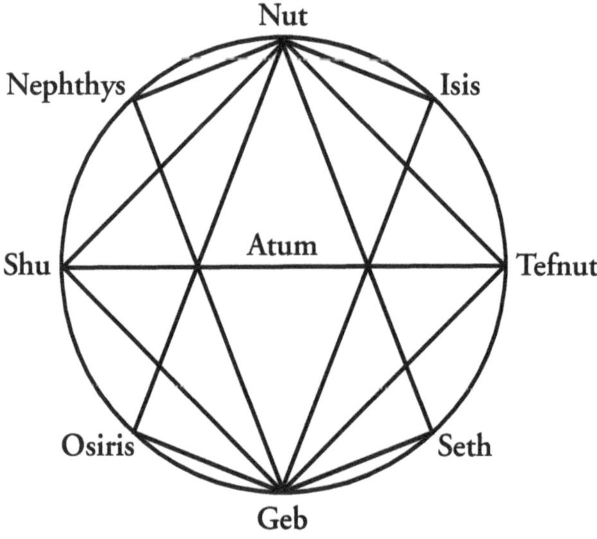

Fig. 4: The Ennead

Each of the lines indicates a god who produces another god. Atum is in the center, unproduced by anything. He produces, of himself, two gods: Tefnut and Shu. Now, each of the gods produced after Tefnut and Shu have two lines leading to them: one from the mother, one from the father. Gods are placed opposite their mates. This diagram illustrates the admirable symmetry of the arrangement of the Ennead.

22 Pinch. *Egyptian Mythology,* 146.

It is clear that this Ennead was selected to slice up the experience of a typical Egyptian at this time. Earth (Geb) and sky (Nut) are the pair between which everything else happens. These arise out of two primal elements: moisture (Tefnut) and air (Shu). We have a god of cultivation (Osiris) and one of the desert (Seth). Finally, we have two aspects of motherhood: one that gives life (Isis) and one that guards, protects, and nurtures us into old age and death (Nephthys).

We could abstract these gods further, and stretching back all the way to Late Antiquity mystics have certainly done so. Atum is the primal light, who gave birth to two movements: drawing together (in Tefnut) and separating apart (in Shu). We have above and below in Nut and Geb. Two types of earth, the wild earth of the desert (Seth) and the cultivated earth of the Nile (Osiris) are set forth below, while above we have two goddesses: one governing life and magic and one governing death and protection. Ultimately, the entire arrangement is a miniature precis of the experience of ancient Egyptian life. Every experience has a place in this divine scheme.

Greco-Roman Pantheons—Dodecatheon

The geometrical symmetry and symbolic completeness of these nine deities—which I have only sketched—shows a sophistication in ancient Egyptian religion that impressed Greco-Roman theurgists who sought such a sophistication for their native gods as well. Yet the imposed order of the Egyptian deities is a result of a trained priesthood living in a longstanding theocratic totalitarian society. The Greeks and later Romans who devised the Greco-Roman gods, while having a "state religion," sometimes lacked the "state" on which to hang it. Until the Hellenistic period, the Greeks did not have a unified country but a collection of loosely affiliated and culturally connected city-states. Only when Alexander conquered the known world did the Greeks come under anything like a central authority. And Alexander, while occasionally worshiped as a god, had no interest in establishing a universal religion. Similarly, the Romans, while having kings in the beginning, moved toward a republic in 508 BCE. While there were state positions of religious authority such as the pontifex maximus and various other priesthoods, there was little hegemony in place to establish or control doctrine.

Despite this anarchic theology, the notion of a company of twelve main gods arose early in Athens, around the sixth century BCE or so, although it may well have had older roots. This scheme wasn't meant to be all-inclusive (important deities like Hades are absent from some conceptions of it), but it was seen as an auspicious number of gods to sit on Olympus. These twelve gods consist, most often, of the list that follows. Quite a bit of controversy arises as to whether or not Hades is in the list, whether Hestia is, or whether she has been replaced by Dionysos. I will address that question later, but you'll notice that my list of twelve gods has fourteen entries, and this controversy—not a failure of my mathematical ability—is the reason. I've added their Roman names after their Greek names to simplify later reference to Roman deities, but the character of the Roman gods is not always the same as the character of the Greek gods, as will be explained as we explore each deity.

Zeus (Iuppiter or Iove) is the king of the gods, usually depicted as a bearded patriarch. He is often holding a thunderbolt, his weapon. The eagle is sacred to Zeus. In mythology he is sometimes a bit of a philanderer, to put it mildly. In religious practice, however, he was the god of justice and good order, and the special protector of strangers and guests.

Hera (Iuno) is the queen of the gods, Zeus's sister-wife, often shown with a peacock. She is the goddess of marriage and social order. In mythology, she's cast as a jealous wife punishing those whom Zeus pursues, but in religious practice her cult seems to have regarded her as less bitter—but then, they also regard Zeus as less philandering. The moral is this: the myths are not accurate guides to the characters of the gods as religious figures.

Apollo (Apollo) is often conflated, in later mythology with Helios (Sol), the god of the sun. But Apollo's domain is larger than that: as a god of light, music, and beauty, he is often painted with a lyre and a crown of laurel, a plant particularly sacred to him. He was also the god of plague and the healing thereof, as well as an important figure of prophesy. His temple at

Delphi acted as the closest thing the ancient world had to a central religious authority able to make declarations of doctrine.

Artemis (Diana), like her brother Apollo, is often conflated with Selene (Luna), the goddess of the moon. But in earlier times, she was the goddess of the hunt and of magic. Her sacred city, Ephesos, has a famous statue of her with many breasts (or maybe they're eggs). Her myths describe her staunch virginity and her loyalty to her brother.

Ares (Mars) is one of those gods whose character differs dramatically depending on whether we ascribe to the Greek or Roman view. In the Greek view, he is an animalistic and bloodthirsty god of war, whose worship was rarely undertaken as a practical cultus. Mars, on the other hand, was central to Rome: as patron of agriculture and empire, he was the protective force that established Rome's expanse. Where Ares is a force of destruction (in Homer, he changes sides in a battle because it looks like the other side is winning), Mars is an agricultural deity and thus a god of civilization and order.

Athene (Minerva) is another virginal goddess, born from Zeus's head alone. She too is a goddess of war, but also a goddess of civilization and wisdom and the patron of Athens. In both the Greek and Roman myths, she is known for her wisdom and modesty, although from time to time—as all the gods—her myths describe her as potentially a dangerous force. When Arachne brags excessively about her skill as a weaver, for example, it is Athene who turns her into a spider.

Aphrodite (Venus) is a goddess of love and beauty over all. In the myths she is somewhat fickle, chasing after Ares while married to Hephaistos, but her nature is always to bring together the disparate. Her symbol is the zona or girdle, which binds together the entire universe; as Aphrodite Ourania, she is a goddess of the sky, and the zona is either the Milky Way or the ecliptic of the fixed stars. In the Symposium, Plato has some of the guests at the philosophic drinking party point out that she has a dual nature: a heavenly love and a common love. She rules, then, pure philosophical love as well as the love of sexual attraction.

Hephaistos (Vulcan) is unusual among Greek gods for having a physical defect: he is lame. Some myths suggest that he was thrown from Olympus by an enraged Hera, while others suggest that he was born from Hera's head just as Athene was born from Zeus's head. He is the god of skill and art as well as fire. The Roman Vulcan was said to live inside of volcanoes, whose eruptions were the stoking of his furnace. He is married to Aphrodite, but she was not always faithful to him in the myths.

Demeter (Ceres) is the goddess of agriculture and nature. She is an earth goddess, whose central myth (and later, a mystery cult) was the kidnapping of her daughter Persephone (Proserpina) by Hades. The earth's cycles are attributed to her pining for or rejoicing in the presence of her daughter, who is bound to dwell for half the year in the realm of the dead with Hades. During this time, the earth is fallow and nothing grows, but when her daughter returns, the earth gives forth life again. She is often seen holding a sheaf of grain.

Poseidon (Neptunus) is the god of the sea and the shaker of the earth. Obviously, he was an important deity to the seagoing Greeks and Romans. He is also the god of horses and, by extension, charioteers. His ire against Odysseus is the driving conflict of Homer's *Odyssey*. His weapon is a trident, and the horse is sacred to him.

Hermes (Mercurius) is the messenger of the gods, and among the Roman gods he is also a deity of commerce. Small statues of him in the form of pillars adorned with his face and an erect phallus were often placed at the crossroads. Called Herms, these pillars were meant to bless and protect the roads and those who travel on them. Hence, he is also a god of travel and transportation. Later he was identified with logos, the ratio that lay under existence, and in that capacity becomes a cosmic deity of order and magic. His emblem is a wand with wings at the top, called a caduceus.

Hestia (Vesta) is a controversial deity. While included in most early lists of the twelve, she is omitted in favor of Dionysos or Hades in later mythology. She is the goddess of the hearth and home, while the Roman Vesta is the protector goddess of the sacred city hearth, whose temple is the origin of the hearthfires of every home in Rome. The hearth itself is her altar. In Rome, her priestesses, the Vestal Virgins, were sworn to virginity and charged with the important task of protecting her sacred fire.

Sometimes, Hestia (Vesta) is replaced by **Dionysos,** a god who is half mortal and half divine. An important mystery religion of Dionysos was established late in antiquity, but even his earliest worship was a relatively late innovation to Greek religion. He is a god of wine, but of course wine is a metaphor for divine inspiration, and Plato allocates one of the three kinds of divine "madness" to him. He is often depicted holding the thyrsis, a wand with a tip shaped like a pinecone. I am not the first author to point out the similarity of this sacred object to a part of the male anatomy.

Other times, Hestia (Vesta) is replaced by **Hades.** Plato at least apparently wished to worship Hades among the twelve, as he assigned him a month in his calendar. Hades is the god of the dead, of course, but he is not death (that is Thanatos, one of his daimones). He is also called Pluton, which means "wealth" because as a chthonic deity it is assumed he has control over the treasures of the earth.

One theurgic way of analyzing the roles of the deities is to assign them cosmological and spiritual functions. Sallustius argues as follows:

> These are four actions, each of which has a beginning, middle, and end, consequently there must be twelve Gods governing the world.
>
> Those who make the world are Zeus, Poseidon, and Hephaistos; those who animate it are Demeter, Hera, and Artemis; those who harmonize it are Apollo, Aphrodite, and Hermes; those who watch over it are Hestia, Athena, and Ares.[23]

---

23 Gilbert Murray. *The Five Stages of Greek Religion.* (Boston: Beacon Press, 1955). Accessed 10 May 2013, http://www.gutenberg.org/files/30250/30250-h/30250-h.htm#Page_207

This passage is a productive one for meditation. For example, when we imagine the creation of anything, we can see that there are three stages: beginning the project, making the project, finishing the project. In the beginning, we lay down the laws of creation according to Zeus. In the making of the object, we draw up impressions and materials from the depths of Poseidon. At the end of the project, we polish it and file off the rough edges as Hephaistos. Similarly, the process of ensoulment or animation follows the three stages of Demeter, Hera, and Artemis, and so on. I'll stop there. To fully elucidate these patterns would rob the theurgist of productive meditations.

The Hermetic Planetary Gods

Astrologers and most magicians are familiar with one final pantheon, that of the seven planetary gods. This pantheon is ancient and survived even the rise of Christianity, because Neoplatonic Christian astrologers and magicians made use of and even personified them as divine forces under the control of the one God of Christianity. Much of Western ceremonial magic is built on this arrangement, and these gods—unlike the twelve or the Ennead—lack mythology. They are purely philosophical, and therefore well-suited to higher forms of theurgy.

Most of my readers are already familiar with the seven, which are Sol, Luna, Mercury, Venus, Mars, Jupiter, and Saturn. These deities are essentially a solar pantheon, with the sun as a central figure or "light" in the midst of them, and the moon or Luna as a consort to Sol. These gods have the same name as some of the twelve, but it's important to recognize their origin to see that they are not, in all ways, the same gods.

The seven planetary gods are one of the oldest pantheons, stretching back to the first written records to Sumer. The Akkadians were a Semitic people who supplanted Sumerian culture around 2270 BCE. They regarded Sumerian culture with a great deal of respect, adopting their writing system and many of their cultural beliefs and practices, including astrology. The Greeks identified the planets with their own gods and gave them names reflective of that identification by the fourth century BCE. The Romans, in an early instance of the syncretism that characterizes Roman approaches to comparative theology, renamed the planets with the names of their cognate deities, and these are the names that we have inherited in English.

Early astrologers observed that only seven visible heavenly bodies moved against the backdrop of the fixed stars in a regular pattern. Of course, other bodies such as comets and meteors also move against the backdrop of fixed stars, but their movement is irregular and unpredictable. The Babylonians took great care in observing not just the paths of the planets but also the events that occurred on earth in concert with those motions. In many ways, this foundation of astrology was eminently empirical, several millennia before the invention of the empirical method. Through this careful observation of heavenly patterns and earthly correlations, the Babylonians assigned personalities and deities to the moving stars or planets.

This observation served as the foundation of our seven-day week. Each of the days of the week is named after one of the gods. If you speak a Romance language, you may notice a clearer correspondence—for example, the Spanish *miércoles* for Wednesday is clearly derived from Mercury. In English, our day names derive from the Germanic gods associated with the Roman planetary gods, in another example of Roman imperial syncretism. Hence, Monday is the moon. Tuesday is Tiw, associated with Mars. Wednesday is Woden, associated with Mercury. Thursday is Thor, associated with Jupiter. Friday is Freya, associated with Venus. Saturday is borrowed directly from the Latin Saturn, and Sunday is, obviously, associated with Sol, through the Norse solar goddess Sunne.

The order and arrangement of these seven planetary powers is reflective of a long-lasting and influential cosmology, or symbolic structure of the universe. In this structure, the earth is in the center of nested crystal spheres. The sphere closest to the Earth is that of Luna. Beyond that is Mercury, Venus, Sol, Mars, Jupiter, Saturn, and the fixed stars. These planets roll about in their crystal orbits according to a fixed scheme of cycles and—identified later—epicycles. Of course, modern understandings of our solar system do not paint such a pretty picture of the universe, but as a metaphor for the operation of these planetary forces, this cosmology still has much use in modern magic.

I suppose it's worth digressing for a moment to point out that while I and pretty much everyone I know fully accepts our contemporary understanding of the astronomy of our solar system, many of us also subscribe to this system as a kind of truth. The planetary cosmology is a psychological and spiritual model of the organization of seven forces or kinds of thoughts in the Nous. They are real but not physical: in fact, they are real because they are not physical. Of course, I don't believe that the Curiosity rover on its way to the lump of rock called Mars punched through crystal spheres. If I wish, however, to arrive at the psychological truth represented by the planetary god Mars which manifests among other things as a lump of rock in our solar system visible from the Earth, then I expect to rise through crystal spheres indeed.

This organization of the seven planets describes a particular progression of ideas in the Nous, the mind of the universe. How this works out requires understanding the nature of these seven gods and how they differ from the descriptions of the gods of the same name given earlier. I see these deities as more abstract and therefore more useful in a wide variety of magic. These seven planets can be arranged in three pairs with one left over.

Let's start with the leftover one first. Mercury as the messenger of the gods is also the mediator of the planets. Sallustius lists Hermes among his harmonizing deities, and here it harmonizes each of the planets with each of the other planets. The planet Mercury is that which communicates, both in the sense of transferring information and in the sense of achieving communion. Since Mercury governs communication, it can be seen as the planet of the mind and the special patron of magic, since all magic is an act of communication.

Sol and Luna are the two lights, both approximately the same size (which by the way is a rather remarkable coincidence; there's no good reason why our satellite should appear the same size as the sun). Where the sun is constant (one of the solar deities of Late Antiquity is called *Sol Invictus*, the Unconquerable Sun), the moon waxes and wanes. In the middle ages, the moon was the symbol of inconstancy and change. As the Carmina Burana, a series of profane songs written in Latin by a group of monks in the eleventh and twelfth centuries, put it: "Oh, Fortune, you are variable like the moon, always waxing and waning. Detestable life! Now it's oppressing, now it's comforting, as the play of its mind takes it. Poverty. Power. It melts them like ice."[24] This is the equivalent of medieval emo music, but it illustrates the changeability of the moon in distinction to the constance of the sun. The sun as the source of life and light is associated with the sense of self, the soul (animus), in astrology. The moon, as the reflection of the sun, is the external personality and the feminine soul (anima). Of course, these are modern interpretations; Sumerians didn't have Jung. In older texts, the sun is a symbol of power and authority, while the moon represents changeability and reflection.

The sun has a particular place in theurgy, as Plato uses it as a metaphor for the Good, or the One, that underlies all other reality. He describes our apprehension of the good as a person who sees an object—let's say an apple—from the light of the sun. The sun casts light on the apple, the eye takes in that light (well, we know this now—Plato didn't), and creates an image in the mind, which is knowledge of the apple. Similarly, the Good casts a certain light, the Nous, which our mind takes in and creates images out of, those images being the philosophical concepts that give rise to our knowledge of the Good.

Venus and Mars are opposites in that where Venus brings things together, Mars pulls them apart. One can see these two planets as ideas about relationships: Venus is harmonious, Mars contentious. But it would be too simple to say that Mars is malefic and Venus is benefic. In fact, too much harmony can be a symptom of weakness, and Mars can serve to strengthen and energize a situation.

Jupiter and Saturn, similarly, expand and contract respectively. Jupiter's expansive idea is represented in our human dealings with generosity and liberality, while Saturn establishes boundaries and borders. We can roughly think of these two planets as representing public policy where Venus and

---

24 My translation.

Mars represent individual relationships. Of course, again, Jupiter's expansiveness can lead to overgrowth and profligacy, while Saturn's borders can define and give structure to the otherwise structureless.

Other than astrology, what can we do with these seven powers? One use of the planets is as sources of meditation in the order of their crystal spheres, a process called "rising on the spheres." One begins with Luna, imagining images of changeability and reflection. Then one moves up to Mercury, and so on, eventually identifying oneself with the fixed stars of the zodiac. Another use, aside from this contemplative practice, is the practical magical use of the planets in creating talismans and amulets, a use that will be addressed in greater detail later in this book.

The Liminal Gods

Additional gods exist outside of these pantheons but are important because they are intermediaries between realms. The goal of theurgy itself is to unite realms, so these liminal deities can act as bridges and helpers. I will examine two particularly important liminal gods, referenced in many works of theurgy.

Hekate

Originally a goddess of the moon and perhaps an epithet of Artemis, the goddess Hekate became associated with crossroads, gateways, and protection from evil spirits in Late Antiquity. She is often depicted as a woman bearing a torch, or as a triple goddess facing in three different directions at once. She is associated with the Roman goddess Trivia, goddess of crossroads, but she has a much greater importance in theurgy than Trivia. Her role is as an intermediary, or key-holder, between realms, and in later depictions she sometimes appears with keys, much as does Janus, whom we will discuss in a moment.[25]

The Chaldean oracles describe her as an intermediary between the sensible world—the world of matter that we perceive with our senses—and the intelligible world—the world of Ideas we perceive through pure reason. As

25 Sarah Iles Johnston. *Hekate Soteira.* (Atlanta, GA: Scholars Press, 1990), 42.

such, she is the soul of the world, because the soul itself serves to link these two realms. The later Christian Neoplatonic idea of the Anima Mundi can be seen as a reworking of Hekate to fit into Christian theology.

Hekate also serves as a psychopomp, having led—by some accounts—Kore into the underworld to become Persephone, the queen of Hades. Hades is sometimes described as the world of matter, so this myth is an allegorical account of the process of animation of matter. Hekate brings soul, as Kore, down into matter, and also reconciled soul and matter so that in their marriage the soul is elevated as Persephone.

As befits a liminal goddess, traditional rituals define Hekate's role in two ways. Hekate figures in theurgic rites as a doorway into the intelligible world, as well as in thaumaturgical rites as an ally and queen of witches. As I will argue later, the thaumaturgical and theurgic are not so sharply defined as one might think. As a thaumaturgical deity, she acts as a deliverer of messages to the world of Ideas. She works in both directions, then: not merely leading the ideas down into manifestation, but leading the theurgist and his or her will back upward into the world of Ideas. This two-way flow of information would have struck traditional Platonists and even some Neoplatonists as impious or illogical. How, after all, could an idea from the many have an impact on the Ideas of the One? The answer, of course, is in the transformation of the theurgist: the ideas of the theurgist become the Ideas of the One, alleviating any paradox of imperfect notions affecting perfect Ideas. In other words, it is not that we affect the gods with our spells but that we change ourselves and our reality in harmony with those gods.

Janus

Janus is the Roman god of doorways and beginnings, usually depicted with two faces that look in opposite directions. As a god of doorways, he is literally a liminal god, as the word "liminal" comes from a root meaning "threshold." Roman rituals usually begin with an invocation to Ianus Pater (Father Janus) or Ianus Bifrons (Two-Faced Janus). In this way, Janus opens the doorway to the gods during the ritual. Like most liminal gods, there are few myths about Janus himself, but his worship is widespread. Perhaps this lack of myth is a function of his not being borrowed from the Greeks, like most Roman mythology. Janus is clearly a native Roman, perhaps derived from an Etruscan god.

Proclus offers a hymn to Hekate that makes an interesting and unexpected connection between her and Janus. He begins and ends the hymn with this refrain:

> Hail, mother of the gods, many-named and giving
> forth beautiful children: Hail, Hekate, standing by
> the door, mighty one: but also, likewise Hail Janus
> the forefather, eternal Zeus. Hail, highest Zeus![26]

He clearly associates Hekate with Janus, and at the same time assigns to both the role of demiurge or world-maker. This association is unusual, but it does lend support to the idea that Janus himself may have been invoked in theurgic rites in the same way that Hekate was: as an intermediary between the sensible and intelligible worlds. Proclus also identifies Janus with Zeus, which is certainly not the usual association (which would be, of course, that Iuppiter is the Roman Zeus). This identification illustrates how important Proclus believed Janus to be to his system of theurgy.

The purpose of these liminal gods is to act as bridges to the divine powers invoked in other theurgic rituals. Therefore, I suggest that any theurgist interested in a particular pantheon begin by developing a relationship with the liminal gods of that pantheon. How to develop such a relationship is the bulk of this book, but a good place to begin is to find or make an image of the liminal deity in question. Small rituals of observance (discussed later) can also be used on a regular basis to establish and maintain a connection. I find the liminal gods quite easy to connect to, so they are a good place to begin when

---

26 Sarah Iles Johnston. *Hekate Soteira.* (Atlanta, GA: Scholars Press, 1990), 147, n. 19. My translation of the Greek text.

first exploring theurgy. Then, of course, they can help connecting to more abstract gods.

The psychological effects of liminal spaces and times should not be discounted in the practice of theurgy. Areas and moments between our categories of time and space can be particularly powerful in breaking down those categories and seeing the reality between them. We can do this intellectually by always seeking a third option when offered a dichotomy. We can do it physically, taking advantage of liminal spaces in nature where two kinds of places interact—sea shores, forest clearings—to create rituals and establish sacred space. And we can do it psychologically, through deliberate invocation and recognition of liminality in our lives.

EXERCISE 2.1: CREATING A PHANTASM

A phantasm is an image in the mind, but it's not merely a visual image. It's sensory in all dimensions—smell, taste, sound, and touch, as well as vision. These phantasms are imaginary images that you will use in your theurgic practice. The ability to construct a detailed and convincing phantasm is the *sine qua non* of practical magic of all types, but especially of practical theurgy.

STEP 1: Study the image of the deity you wish to work with. A lot of occultists like to work with Egyptian deities simply because they are easy to visualize and distinguish from one another. But keep in mind that Greek deities also have distinctive emblems and features. A bearded man with an eagle is Zeus, for example, and a similarly bearded man with a trident is probably Poseidon. You can learn about such identifying characteristics in any good book on mythology or even the Internet if you employ a small amount of care to distinguish the good historical information from fantasy.

STEP 2: Study, as well, any traditional scents or other sensory factors that might be considered. If you cannot find historical perfumes or odors assigned to the deity in question, you can assign scents based on reason. For example, the smell of ozone after a storm is clearly associated with Zeus, while the earth-smell of fresh rainfall is very much a scent associated with Tefnut.

STEP 3: Finally, seek out sounds associated with the deity or the deity's domain. Soft rain for Tefnut, thunder for Zeus, and so on.

STEP 4: Every morning, for a few minutes, cast the image of the deity before your mind's eye along with the scent and sound in your imagination. Try to make the image as detailed as possible, and see it from all possible angles. Mentally repeat the name of the god as you do this; this is very important, because it serves as an anchor and a protective device.

STEP 5: When you can do this easily, do it throughout the day, especially in situations associated with that deity's domain.

STEP 6: You will succeed in building a powerful phantasm when it begins to move and react on its own. When the phantasm no longer seems like a thing you are doing, but a thing you are watching, you have succeeded in making a strong phantasm.

This exercise is a central one to most of the work that follows. Practice it diligently until you can construct a phantasm easily. It would be a good idea to select a pantheon either from those listed above or from your own research and begin to work through it, devoting a week or so to building a phantasm to each of the gods in turn. Be careful with this exercise, though: it's not just pretending. If done well, you will create a connection to the gods that will affect your life, so be aware that by beginning this practice you will begin to transform yourself. Also, it's not wise to create this kind of phantasm out of spiritual beings that are not gods unless you know what you are doing. It would be downright idiotic to start doing this with Goetic demons, for example.

Myth

We moderns have a strange idea of myth.

Part of the problem is that we need to learn about myth to understand a lot of the literature we value as a culture. But in learning about myth, we are told that "of course" no one believes in these gods anymore. Moreover, we're told that myths were a clumsy attempt to explain the origins of natural phenomenon, before the invention of science. But all of this is nonsense. If myth were just a clumsy groping after knowledge before the invention of science, we wouldn't still have myth—and we do. And good thing, too, because myth serves much more interesting purposes than a stand-in for science. Myth defines meaning.

The first thing to understand about myth is that there are different kinds of myth: there are myths that reveal truth, and myths that tell interesting or amusing stories. Even the ancients were disturbed by myths describing the gods as philanderers and liars, cheaters and rapists; but the myths treat the gods with a double-consciousness. If you read *The Iliad*, you'll see that Homer describes the gods as somewhat ridiculous when interacting with humans, but as majestic when dwelling in Olympus. The literary figures of the gods who drove the human plot are petty and destructive, but the gods on Olympus, the forces that governed the world, are worthy of worship. Homer understood that the stories we tell about the gods depend upon our perspective. From the human perspective, a hurricane might destroy a city and kill many people; from a divine perspective, this hurricane may mean something we cannot comprehend. As Sallustius explains:

> Now the myths represent the Gods themselves and the goodness of the Gods—subject always to the distinction of the speakable and the unspeakable, the revealed and the unrevealed, that which is clear and that which is hidden: since, just as the Gods have made the goods of sense common to all, but those of intellect only to the wise,

> so the myths state the existence of Gods to all, but who and what they are only to those who can understand.[27]

The value of myth for us is in discovering the hidden rather than just enjoying the story—although that's often a good place to start.

We can just approach the myths as stories, perhaps even as historical stories. Euhemerus, a late fourth-century-BCE historian, argued that myths were merely histories retold and distorted. The gods were just powerful men and women of the past. You will occasionally still find those who espouse Euhemerism, but Plato argues against it. For Plato, the myths are more powerful than mere stories: they are power that are to be treated carefully. Plato's ambivalent attitude toward myth can be seen in his banning it from his imaginary ideal Republic.

Where Euhemerus sought a way to rationalize myth as historical, Theagenes (sixth century BCE) understood myth as allegory: each of the gods is a personification of a natural force, and the actions of the gods in myth represent truths about those forces. Zeus's philandering ways are therefore not an endorsement of morally reprehensible behavior but an allegory for the fructifying power of the rain that falls upon the earth without regard for difference. The value of the myths for Theagenes is that they hide truths about the world.

Later philosophers extend this allegorical interpretation into moral allegory. The Neoplatonist Porphyry, in his "Cave of the Nymphs," interprets an episode in *The Odyssey*, converting the myth into a moral allegory. We can see, then, the figures of the myths standing in for moral vices and virtues and their interaction offering moral teaching. This kind of hermeneutic is not far from the common idea that stories must have morals that teach us something of value.

---

27 Murray, Gilbert. *The Five Stages of Greek Religion.* (Boston: Beacon Press, 1955), 201. Accessed 10 May 2013, http://www.gutenberg.org/files/30250/30250-h/30250-h.htm#Page_201

On the other hand, the value of a story isn't the moral it gives us, and the value of a myth isn't its allegory. John Michael Greer puts it succinctly, saying that a "pitfall that must be avoided in making sense of myth is the perception that myths are 'about' something other than themselves."[28] Myth, in his reading, is not a story about the world, but a story that gives meaning to the world. In other words, myth is primary and fundamental, and all the other narratives we tell ourselves about are experiences or reflections of these underlying myths.

I find the notion espoused in Jewish hermeneutics of four different readings of each text to be particularly useful in understanding these underlying myths. In this method of hermeneutics, each text can be read in four ways:

1. **The literal reading:** What do the words mean in the literal context of the myth? Here we see that the gods live on Olympus, and we recognize that there is a Mount Olympus in Greece that is a very tall mountain. Or we see that Tefnut and Shu are born out of the semen or spit of Amun, and understand them not to have a second parent. We don't necessarily *believe* in the literal truth at this level, but we see the facts of the case, as it were, laid out before us. We read it as a story on its own terms, just as we might read a novel for pleasure.
2. **The symbolic reading:** What do the symbols of the text mean to the original authors and to us? A mountain like Olympus rises up into the sky while still connected to the earth: from it, we understand that the gods transcend humanity but nevertheless remain connected to our world. We see that Tefnut, moisture, and Shu, wind, both derive from Amun, the light: indeed, it is the light of the sun that powers the winds and the water cycle. The reader at this level is like a student of literature, analyzing the symbolism of the text and its historical and cultural context.

28 John Michael Greer. *A World Full of Gods.* (Tucson, AZ: ADF Publishing, 2005), 165.

3. **The moral reading:** What does this myth say we should do? Here is the dangerous bit, requiring a specific rule: humans should not strive to be like gods in the moral sense. Zeus turning into a swan and mating with a human does not mean we should do the same thing or anything like it. We can understand the moral teachings of myths in several ways. That the gods live on Olympus tells us we should look up toward them but not forget our own world; they do not live in the sky, disconnected from the earth, and so to reach them we must keep our feet on the ground no matter how high we rise. If Tefnut is life-giving moisture and Shu is separation, we understand that both generosity and our own limits should be defined in the light of wisdom.
4. **The mystical reading:** This one is the hardest: in what way does this myth tell us how to return to the gods? What paths does it lay out for our henosis? Here rather than instructions for living the myth becomes instruction for ritual and contemplation. This is what Greer speaks of when he says, "The most productive way to view myths . . . is as fundamental patterns of human experience, from which a host of possible applications unfold."[29]

Consider our lives to be like songs in harmony with particular myths. The psychological theories of C. G. Jung, while not particularly relevant in contemporary psychology, can be useful to our theology. He teaches that we play out particular characters, archetypes, that recur in the stories of our culture. We learn our roles at an early age from those stories and our experiences of the world, and as we go through our lives we play those roles out. For example, think of all the myths our culture tells about the attractiveness of the Rebel archetype. How many of us, then, chose our clothing in response to that archetype, perhaps trying to appear to be a Rebel or

29 John Michael Greer. *A World Full of Gods.* (Tucson, AZ: ADF Publishing, 2005), 166.

Trickster because we find such an image attractive? You can see such appeal to archetypes in advertisements for everything from cars to body spray. The old cigarette ads that used a cowboy as their image appealed, for example, to the Rootless Adventurer archetype of American cultural mythology.

And on the mystical level, we often play out the figures in myths on our own, even outside the allegory of Jungian psychology. This myth-making can be dangerous, because many of those old myths are tragedies. It's useful to recognize when we're playing ourselves into a disaster and choose to step out of our archetype. One of the powers of theurgy is the ability to select our archetypes based on the situation. Even if the gods didn't exist, theurgy would be an incredibly powerful form of psychological therapy.

Perhaps these approaches to myth would be clearer if laid out with a particular example: the story of Hermes stealing Apollo's cattle is told in the Homeric Hymns. On the surface, it is an amusing story about a precocious deity. Does it have theurgic significance beyond that? I encourage you to read the entirety of the poem, available online in several places as well as in print. I like Thelma Sargent's verse translation.[30]

First, on the literal level we see a story about two characters. Hermes, newly born and laid in his crib in a cavern, climbs free of the crib and finds a tortoise. Using sinews and horns from a cow, he fashions the shell of the tortoise into a lyre and plays it. Growing hungry, he goes in search of food and finds the cows of Apollo untended. He teaches fifty of them to walk backwards and upon passing an old man, cautions him to be silent about what he's seen. After gathering the cattle, he kindles a fire and portions out twelve offerings to the gods. After enjoying the scent of meat but not tasting it, Hermes returns home.

Apollo discovers his cattle missing and goes in search. The old man recounts the sight of a child leading the cattle backwards and by omens Apollo discovers it was Hermes. He argues with the infant god, eventually ending up

---

30 Thelma Sargent, trans. *The Homeric Hymns: A Verse Translation.* (New York: W. W. Norton, 1975).

before the throne of Zeus for judgment. Zeus sees through Hermes's deception but just laughs, and Apollo's attempt to bind Hermes with willow fails because the willows fall from his wrists and take root. Hermes plays his lyre for Apollo, and entranced, Apollo agrees to take the lyre in payment for the fifty cattle. He takes up the lyre and gives Hermes the golden rod of the cowherd.

We could read this myth as a just-so story about how cattle herding became part of the domain of Hermes rather than Apollo, and possibly there is some such prehistoric impetus behind the myth. But we also have to understand what these things mean in the original culture: this is the symbolic reading that opens up the allegorical, moral, and mystical readings. First, consider the tortoise, a creature whose back is patterned in hexagonal tiles symbolic of geometric order. Hermes says of it, "Alive you will be a shield against baneful enchantment,/ But if you should die, then would you sing with great beauty."[31] The orderly patterning of the tortoise's shell is a symbol of mathematical precision, and the silence of the tortoise is a contrast to its eventual fate as a singer. Similarly, the cattle can represent wealth and power. We can understand Hermes as the logos, the reason, which is newborn: this myth is about the beginning of consciousness. Apollo is the god of harmony and prophesy, a god partially outside of time.

On the moral level, we certainly would not want to read this myth as an encouragement to steal. The gods have moral rules that do not apply to humans; we can see this in the fact that the willow did not bind Hermes. But we do see the reflection of moral values held dear by the original tellers of the story: cleverness, fairness, beauty, and in this story above all, humor. These things are endorsed for both gods and humans.

Finally, on the mystical level, we can bring together the other three levels and really begin to dig into the meaning of particular passages. I want to look at two specific passages in detail: the invention of the lyre and the forgiveness of Apollo. In both passages, the lyre figures:

31 Thelma Sargent, trans. *The Homeric Hymns: A Verse Translation.* (New York: W. W. Norton, 1975), 31.

He fixed at measured intervals cut stalks of reed
Through the clean-scooped shell of the
tortoise and spanning his back,
And, by a stroke of wisdom, stretched
oxhide over the hollow.
He added two horns to the sides
yoked by a crossbar,
From which he stretched taut seven
strings made of sheepgut.[32]

On the literal level, this passage describes using a tortoise shell as a sounding board for a lyre. On the mystical level, if we see the shell's regular pattern as a symbol of divine order, the creation of the lyre is the establishment of harmony out of underlying order. When we understand Hermes as the logos, the rationality of the Nous itself, we can see that this myth can be about the role of rationality in creating harmony. We move into this mystical layer of interpretation when we begin to see ourselves as playing out this noetic harmony in our lives.

Now, when logos or divine order confronts the beasts of Apollo, he controls their bestial nature and drives them backwards. Then he offers them up to the twelve gods. From this, we see a way to overcome our bestial nature. The divine logos in our own minds can order and control our bestial nature and offer it up to the gods. And the fact that the god who owns the cattle is Apollo signifies that the rational logos of the human mind is offered up to the divine intuition of inspiration. Apollo is the god of the divine inspiration represented by the Muses, an inspiration that Plato describes as a kind of madness in the Phaedrus.[33]

---

32 Thelma Sargent, trans. *The Homeric Hymns: A Verse Translation.* (New York: W. W. Norton, 1975), 31.

33 Jowett, Benjamin, trans. *Phaedrus by Plato.* Accessed 10 May 2013, http://classics.mit.edu/Plato/phaedrus.html

The result of imposing this order is a conflict—a conflict between human rationality and divine inspiration—but the conflict is resolved in a trade: the lyre for the rod: "Wrought of gold, triply entwined, to protect you, unharmed."[34] This wand is the caduceus, a rod surmounted with wings and twined with two serpents. (The caduceus is often mistaken for Aesclepius's staff, a symbol of medical professionals, but they are not the same thing.) Interestingly, the rod is described as "triply entwined" in Homer, implying either one snake woven about it three times, or three snakes entwined on it. Apollo took over the temple of Python, which became the temple at Delphi after killing the sacred serpent for which it was named. This caduceus therefore links Hermes to that prophetic myth as well.

If we choose to assign allegorical values to these three divine figures, we might say that Hermes is the logos, the divine order underlying consciousness. Apollo is light, illumination, and divine inspiration. And Zeus is of course the judge of fairness. Tracing the progression of the lyre reveals the nature of divine harmony: it is created by Hermes, delivered to Apollo, and blessed by Zeus. In other words, it is founded in rationality, given over to inspiration, and sanctified by divine law. Moreover, the "divine word" of the caduceus moves from Zeus's mouth, to Apollo's wand, to Hermes: from divine balance to divine light to the logos.

We could assign any number of allegorical meanings that would be just as useful—and this, in fact, is one of the drawbacks of a purely allegorical reading of myth. The real purpose of this exercise is not to write a college essay on symbolism in Homer. The purpose is to begin to interact with the complex underlying realities of the myths for yourself. The best method for this is discursive meditation,[35] a useful tool for exploring ideas and building a path to henosis.

---

34 Thelma Sargent, trans. *The Homeric Hymns: A Verse Translation.* (New York: W. W. Norton, 1975), 44.

35 I am indebted to John Michael Greer for teaching me this method of meditation.

Exercise 2.2: Discursive Meditation on a Myth

In contemporary spiritual traditions, discursive meditation is a Christian practice in which a passage of scripture is the object of meditation. But discursive meditation is much older than Christianity. When Plotinus speaks of meditation, he may mean something like discursive meditation. Yet most contemporary occultists prefer Eastern systems of meditation like mindfulness meditation (and, in fact, I don't blame them: I find mindfulness meditation useful as well).

Discursive meditation differs from Eastern methods of meditation in that it seeks focus upon a single idea. A lot of people find it easier in that it is does not have the tendency to be boring that some forms of meditation do, like zazen. Of course for zazen and related meditations, working through the boredom is part of the point, and one could argue—with quite a bit of justification—that Eastern mindfulness meditation is actually discursive meditation with the breath as an object. Ultimately, the goal of discursive meditation is to see into the essence of an idea: in that regard, it is a bit like insight meditation in Buddhism. Yet the objects of contemplation in discursive meditation are selected from a wider variety.

So what does this kind of discursive meditation look like? How does one go about it?

Step 1: Select the object of meditation. Myth is a rich field for objects of meditation, but one may also meditate on particular lines of scripture or poetry, mathematical and geometrical truths, a musical passage, an image of a deity, an esoteric symbol, or any number of other things. Almost anything can be the subject of discursive meditation. We will focus on myth for now. Select a myth that speaks to you and that you know well. Prepare for your meditation by reading the myth several times, ideally in the original if you can find it rather than an adaptation (look for either a good translation or in the original language if you're lucky enough to know it).

STEP 2: Relax. In this kind of meditation, your position does not matter—you can sit upright in a comfortable chair or lie back if you are well-rested enough that there is no danger of falling asleep. If sitting, sit with your spine naturally upright. The best advice I've heard for this is to imagine a hook on the top of your head, pulling you upward. This will align your spine correctly. You may employ any technique you like for the relaxation itself, including the four-fold breath (inhale for a count of four, hold for a count of four, exhale for a count of four, hold for a count of four, repeat), or progressive relaxation (starting with your feet, work up to your head, relaxing muscles in sequence). The goal is to be comfortable and relaxed.

STEP 3: In your imagination, work through the myth step by step, as if you're watching a movie. Experiment with the third-person perspective of a disembodied camera, and the first-person perspectives of various participants in the myth. You may run through it several times, adding or refining details each time.

STEP 4: When your mind wanders—and it will wander—bring it back to the myth. That is the object of your concentration. In this process you will learn that concentration is like riding a horse: the trick is to learn to move with it and gently bring it back under control, rather than bear down and try to master it by brute force. Be gentle with yourself; if you find yourself getting frustrated, please remember that even experienced meditators have to bring their minds back repeatedly during a session.

STEP 5: As you work through the myth perhaps over a period of several days, you may find your mind catching on a detail. For example, perhaps I keep thinking of the tortoise and the cattle. Why these two animals? Let your mind explore the relationship between them with a mixture of reason and intuition. What does Hermes do to the tortoise that's similar to what he does to the cows? He kills them, of course, as sacrifices, one to music and one to the other gods, creating a link between music and divinity. He also pulls them out of their ordinary way of being: the horizontal and silent tortoise becomes vertical and capable of song, while the cattle are driven backwards. He also uses parts of cattle to modify the tortoise, which could link the two animals even more... As you trace this idea, try to keep track of the avenues you go down. This is the moment that requires the most concentration, because the mind is an expert at turning this sort of metaphysical consideration into the construction of a grocery list or a litany of anxiety about bills. You may begin with the allegorical level of interpretation, but the goal is to arrive at the mystical level and begin to see how you yourself play out parts of this myth in your life. However, when I say that is the goal, I do not mean that you must achieve that level of insight in every meditation or the meditation is a failure. I always tell myself that sitting down and just breathing is already victory enough whether or not I achieve any insight.

Step 6: Finish your meditation with a prayer or affirmation of what you have learned or understood, if anything. Remember that there are no such things as bad meditations: a meditation is good even if you break concentration a hundred times and come away with no insight other than that Hermes must have some stain-resistant baby clothes to sacrifice fifty cattle and come away clean.

Step 7: The next morning (or evening, or lunch hour), come back and do it again. This is important: meditation works best when you make it a habit. Stick with one myth or topic for at least a week. When you find yourself getting bored with it, that's when you know it's about to produce something interesting, so stick with it a little longer.

If, like me, you already find other meditative practices productive, you can mix and match to some degree. For example, I like to begin the discursive meditation with a few minutes of mindfulness meditation; I find it clarifies the entire experience.

Do not be surprised if during your day your mind returns to the topic of your meditation. If you catch yourself contemplating myths during the day, that's a good sign: it means you've begun to train your mind in contemplation and concentration. You've begun to make the gods a part of your life and yourself, which is the first step on the path of theurgy.

CHAPTER 3

The Addresses of the Gods

If you wish to contact me, a mortal, there are many ways you can do it. You can write to my publisher, whose address is in the front of this book. You can ask me for my home address and write me there. You could find my email address and email me.[36] You could look up my phone number and call me. What do these modes of communication have in common? Each of them requires a sort of address: a symbolic representation of my location to which you can appeal. Without getting the right symbols, you won't reach me. Add one wrong letter to my email, leave off the city on your letter, and nothing will happen.

While theurgists like Iamblichus didn't have email or addresses in the conventional sense, they understood very well the importance of these symbols as a means of communication. And just as I would have to give you my home address, the gods give us their symbolic addresses. The author of the Chaldean Oracles writes: "The Paternal Intellect has sown symbols

36 pwdunn@gmail.com

throughout the cosmos."[37] In the psyche, then, both the individual soul and the Psyche of the world are symbols sowed by the demiurge, just as I sowed my email in an earlier footnote. These symbols are addresses back to the gods, and can be used as points of contact.

Iamblichus defines three levels of these addresses, or *synthemata*: the material, the intermediate, and the noetic. The material synthemata are those that exist in the world of hyle, the matter that we (think we) know. Iamblichus uses the example of Helios, the sun, but let's instead use Selene, the moon, as our example, just to mix it up a bit. We have this goddess whose domain is change and reflection, perception and transformation. We want to understand her better, so we look around the world of matter and look for items that reflect this idea. The most obvious is that pretty hunk of rock orbiting the earth, of course. This is a synthema of Selene. To say "Selene is the goddess of the moon" is to make an error from a strictly theurgic perspective: the moon, the object, is a symbol of Selene.

But we don't have to stop with that symbol, especially since it's hard to manipulate the moon in our rituals (although not hard to time our rituals with the moon). So we look in the world of matter for manifestations of the gods which Iamblichus enumerates as "stones, plants, animals, aromatic substances, and other such things that are sacred, perfect and godlike."[38] Among stones he includes other such materials like metals, and when we look at the world of metals we find a metal that is silvery and tarnishes black over time, but can be wiped clean again. Silver is much like the moon and hence a synthema of Selene. Among herbs we find night-flowering plants, among animals the dog, the cow, and the cock, and among aromatics I suggest gardenia.

There are two ways to identify the synthemata of a particular god: the doctrine of signatures and the weight of tradition. The doctrine of signatures

37 Ruth Majercik. *The Chaldean Oracles: Text, Translation and Commentary.* (Leiden, NL: Brill, 1989), 91.

38 Emma C. Clarke, John M. Dillon, and Jackson P. Hershbell, trans. *Iamblichus: On the Mysteries.* (Atlanta: Society for Biblical Literature, 2003), 269. DM 233: 9–12.

suggests that every idea or form in the Nous imprints itself on matter more or less distinctly. In the above example, silver shares the signatures of Selene: changeable, reflective, and so on. Understanding the doctrine of signatures allows us to innovate when the materials we might want are not easily at hand. Often, at least in English, the names of particular herbs and stones can be an indication of their signatures: moonstone, for example, or artemesia, signify that people at one point or another saw such things as containing the signatures of goddesses like Selene or Artemis. On the other hand, the weight of tradition offers traditional associations: for example, the association of the dog with Selene is perhaps obvious: the dog tends to howl at the moon. The cow's horns share its shape. The rooster, like the dog, may well crow at a full moon. But fundamentally, these associations are traditional; they come from ancient sources, and we may not immediately see the logic or signature of them. The association of the dolphin with Apollo, for example, arises from a particular myth, rather than any obvious signature the dolphin displays of the god.

The intermediate synthemata are those symbols which partake not just of matter but of the soul. They are matter embodied and deliberately shaped with some feature of the god. Where material synthemata arise naturally out of nature, the intermediate synthemata require some participation of human intelligence. Here are images of the gods, their names and conventional appearances, statues, drawings, and hymns.[39]

The names of the gods come from tradition, but there is also a tradition that secret names of the gods may be given to some theurgists, personal only to them, just as we give particular nicknames to our friends, or permission to call us in certain ways to certain people. A god may have many names and epithets. If we look at Apollo, we can find that not only does he have the name Apollo in Greek, but this name appears in Etruscan as Apulu, in Doric as Apellon, and so on. In addition to their names in various

---

39 Gregory Shaw. *Theurgy and the Soul: The Neoplatonism of Iamblichus.* (University Park, PA: University of Pennsylvania Press, 1995), 170–188.

dialects and languages, most gods have epithets of two varieties: characteristic epithets, and toponymic epithets. Characteristic epithets recall one of the features of the god: For Apollo, he is sometimes called Phoebus (meaning "bright"), Phanaeus ("light-bringer"), Hekaergos ("far-shooter"), and so on. One could literally fill a page with the characteristic epithets of Apollo, an important and popular god. Toponymic epithets recall particular locations where the god performed some feat or was worshiped in a particular way or with particular devotion. Apollo can be referred to as Delphinius, referring to his oracle at Delphi or Actiacus after the promontory of Actium, where there was an important temple to the god. Sometimes, toponymic names can be reinterpreted, such as Sminthius which originally referred to a town of Sminthe, becoming confused with the Greek word for mouse, *sminthos*, thus leading to Apollo becoming a mouse-god.

With such a proliferation of names, it stands to reason that there might be some names of the gods that worshipers are not aware of, so a common formula in ancient Greek and Roman prayers is something amounting to a list of names followed by a phrase like "or whatever name it pleases you to be called." They recognized that the names of the gods are not what the gods might call themselves: their names among themselves might be nonlinguistic labels of which we cannot even conceive. And, of course, for those highest ideas of the gods in the Nous, no name can symbolize them: they are, themselves, what the names symbolize.

Just as names are multiple and unbounded, so are images. The earliest cult images of deities were bare pillars or planks, although small representative cult images were not unknown.[40] The large marble statues that we know from our museums are a later innovation. In ancient Greek religion, the gods were thought to dwell within the statue: by taking on the form of the god, the statue invited the psyche of the daimon to dwell within it.

---

40 Walter Burkert. *Greek Religion.* (Cambridge, MA: Harvard University Press, 1985), 88.

Much of what we know about the use of cult images in Late Antiquity comes from the writings of Christians very much opposed to the practice. The term "idol," originally an ordinary Greek word meaning "image," became an insult. The Christians inherited this attitude toward cult images from the Jews, of course, whose deity was—at least at this late stage—so perfectly transcendent of matter that to give Him an image was insulting. Psalm 135:15–18 condemns the use of idols because they lack clear signs of life; they are mere objects unworthy to represent the perfectly transcendent God whose only image is the human form itself. The Pagan gods, however, are not perfectly transcendent: as we've already discussed, they are the immanent part of an ultimately transcendent reality. Their very immanence is what gives them the power to affect us for the better. The Pagan worship of idols, then, is not mere ignorance as it's often painted but a profound philosophical statement about reality.

The Greek and Roman attitude toward images of their gods was quite practical. A worshiper could pray anytime, anywhere, without an image. But if a worshiper wanted to pray specifically to a particular god, the prayer could be more efficacious if he or she attended a temple. Temples were not places of congregation; festivals and religious ceremonies took place outside of the temple itself. Temples were locations where the gods were particularly immanent, and one could look upon the image and speak to it directly.

The dual nature of the divine, that it straddles immanence and transcendence, lends an interesting tension to Neoplatonic and later Hermetic thought. Plotinus argues that the efficacy of statues is built upon the Neoplatonic theory of forms:

> IV. 3, 11. The olden sages, in seeking to procure the presence of the Gods by erecting temples and statues, seem to me to have possessed deep insight into the nature of the universe: They felt the All-Soul to be a Principle ever at our call; it is but fitly preparing a place in which some phase of it may be received, and a thing is always fit to receive the operation

> of the Soul when it is brought to the condition of a mirror, apt to catch the image.[41]

For Plotinus, the statue is a site of contemplation of the One, through the intermediaries of the gods. As Algis Uždavinys explains it, "Since all manifested reality is established as theophany, a deity... is a priori present in the raw materials gathered to create the image."[42] Which is to say, since matter itself is a function of the divine, a sort of divine appearance or manifestation, then forming a statue out of that matter exalts it and brings forth its divine qualities.

The *Asclepius*, a hermetic tract written in Latin, instructs the hermetic student how to make an efficacious cult image, and where its divine power comes from:

> "It comes from a mixture of plants, stones, and spices, Asclepius, that have in them a natural power of divinity. And this is why those gods are entertained with constant sacrifices, with hymns, praises and sweet sounds in tune with heaven's harmony: so that the heavenly ingredient enticed into the idol by constant communication with heaven may gladly endure its long stay among humankind."[43]

---

41 Plotinus, *The Ethical Treatises, being the Treatises of the First Ennead, with Porphry's Life of Plotinus, and the Preller-Ritter Extracts forming a Conspectus of the Plotinian System, translated from Greek by Stephen Mackenna* (Boston: Charles T. Branford, 1918). Chapter: X: Soul and Body. Accessed from http://oll.libertyfund.org/title/1272/6766 on 2013–05–08

42 Algis Uždavinys. *Philosophy and Theurgy in Late Antiquity.* (San Rafael, CA: Sophia Perennis, 2010), 173.

43 Brian Copenhaver, trans. *Hermetica: The Greek Corpus Hermeticum and the Latin Asclepius in a New English Translation with Notes and Introduction.* (Cambridge: Cambridge University Press, 1992), 90.

For Trismegistus in the *Asclepius*, the statue is a synthema of the gods, and it brought into greater focus and harmony by uniting it with the material synthemata as well. The statue therefore represents two levels of the reality of the god: the material things that bear the god's print in the realm of hyle or matter, and the ideal form of that god in the mind that appears in the statue itself.

Yet one needs more than just the matter to "fashion a god." More rarified intermediate synthemata—songs, hymns—are added to the mix, with acts of sacrifice in accord with even more rarified, noetic synthemata of "harmony." I will address the noetic synthemata more fully in a bit, and we will explore the ritual of sacrifice and how we can reap its benefits without staining our carpets or calling down the wrath of the ASPCA. Suffice it to say that the chickens and goats are safe from me.

The ultimate goal is to harmonize all the realms of synthemata— the material, the intermediate, and the noetic—all in one place. The statue becomes a god then not in the physical sense, but in the sense of being a locus of the god's forces in all three worlds. The statue is a line drawn through the worlds, touching on the nature of the god at all levels, and that line acts as a phone cord back up to the divine.

Exercise 3.1: Creating an Image

Step 1: Select a deity with whom you wish to have a closer relationship. If you have been contemplating the deities, you may very well already have one in mind as a possible patron, but it could also be a god outside of any pantheon. If in doubt, solar and lunar gods are good places to start, and liminal gods are often helpful places to begin.

Step 2: Research the deity in question. You can find tables of correspondence about the gods in several places, but the best way to find what you need is to dig through the myths, either in their original forms or in condensations like Edith Hamilton's or Bulfinch. Ultimately, you are looking for the material synthemata of that god in the form of metals, stones, herbs, and animals.

EXAMPLE: In researching Artemis, I discover that she is associated with wormwood, silver, and traditional magical correspondences that link her to the moon and all of its relevant correspondences. But she also has a traditional association with the temple of Ephesus, where in addition to her statue there was a sacred stone believed to be a meteorite.

STEP 3: Gather what synthemata you can. Ideally, you want at least something herbal and something mineral. Animal parts, if used, should be collected respectfully, humanely, and legally, and make absolutely sure that the god is not likely to find it disgusting that you have taken apart one of its sacred animals (I do not think that Apollo would look kindly on your using a dolphin bone, even if you somehow got it legally, and breaking the law to get a bald eagle feather in the United States would probably do more to annoy Zeus—as a god of law—than please him).

EXAMPLE: As I wish to create a statue to Artemis, I gather herbs sacred to her from her myths, specifically some wormwood. I find a small meteorite to use as a sacred stone, and a strip of deer leather gathered from a hunter friend who got the deer hunting it, rather than hitting it with his truck.

STEP 4: Acquire or construct the image. If you lack artistic talent, it's okay if your creation is crude. Such crude statues, called *xoana*, were often used in archaic temples and were sometimes as simple as pillars draped with cloth. If you have artistic talent, you can sculpt your own out of clay; even oven-baked polymer clays will work fine. Alternately, you could draw or paint the image. And yes, you can even buy the image if you want a particular one.

EXAMPLE: Since I'm interested in Artemis of Ephesus, I acquire a replica of the famous statue of her there.

STEP 5: Create a receptacle somewhere on the image for the material synthemata. You can bore a small hole in the back or the bottom of the base. If you sculpted the image yourself, you can create a hole as part of the process of sculpting. One of the unsung tools of the modern occultist, a rotary tool is handy for creating holes in purchased statues. Remember, for store-bought statues, especially those made of stone rather than resin, slow and easy does it.

Step 6: At a time appropriate to the deity, if possible, fill the receptacle with the objects and attach them in some way. You can seal over the hole with clay, or you can just use a blob of silicon epoxy.

Step 7: If you wish, dress, decorate, or drape the statue in appropriate materials. Example: I tie a thin thong cut from the leather around the shoulders of my statue.

Step 8: This last step is animating the statue, but we will leave that for a later exercise. For now, feel free to use the statue in your devotions and as an object of contemplation. Simply interacting with it as a representative of the god is enough to begin the process of animating it, because the god is already present in the materials used. Of course, treat it with respect. You should keep it clean and not let people treat it with disrespect; roommates, children, and parents can be respectfully and politely informed to keep their hands off. If you wish to lock it away, you can put it in a small and attractive box with appropriate offerings (such as flowers, please, and not food—roaches tend not to inspire pious thoughts).

Noetic Synthemata

Material synthemata are those objects in the world of hyle or matter that take on the imprint of the gods. Alternately, we might say they are the pieces of matter we ascribe to the deity through some process of association or analogy. Intermediate synthemata are those symbols that we ascribe to the gods more directly and are more culturally determined: names, images, hymns. But a third kind of synthema, the kind that Iamblichus argues is the highest and most powerful of the synthemata, are those which reside not in human consciousness but in the consciousness of the universe itself. These are things like geometry, time, and the abstract divisions of the sky known as the Zodiac. In order to anchor us on the ground and not fly away into mystery, let's once again drop in on Philanike and her student Euthymios.

Euthymios: What's in the oven?

Philanike: Cupcakes. What's more important is, what's on the table?

Eu: Looks like a ruler and a drawing compass. And lots of paper. And some pencils.

Ph: Good. What else do you notice?

Eu: I notice that it's a crappy ruler, since it has no markings. Otherwise, that's it.

Ph: You're right: it has no markings, because it's not a ruler. It's just a straight-edge. If I hold it up here and you extend the end far beyond where the straight-edge ends, what do you get?

Eu: An imaginary line?

Ph: And where does it end?

Eu: It won't end, unless it's stopped by something.

Ph: And if we take up the compass, we notice it has two parts. What are the parts?

Eu: The writey-bit and the stabby-bit. You poke the cute girl in math class with the stabby-bit because you secretly like her. At least, that's what I did.

Ph: What did I ever do to deserve—fine, it's the stabby bit. When you stab little Susie—

Eu: Kate.

Ph: When you stab little Kate with it, what does it leave?

Eu: A mark on her skin. A little one. And then I ended up in detention and learned how not to talk to girls.

Ph: Like the mark, the point, I've made on the paper. And if I swing the other arm around, I make a circle.

Eu: Sure.

Ph: If I draw a line from the point to the edge of the circle, what's the result?

Eu: Um. I don't know.

Ph: What if I make another circle, with the line equal to that length, and my stabby bit on where the first circle cuts it off. Voilà. What's this?

Eu: Two overlapping circles.

Ph: Not just overlapping. They overlap in a very specific way. The center of one is on the circumference of the other.

Eu: What does this have to do with theurgy, now?

Ph: Wait for it. Now, I can draw a line from the point where each circle touches the other. And a line connecting the ends of that longer line to the ends of the smaller line.

Eu: Two triangles.

Ph: Two equilateral triangles.

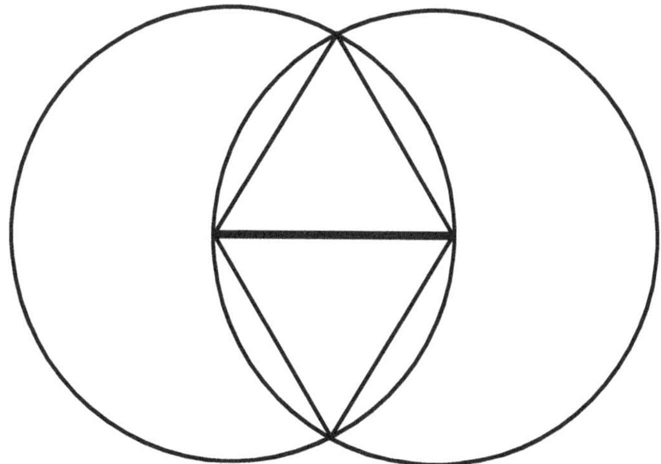

Fig. 5: Construction of a Triangle

Euthymios: Your point is?

Philanike: Our two tools are the straight-edge, which makes an infinite line, and the circle, which makes a point and ascribes a limit around that point. We have, therefore, the infinite and the limited. We start with one thing: a single point. That point implies a plane of possible points, and if we choose to mark those points a certain set distance from that first point, we get a circle.

Eu: I hope there won't be a test.

Ph: Life is your test. But listen: Within that first circle, there is the implication of a second circle—or rather, an infinite number of second circles, all taking their centers from those new points.

Eu: And in that overlapping circle—

Ph: The *vesica piscis.*

Eu: Gesundheit. In that overlapping circle, there's the implication of two lines.

Ph: Which themselves imply…

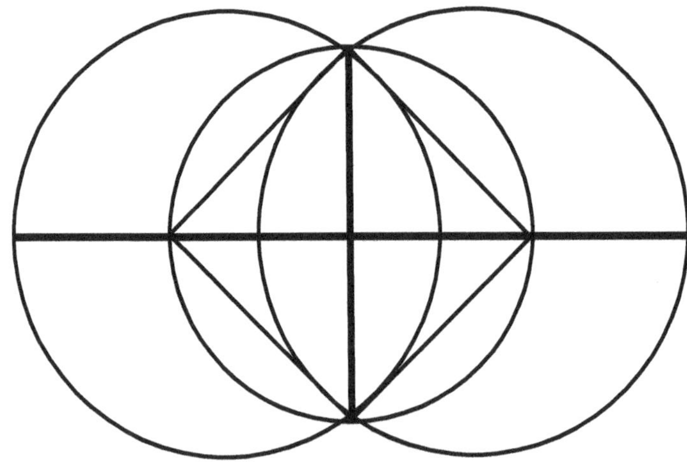

Fig. 6: Construction of a Square

Euthymios: Two equilateral triangles.

Philanike: Where else do you see a right angle like this?

Eu: In a right triangle or—oh, a square.

Ph: Go ahead. Extend the horizontal line at the base of our triangles outward. Now draw a circle from where they cross, to cut them off at an equal distance. Connect the corners.

Eu: So a single circle implies a second circle, a line, a triangle, and a square.

Ph: A single point, not a single circle.

Eu: So all these structures come out of a point that has—

Ph: Nothing at all in it but location. It's featureless. It's just One. But out of it comes the two points that define a line, the three points that define a triangle, and the four points that define a square.

Eu: So order can derive from featureless unity.

Ph: Exactly. Oh, good, the cupcakes are done. Not yet, they're too hot.

Eu: I see what you're doing. You're arranging them in a triangle. This is a lesson I better get to eat.

Ph: Once I frost them, yes. But they need to cool anyway. How many have I baked?

Eu: Ten.

Ph: And how have I arranged them?

Eu: In rows of one, two, three, and four. I get it. Ten is completion, and the four elements and so on and so forth. Is it cream cheese frosting?

Ph: Better than that. So these first two rows are in a ratio of—

Eu: One to two. Then two to three. Three to four. Buttercream is good too.

Ph: Ever see a monochord?

Eu: Is that what that is? I thought it was a cheese-slicer.

Ph: Nope. It's an instrument with a single string and a movable bridge. We can divide this string into any proportion we like. I've marked a few on the sounding board. Here, let's move the bridge to the halfway point, which divides the string in what proportion?

Eu: One to two. Oh, clever. Where are you going with this?

Ph: Pluck.

Eu: Pardon me? Oh, *pluck*. Yes. Sounds nice.

Ph: It's harmonious to your ear: an octave, to be technical. If I play the whole string, then cut it in half and just play half, I get an octave. Now let's set it to a proportion of 2/3.

Eu: Again, nice sounding.

Ph: It's what's called a fifth. And now for 3/4.

Eu: Pretty, once again.

Ph: A fourth. Now let's just pick any ol' random proportion.

Eu: Less pretty.

Ph: Quite. Now, Pythagoras noticed that these three proportions are harmonious, and also the proportions represented in my cupcakes, which Pythagoras called the *tetrakys.*

Eu: He called your cupcakes tetrakys?

Ph: ...He concluded that harmony, the experience of beauty itself, was inherent in the very nature of number. It's in the very mind of the universe itself.

Eu: Trippy.

Trippy indeed, but what's the point? The point, of course, as Philanike well knows, is that harmony is not only inherent in the system of mathematics that governs geometry and arithmetic: it is demanded by it. Of course, perhaps we only perceive harmony because we get used to it: but why do we get used to it? Take the well-used and well-abused golden ratio of 1:1.618. We see this ratio in a number of proportions of the human body, in the growth of some plants, in some crystals, and all over art. Why do we like the proportions of the golden rectangle? We like it because we see it all the time and are used to it, but we see it all the time because it occurs all the time in nature.

Skeptics of this kind of mathematical mysticism rightly point out that the golden ratio does not, actually, occur *all* the time in nature. It occurs often, but so do other proportions. The famous claim that the nautilus shell grows in the golden ratio is easily debunked by measuring some nautilus shells, and while the proportion occurs all over the human body, so do many other ratios and proportions, depending upon what you wish to measure. The reason it seems so mystical is that we notice it.

With all due respect to the skeptics of this sort of number mysticism (for whom I have some sympathy), they are missing the point. Of course, so are a lot of would-be mystics. The golden ratio, the harmonies of 1:2, 2:3, 3:4, and other important ratios are not important because they show up all the time, but because they don't. Things take on meaning because of difference. If every proportion in the universe were the golden ratio, it'd mean nothing. Instead, because it occurs in some proportions and not others, we can take it as a mark—or, in Greek, a *synthema*—of a certain kind of harmony.

The full exploration of this kind of sacred geometry and number mysticism would quickly eat three hundred pages of this book and leave much left undone. But it's important to know that the theurgists of Late Antiquity regarded the synthemata of number and geometry as the highest, most perfect synthemata, and—for those with the inclination and ability—the fastest way to understand the mind of god. Those theurgists took their inspiration ultimately from Pythagoras and Euclid. For Pythagoras, numerical harmony was the underlying structure of the universe: perceiving this harmony would make a person's mind over in the shape of the divine. For Euclid, the principles of the extended line and the bounded definition was all that was necessary to construct reality.

We now know that certain activities cannot be performed by Euclid with his simple tools of straight-edge and compass. For example, Euclid could not trisect an angle, or square a circle—and, using his rules, neither can you. Seriously, you can't. It's mathematically impossible.[44] Which means it's not in the idea of the Nous that such a thing can be done using only the principles of extension and circumscription. This means that while certain geometrical shapes can be constructed by straight-edge and compass—we've seen the triangle and square, but you can also construct a pentagon (and the pentagram inscribed within it), the hexagon (6gon), an octagon (8gon), and a decagon (10gon). You cannot construct a 7gon or a 9gon using just a ruler and straightedge. Of course, you can come close and approximate, but Euclid's rules are about exact relationships, not approximations. You may notice that you rarely see 7gons or 9gons in nature, while 6gons and 8gons are common enough, and 5gons are almost everywhere you look.

What leads to this impossibility? From a mathematical standpoint, the math inherent in the tools. Analog computers are limited, and compass and straightedge are early analog computers for doing complex arithmetic. From a mystical standpoint, these impossibilities are worthy of contemplations because not only is the mathematical explanation true, but we can assign mystical significance to it as well. There's one particular number encoded in the compass itself that opens up entire worlds of impossibility: pi.

Pi is what mathematicians call an irrational number, not because it's crazy but because it cannot be described by a ratio of whole numbers. Another irrational number, the square root of two, is the ratio of a side of a square to its diagonal. And a third, the square root of three, is the ratio

---

44 Really. No, you didn't. Please don't write me, or worse, random math professors, saying that you did.

of a side of an equilateral triangle to its height. These numbers can never be described as a fraction of integers. Pi has another quality as well, which mathematicians name "transcendental," an appropriate name although they mean nothing mystical by it. Pi not only cannot be described as a ratio, it cannot be derived from any arithmetic operation. There are algorithms that can derive pi, of course, but arithmetic—addition, subtraction, division, multiplication, and their extensions of powers and roots—cannot derive pi. Since the straight-edge and compass constitute a computer designed to do arithmetic, we cannot derive pi. Pi is automatically created by every swing of the compass, but any operation that requires us to derive it by some other means is impossible. We can actually bisect an angle: this only requires arithmetic. But trisecting an angle means trisecting an arc, and trisecting an arc requires us to arithmetically derive pi with tools unsuited to it. Now, we can cheat—we can mark our ruler, for example—and then trisection becomes trivial. And this is an analogy for creation.

In order to create all the polygons using a ruler and straightedge, we need to impose our own order upon the tools. Order arises out of the structure of the mind of universe, and we speak back to it. We contribute something, potentially, to creation. Of course, heptagons (7gons) and trisected angles occur in nature—but not often. And so we as conscious beings, reflective of the Nous, can fill in the gaps. Yet it's important to remember that even the order we impose upon the tools is inherent in that point: it all comes out of a single dot, a location without magnitude.

All these meditations are inspiring and worthwhile, but as I said, I could spend hundreds of pages on them and never scratch the surface. For our more practical theurgic purposes, we can make some use of these geometrical shapes as synthemata without necessarily learning the whole of geometry in the process. I would encourage you, in using these geometrical shapes, to construct them yourself out of compass and straightedge (or string and chalk line) according to the ancient fashion; geometrical construction is itself a ritual invoking the gods. You will not receive the same effect just copying them out of a book.

The best use to make of these noetic synthemata is as objects of meditation. For example, if you were to construct the triangle in your mind (after having practiced it on paper a few times), you can use this mental construction as a contemplative device. Where, for instance, does the complexity of the triangle come from? The simplicity of a featureless point. What does that tell you about existence of the divine? At more advanced levels, you can begin to play with the constructions. Once you construct a triangle, it's fairly simple to construct a hexagon. What does the process of doing so tell you about the nature of the hexagon? My mind is immediately led to the fact that the process involves connecting the corner of the first triangle to its center, and then extending the line outward to the circle, which makes me think that the hexagon is latent within the triangle, and is therefore a symbol of reflection and balance of the hidden and the apparent. You, of course, will arrive at different ideas as you contemplate these symbols.

As you do this contemplation, you will begin to build up a vocabulary of geometrical shapes that will be more alive and powerful for you than any list of correspondences. I could tell you that a certain god relates to a certain shape, but you will more productively make such connections yourself, through construction and contemplation, because then they will become living symbols. At the same time, you will also gain insight into the nature of the mathematical universe, and therefore—from a theurgic perspective—the world of Ideas.

Time

The timing of our lives is determined by the regular geometrical movement of the earth and various heavenly bodies. We often forget it, those of us who live in cities, but the sky is a giant clock (or rather, our clocks are miniature skies) that moves through a bewildering array of sweeping and interlocking cycles to spell out particular times. One of the original schools of mathematics was calendrics: the study of these cycles, intimately connected to astronomy and hence astrology. Our current popular understanding of astrology as mere sun signs is a pale reflection of the sophisticated system that once existed, and I find myself joining the skeptics in sneering at it. But there are insights in the movements of the planets and the earth that can help us understand the nature of the divine, and time itself is a noetic synthema.

If we take the wheel of the year, we can chop it into four chunks, which mark the longest and shortest days, as well as the two day/night pairs that are absolutely even. We know these four points as the turning of the seasons, and we have assigned the name Aries to the turning of the spring season, then divided the sun's motion into thirty-degree chunks throughout the sky, assigning a sign with a name taken from a related constellation to each. It's a common misconception that the astronomical constellation Aries marks the beginning of spring. At one point this was true, but now the sun does not enter the constellation of Aries on the first day of spring. Instead, it enters a space in the sky we call "Aries," in honor of where that astronomical constellation once was. It's common every few years for some reporter to breathlessly announce that our astrological signs are "wrong." This isn't news for any astrologer, nor is it true. The astrological signs are named after, but not contiguous with, the astronomical constellations of the zodiac.

These four seasons have a large influence on the earth. For much of North America and most of Europe, winter is the season of quiet and rest, spring the season of fecundity and new growth, summer the season of heat and activity, and fall the season of dying and harvest. This cycle of seasons is particularly significant to fertility and vegetation deities, such as Osiris, who can be seen to be living out his life cycle over and over, promising resurrection in the spring.

Interlocking with this cycle of four is the natural lunar cycle of 29.5 days giving us months (named after the moon). This cycle can itself be divided into four points: new, first quarter, full, third quarter.

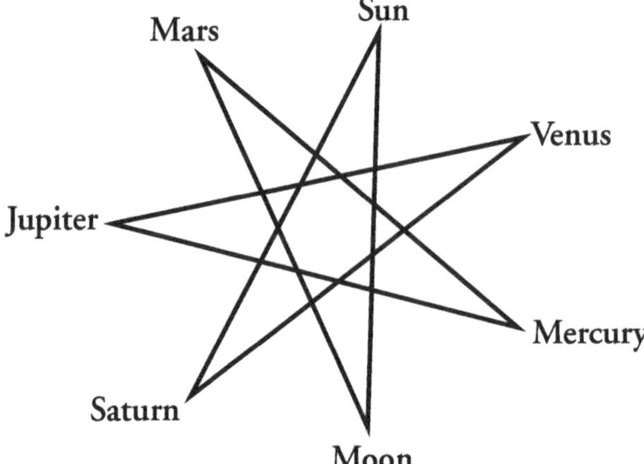

Fig. 7: Order of the Planets

Often it is thought that the full moon is more propitious than the new, and that the moon increasing through first quarter is better for growing and increasing than the moon falling from full through its third quarter to new.

We have an association of each of the seven days of the week with the planets dating back to the second century, which I've previously mentioned. Each day is sacred to one of the planetary gods, and activities and rituals dedicated to that god may be done on that day.

Finally, we have a later innovation: the division of the day into hours, each of which is sacred to a god. These hours are divisions of the period between sunup and sundown for each day, so they are of uneven length most days of the year; they rarely are sixty minutes in length. Many computer programs exist that can calculate these hours for you, some of them online and most of them free. In brief, the hours follow the Chaldean sequence of the planets. You will notice if we arrange the planets in a heptagram, we can see an interesting relationship between the sequence of the planetary days and that of the hours. Following around the circumference of the circle reveals the sequence of the days, while following the line of the heptagram gives us the order of the Chaldean hours.

Another set of sacred days we can use to time our theurgic workings can be gleaned from the ancient calendars of antiquity. Here, rather than geometrical divisions of the sky and the motions of celestial bodies, festivals are established by human cultural convention. These, then, are intermediate rather than noetic synthemata, but they still have their uses as a gesture of recognition of original contexts. At the same time, we as theurgists are not reconstructing ancient religion. Reconstruction is a worthwhile goal but not the goal of theurgy, so I would not be bound by the traditional holidays and ceremonies of the gods.

Because Roman festivals followed a solar calendar like ours—in fact, Romans invented our solar calendar—they can be dated with some precision. Most Roman festivals were several-day affairs, and they had many, many more holidays than we do. It is not unusual for a single month to have, potentially, a week or two of festival days. Of course, just like most Americans do nothing more on Flag Day than put up a flag, many of these festivals were probably relatively cursory affairs, excuses for barbecues. And since the only meat many people got on a regular basis was that served at the sacrifices, the needs of protein may have driven the festival calendar more than any particular religious feeling.

Greek festivals, on the other hand, were set on a lunar calendar, and individual city-states had their own festival calendars. Because these lunar calendar days do not coincide with the seasons, they are hard to pin down on our modern calendar. Moreover, it's almost impossible to make a full list of all the festivals of all the city-states without filling in almost every single day of the year with a sacrifice or ritual game. Not all festivals occurred every year: some occurred every so many years, some occurred when the local government decided it was time. The only one of these festivals we still celebrate is the Agon Olympikos, the Olympic Games, in honor of the gods of Olympus, held every four years. The games themselves were a tribute to Zeus, showcasing the most perfect and beautiful achievements capable of the human body. But not only physical achievement was displayed: artistic and poetic talent also had their competitions. The festival was an offering of human beauty to the gods. Our modern Olympics, restored after the ban on the games in the fourth century, are quite different.[45] We have more different kinds of events, the athletes are clothed, and the games travel from country to country.

We could easily revive the practice of some of these festivals, although others would require a larger cultural participation. It's ill-advised, for example, to slap a crowd of girls with raw-hide to increase their fertility if you don't have a willing crowd of girls. The reestablishment of the ancient holidays is more the project of a reconstructionist. I have experimented with adding in elements of holidays to existing holidays in our culture—adding, for example, offerings to Saturnus to Christmas, a holiday the ancients called Saturnalia. Overall, I have not found this particularly religiously significant for my own practice. I have found it more useful to time my religious practices to astrological phenomena.

It would be convenient, therefore, if we could simply assign gods to months or astrological signs and thus have a series of theurgic festivals for our own devotional use without having to rely on translating a lunar calendar to a solar one, or cultural traditions from antiquity to contemporary times. Plato, in the Phaedrus, indicates a possible correspondence between thirteen gods and the astrological signs, with an explanation of how to arrange thirteen gods on twelve signs:

> Zeus, the mighty lord, holding the reins of a winged chariot, leads the way in heaven, ordering all and taking care of all; and there follows him the array of gods and demigods, marshaled in eleven bands; Hestia alone abides at home in the house of heaven; of the rest they who are reckoned among the princely twelve march in their appointed order.[46]

45 Historical information about the Olympics may be found at http://www.worldatlas.com/aatlas/infopage/olympic.htm.

46 Benjamin Jowett, trans. *Phaedrus by Plato*. Accessed 10 May 2013, http://classics.mit.edu/Plato/phaedrus.html

The Phaedrus is an important text to later Neoplatonists because it establishes some of the methods and metaphors that permeate the practice of theurgy in the West. Here we see a hint of the organization of the gods on the zodiac, with Hestia remaining in the center and Zeus leading the eleven other gods around the ring. Sadly, Plato never adequately explains what gods fit what signs. Perhaps he thought it would be self-explanatory, or perhaps it was esoteric knowledge only given to members of his school.

Some evidence for the latter explanation exists throughout the later Roman period in the form of various mosaics establishing correspondences between the gods and the signs or months. Unfortunately, few of these correspondences agree with each other.[47] Evidence for the former conjecture, the idea that this correspondence was common knowledge, exists in the names of some of the months themselves.

The earliest Roman calendar, that of Romulus, consisted of ten months of thirty or thirty-one days each. Obviously, since the year is 365.256 days long, this calendar is not going to work long term, which is why we have uneven month-lengths in our current calendar, as well as two extra months. The names of the first four months—starting with March—are associated with Etruscan deities, the precursors of many of the Roman deities not borrowed from the Greeks. Later months were named for the numbers from five to ten (of these, only four of them—September the seventh month, October the eighth month, November the ninth month, and December the tenth month—preserve their numbers, the earlier ones having been renamed after Julius and Augustus Caesar). Clearly, this was a calendar of agricultural people, beginning in the spring and consigning other months to mere numbers. The first month, Martius, is named after Mars, who is both an agricultural god and a god of war. It makes sense that the first month of spring is a time of planting as well as a time of beginning military campaigns. The second month, Aprilis, may be named after the Etruscan god Apru, while the

47 For a thorough treatment, see Ken Gillman. "Twelve Gods and Seven Planets." http://cura.free.fr/decem/10kengil.html. Accessed 8 May 2013.

third month, Maias, is named after Maia, a goddess of fertility and the earth. Finally, the fourth month, Iunius, is named in honor of Iuno.

Where to place the gods if we wish to align them to the calendar? One could, of course, simply assign the gods to the months on the basis of their public festivals, but the Roman and Greek festivals were not evenly spaced around the year, as those of Wicca are, so this correspondence can prove more troublesome than it appears, especially since different cities honored different customs at different times. Alternately, one could import one of the existent correspondences wholesale, which may appeal to reconstructionists even if the immediate logic is not quite clear. Some of the correspondences, however, do offer some reasoning. For example, Manillius arranges the gods according to the zodiac, as follows:

> Pallas (Minerva) watches over the Woolbearer (Aries);
> Cytherea (Venus) over Taurus;
> Phoebus (Apollo) the shapely Gemini;
> You, Cyllenius (Mercury), over Cancer;
> and Jupiter, you yourself rule Leo
> with the Mother of the Gods;
> Virgo who bears ears of grain belongs to Ceres;
> and the forged scales to Vulcan;
> quarrelsome Scorpio clings to Mars;
> Diana cherishes the hunting man part horse (Sagittarius);
> and Vesta the contracted stars of Capricorn;
> opposite Jupiter is Aquarius, the star of Juno;
> and Neptune acknowledges his own
> Pisces in the upper air.[48]

There is, at least, a certain logic to this arrangement, and it is the one that I prefer.

---

48 Gillman. "Twelve Gods and Seven Planets." Accessed 8 May 2013, http://cura.free.fr/decem/10kengil.html.

I prefer this arrangement for its symmetry as well as its logic. In Figure 8, you can see that each pair of male and female deities is set opposite each other. And there is some rationale given for each of the correspondences. Astrologers may find it itches their mind to place, for example, Mercurius in charge of Cancer, but remember that the planetary gods are a separate arrangement from those of the twelve.

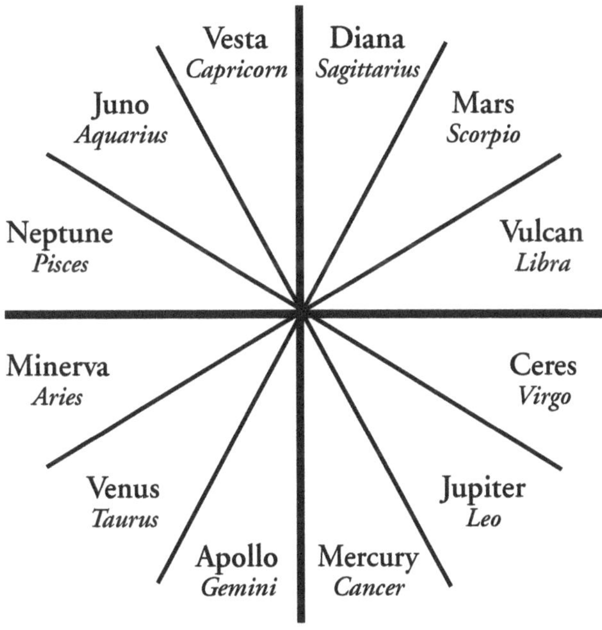

Fig. 8: Gods and Astrological Signs

For those with a less ceremonial bent, this arrangement may not be of much use. But it can help us time particular theurgic rituals to coincide with auspicious seasons. For example, the Spring equinox, when the sun enters into Aries, is especially useful for the worship of Minerva. And if you wish to cultivate a particular relationship with a god, then performing rituals during their month is a good way of aligning your theurgic goals with cosmic timing.

The Theurgist as Synthema

Saturday Night Live, a comedy show running since 1976, had a skit several years ago in which a pious housewife—played by Sally Field—goes through her morning praying for her daughter at school, her husband at work, and finally for the characters on her favorite soap opera. At that moment, Jesus appears and asks her to stop praying so much, since it requires him to do a lot of work just to keep the rice from getting sticky and helping her vacuum the stairs. The skit ends with Jesus feeling a bit guilty and erasing her memory of the event, whereupon she goes back to praying about trivial things.

We all know people who are so enthusiastic about their religion that they tie it to all aspects of their lives, and while we might find that a bit ridiculous and risible, especially when those facets of life include trivialities, we also—I think—kind of admire it. After all, who can be so dedicated and single-minded but a saint? The pious housewife that Sally Field plays in that skit is earnest and likeable even as we laugh at her.

I think what I find ridiculous in that attitude is the abdication of life involved in giving over every daily activity to a deity. Humans are creatures that choose and create, and when we decide to give up choice in order to subject our entire will to a deity, we reduce ourselves to programmed robots. I cannot imagine that's what the gods want or find appealing. After all, what good is a praise from a robot? So in writing this section, I put myself in a sticky position: I want to suggest, even advocate, an enthusiastic immersion into your theurgy without necessarily becoming a Pagan update of the old skit.

Another reason the pious housewife in the *Saturday Night Live* skit seems ridiculous is that she's asking a transcendent deity for help in housework and cooking. At one point, she suggests that perhaps she has gone too far in asking for help for her daughter in her algebra class, to which Jesus replies something like, "No, that's okay, she's going to need algebra in her later life." This sends her into confusion: how can a transcendent deity support the study of algebra but not care about the vacuuming?

As theurgists, we have no such problem: the gods do work, and we do work with the gods. They are not transcendent or not purely so. Their immanent part is present as synthemata in our daily life, and in our practice of theurgy we can strive to make ourselves synthemata of the gods.

Consider your daily activities. When you cook dinner, you are in the immanent presence of Hestia, goddess of the hearth, even if your modern hearth is a microwave. If you are locking your door in the morning, you are honoring Janus Bifrons, god of doorways. If you are driving to work, you are in the temple of Hermes. If you are drafting a memo about a new policy, you are making an offering to Zeus. If you are, either as father or mother, caring for your child, you are doing the godwork of Hera. And when you sleep, you enter the domain of Hypnos. Every act, every area and domain of life, is a *temenos*, a sacred precinct of one or more gods. When we overtly recognize this fact, we begin to make our lives a synthema.

This doesn't mean you must change your life to become a saint (although it might lead to you changing your life to become a more effective father, a more caring partner, a more honest businessperson). It means that your life as it is, as it currently stands, is a synthema of the divine, a manifestation of the logos that guides and undergirds the cosmos. Even the dull, everyday details of your life are under the gaze of a god. As the old occult maxim has it, there is no part of you that is not of the gods.

The theurgist recognizes this and makes of these activities an opportunity for contemplation. We don't need to drop to our knees. In fact, no one needs to know what we're doing at all for most of these activities. In the next chapter we'll talk about more overt ritual actions we can take such as libations and offerings. But here are some gestures we can make to recognize the domain of the gods in our lives and begin to act as a synthema in our own right.

The simplest and quietest way of recognizing the gods' actions in our lives is to call up a phantasm, even for just a second, of the god or goddess connected to any given activity. For example, while cooking we can imagine the image of Hestia at her sacred hearth, just for a moment. If that's too much, one can simply recall the god's emblem: Hestia's fire or Hermes's staff, for example.

If you wish to audibly or silently recognize the deity, you can do so with a short verbal formula. For Greek gods, you can say *khaire* (pronounced, approximately, "hhai-reh" with a harsh h) and the name of the god in the vocative. For Roman gods, you can do the same after saying *io*, pronounced "ee-oh" or "yo." For Egyptian gods, the introductory word is *dua* pronounced however you darn well please, since scholars really have only a vague notion anyway. You can say these formulae aloud or to yourself. I tend to mutter a quiet "khaire Herme" if I find a coin on the ground, but mostly I keep it to myself. You can also use your native language to recognize the god by name; don't worry excessively about linguistic authenticity.

One useful traditional formula is a quick blessing of Janus on leaving home. The phrase "*Io Iane, pro itu et reditu*" means "Hail Janus, for going out and coming back." If you keep in mind Janus's cosmic role as not only god of your personal doorways but also the doorways of the universe, you'll find this a useful way to train yourself to recognize those liminal spaces in which magic can occur.

Certain physical gestures, traditional salutes to the gods, can also be used to subtly invoke a god at the appropriate moment. For example, ancient Greeks might kiss the fingertips of the right hand on seeing the sun or the moon for the first time in a day. Socrates mentions saluting the sun this way, and Burkert describes it as a common salute to the images of the gods.[49] It's easy enough to perform unobtrusively and good practice in keeping conscious of the movements of the heavenly bodies, as well as the gods they represent. A clockwise circumambulation of a sacred object is also a symbolic salute to the deity it represents or houses. This may be a sacred spring, tree, or an artificial object like a statue. In doing both of these gestures, the theurgist identifies himself or herself symbolically in relationship

49 Walter Burkert. *Greek Religion.* (Cambridge, MA: Harvard University Press, 1985), 75.

to the god. The kiss is a small offering of breath, a dedication of the soul to the divine presences of the moon and sun. The circumambulation identifies the theurgist with the path of the sun, of course, and it also inscribes a circle with the sacred object at the center and the theurgist describing its circumference. As we know, a circle is a powerful geometrical shape, representing the emanation of the world from the elaboration of the One. The choice of the sun and the moon as primary objects of this kind of veneration is also significant: the sun is a metaphor for the One, and the moon is therefore the Nous that reflects the One. These simple gestures are—to those in the know—profound philosophical and metaphysical statements.

Other more elaborate physical rituals may be undertaken, but we will cover them more fully in the next chapter. So far, these are all intermediate synthemata that have the benefit of bringing our bodies into accord with the divine and making our actions synthemata of the gods. Secondarily, they are easy to perform: it requires no particular training to kiss one's hand. We know, however, that noetic synthemata also exist and are in some ways more powerful. Iamblichus argues that the material and intermediate synthemata are starting points for theurgy given to those with little training or skill, while the more skilled theurgist works with the mind. I lean toward a blended position in which all these forms of theurgy work best when in harmony: when the material synthemata are chosen well and the intermediate synthemata are performed mindfully, all guided by a mind shaped by the noetic synthemata.

Plato describes a simple meditation that can lead one very far into becoming a synthema of the gods. Plotinus, we are told by his biographer Porphyry, used this meditation to achieve henosis.[50] Plato presents it in a dialogue in the *Symposium*, in which Socrates reports the words of the wise woman Diotima. She suggests an exercise by which one climbs a ladder of abstraction toward the Form of beauty:

---

50 Mark Edwards, trans. *Neoplatonic Saints: The Lives of Plotinus and Proclus by their Students.* (Liverpool: Liverpool University Press, 2000), 44.

Exercise 3.2: Contemplation of Beauty

Step 1: Select a single beautiful object, one that you love intensely. This can be a person or an object. Contemplate this beauty discursively, seeking out what it is that makes this particular form beautiful. Identify its abstract, rather than physical beauty. Perhaps you admire the way your lover's hair falls: recognize that it's not the hair, but the grace of the hair, that you find beautiful.

Step 2: You will begin to see that this beauty exists elsewhere in other things as well: the fall of a waterfall, the movements of a cat, and so on. Recognize and contemplate the nature of these beauties, all of a kind together with each other, each representing some instantiation of the same ultimate beauty.

Step 3: As you continue with this contemplation, you will begin to see the beauty of virtue superseding that of the body itself. Contemplate those virtues that are beautiful, leaving behind physical form. Muscles are beautiful because they are power in control: the control of power is a virtue separate from any physicality, so contemplate the virtue of self-control or balance and harmony.

Step 4: As you do so, you will begin to see the beauty of systems of knowledge, ideas, and laws. Contemplate the beauty of these until you begin to recognize that what is beautiful in a society or a system of knowledge is the same thing, no matter how it is instantiated. Recognize that cultural customs may change but they reflect ultimately the same underlying values of the family that is humanity.

Step 5: Ultimately, you will begin to move up to realize that all beauties, all virtues, all beautiful customs and systems of knowledge partake of a single ineffable beauty, the Good. This experience is henosis, and achieving it, even for a moment, makes your mind the same as the Good, which is the One.

The Noetic Synthema of Memory

The art of memory was a central part of Renaissance esoteric practice, and the Greeks also honored and admired the power of memory, so much so that Socrates, perhaps ironically, calls writing a poison that kills memory and suggests that we shouldn't write down the things he says. Of course, he does this in a dialogue that Plato did, fortunately, commit to writing.[51] Training your memory is also useful in the rituals of the next chapter, so you can memorize how to do them rather than reading them off of notecards. Since the Logos is organized, training the human mind makes it a synthema of the universe.

The goddess of memory is Mnemosyne, a Titan or primordial deity and mother of the nine muses who inspire all knowledge and art in humanity. She is a personification of memory itself, and she had no cult, no temple, and few myths. In later Neoplatonic and Hermetic religious beliefs it was thought that she presided over a spring in the underworld, the Pool of Mnemosyne, whose waters countered the forgetful effect of the waters of the river Lethe. Those who died usually drank of Lethe, and forgot their lives before being reborn. Initiates in the secrets of the underworld, however, could choose instead to drink from the Pool of Mnemosyne, and thus remember who they had been in their previous lives. Memory was a type of religious salvation.

The basic key of memory is this: we remember phantasms to which we have an erotic link, and we do not remember things that are not linked to a phantasm by an erotic connection. Now, by "phantasm" I mean sensory image, and by "erotic" I mean emotive, not necessarily sexual. I use these particular terms rather than more contemporary psychological terminology, because they are evocative of the way in which the training of memory creates a synthema out of the mind. Eros is a god: you see supposed depictions of him on Valentine's day, a cute cherub with a bow and arrow. But in the Orphic tradition, Eros is not just a cute cherub, but another name

---

51 Benjamin Jowett, trans. *Phaedrus by Plato*. Accessed 10 May 2013, http://classics.mit.edu/Plato/phaedrus.html

for Phanes, a fundamental god that orders reality and establishes the "first origin": he is the god that brings things together, the god of gravity, magnetism, sympathy, and love.[52] In modern terms, he is the god of the fundamental forces that bind atoms. He also lends structure to the mind, making memory possible. One of the easiest ways to make these erotic links is by using the method of loci, or places.

Since I mentioned the method of loci, I am now required by law to tell a particular story. Every book on memory tells this story, so I assume there must be a law requiring me to tell it: Once, during a banquet, Cicero tells us, the blind poet Simonides was called out of the hall to answer a message. While gone, the hall collapsed, killing everyone inside. When they cleared the rubble, they could not identify the dead, so Simonides walked among them naming the bodies, because he had memorized their locations in the short time he had been in the hall.[53] I don't find this a particularly unlikely story, and it has very little to do with the method of loci, so—there it is. My obligation is fulfilled.

The method of loci takes advantage of our sense of space to create an orderly mental framework upon which we can hang ideas. You can use any space with which you are familiar, or even an imaginary space, as long as it matters to you in some way. If you wish to remember a sequence of things—a grocery list, ritual actions, the names of your nephews—you simply enter in the imagination into a space you are familiar with and begin placing phantasms of those things to be remembered in various orderly locations.

This is easier exemplified than explained. Let's imagine I wish to remember my grocery list: eggs, butter, apples, cherries, tuna, bread. I enter—in my imagination—my front door, which I imagine dripping with broken eggs, the yolk running down over the threshold and the front steps. The tea

---

52 W. K. C. Guthrie. *Orpheus and Greek Religion.* (Princeton, NJ: Princeton University Press, 1993), 80.

53 This account is found in Cicero's *de Oratore 2.74.299–300,* which is available online at http://www.utexas.edu/research/memoria/Cicero.html, accessed 11 May 2013.

table inside the front door has been spread with a thick coating of butter; I'll never get it cleaned off the glass top. My piano has had all its white keys replaced with apples, all its black ones with cherries. The bookshelf against the wall has flopping tuna-fish between the books, and the couch has been replaced with a comfortable-looking giant loaf of bread.

This example exemplifies four essential principles of this technique:

1. **Order:** The items are placed in a specific sequence, set by the pattern I walk into the house when I enter the front door. This pattern never varies. These locations are called loci.
2. **Phantasm:** Each item to be remembered is remembered not as a word but as an image, a phantasm, with as much sensory detail as one can call up. The more vividly they can be imagined, the more successfully they will be remembered.
3. **Brevity:** Objects with natural groupings can be grouped together: it makes sense to include apples and cherries in the same locus. One can cluster a large number of objects together, up to eight or even more, thus expanding a relatively small number of loci.
4. **Eros:** Each image is arresting. They are not particularly erotic in the usual sense (although they could have been) but they cause a reaction of attraction or repulsion that helps them stick in the mind. The objects interact with or replace the objects in question: the connection is active, not passive. An object changing, replacing, or modifying a locus creates a stronger erotic link than merely having an object sit in a particular locus.

Your home is one simple set of loci you already have, and the Greeks and Romans used other systems as well. Later Renaissance thinkers elaborated into very large, abstract collections of loci. A common set was the twelve signs of the zodiac, which already come with specific images that are easy to incorporate into phantasms. Other masters of the art of memory created elaborate temples or palaces called memory palaces where they could store their ideas.

Renaissance Neoplatonists like Giordano Bruno structured memory palaces out of geometrical relationships so one could not only store ideas but link them together in geometrical relationships: their memory palaces became engines for thinking.

The point of all of this was not simply to memorize shopping lists or the points one wished to make in a speech. The point is to construct and order the mind according to principles of order or cosmos, thus putting the mind in order to mirror the order of the universe. Doing so brings the mind closer to the Nous wherein dwell all the ordering principles of the universe. The beneficial side effects of memory should not be discounted (with my native memory being what it is, that I have these techniques is a godsend). They are, however, side effects: the real result is an ordered mind which can see more clearly into the world of Ideas.

EXERCISE 3.3: ORDERING THE MIND

You can, of course, simply use your home as a source of loci, but unless you are careful to walk through it exactly the same way in your imagination each time, there is room for confusion. A more elaborate and useful temple can be constructed in the mind that can hold any number of objects. We will construct such a temple now.

STEP 1: Sit comfortably and close your eyes as you imagine the loci I describe. Place them in the spatial order described, as if you are walking through the space. You'll need to get in the habit of walking through this space many times, each time visualizing each of the details as the same. This exercise will be easier if you already are familiar with occult symbols: otherwise, you will need to memorize the symbols as described for the first time. This will require native memory to some extent, but you will find it easier if you can imagine yourself viewing them in space rather than memorizing them in the abstract.

Imagine a door of wood, with a brass handle. Open it and step into a foyer. On each of the walls of the foyer is a mural. Begin with that behind you and go clockwise around the room.

Behind you is a mural of three parts. On the bottom is a rocky environment, with plowed fields in the distance. Standing above this environment is a gnome, a small man in a peaked green hat. Above him stalactites hang down. To your right is a similar mural of three parts. This one has waves on the bottom part, a beautiful naked woman standing on the waves in the middle part, and a sky of heavy rainclouds above her. The wall to the right of that wall, the one facing you as you enter the room, also has three parts. On the lower half is a lake of lava, smoking. Above that stands a curling lizard. Above him, the sky is lit red with lightning and smoke. To the right of this mural (on the wall to your left as you enter the room from the outside) is another three-part mural: on the lower part, white fluffy clouds float through a blue sky. Above those clouds is a young man with wings, rising upward with a satisfied look on his face. Above him is a soft yellow glow, as if the sun is just out of the frame.

The center of the room contains an altar with a golden lamp and an offering dish.

STEP 2: Once you have built this structure, you will find it easy and useful to employ in your daily life. For example, if I am going shopping for the ingredients for a cake, I need sugar, vanilla, eggs, milk, lemon juice, cocoa powder, flour, baking soda, and salt. These are nine items, so I can place them on the murals by starting with the earth mural. I call up the scene I've built on that mural, then place sugar on the lower part: in the rocks there is a visible vein of glittering sugar, rather than precious stones. The gnome is swigging from a brown bottle of vanilla extract with visible delight. The stalactites have round, white eggs dangling off their ends. In the mural of water, the ocean waves are white and frothy: they've become milk.

The undine is biting into a lemon and making a face, and the rain clouds in the back are dropping cocoa into the milky sea. The mural of fire takes the next three items: the lava has been sprinkled with flour and so has become breaded and browned; it looks tasty. The salamander has swallowed baking soda, and so he is rising like a biscuit: he's all puffy. The smoke in the sky has crystallized into square salty crystals.

Obviously these images are weird, and you may feel strange taking what are essentially sacred images and applying often ridiculous phantasms to them. In fact, one of the reasons the art of memory finally died out in the middle ages is that theologians felt much the same way: applying vain images to often holy scenes was seen as impious. I would encourage you to think of it otherwise: the universe has a sense of humor, and by ordering these things in whatever way helps us remember them, we too begin to understand the humor of such incongruities and their underlying reason.

STEP 3: The altar in the center of the room has another use: to sacrifice those memories and thoughts that cause us pain. We can use it to offer our flaws, our painful memories, and our weaknesses to the gods to take care of. Essentially, you can imagine the source of your pain as an object in the offering dish, then burn it to white ash with the flame of the lamp. You will not forget painful memories this way, but it is a way to understand the alchemical process of transforming pain into something more useful.

As this last step implies, the palace of memory is also a place where we can work on ourselves in a safe mental environment. It becomes a psychological tool as well as a practical tool, and in bringing it into order we bring our own minds into order. The more ordered our minds, the more we are able to think and consider and hold, the more we become like the universal Nous.

You don't need to build this kind of esoteric memory palace in order to have an effective place to store and organize ideas as well as a space for psychological work. Any structure will work. This particular example has some advantages: it's organized already, built out of already available esoteric symbolism, and not tied to a particular place. One disadvantage of using a physical place is that those places change and move about. I was using my childhood home for years after it was torn down, and now I often use the front room of my house with the awareness that it might well no longer resemble that in the future. You can also build different palaces. For example, you will eventually find twelve slots to be a bit crowded (although you can double or even triple up the things you store in those slots), so you can add additional murals—the seven planets, the twelve signs, and so on. Essentially, any ordered system of easily visualized symbols can be used as a memory palace.

The method of loci isn't the only means of memorization, of course, and in fact I use it much less often than I use more versatile methods like the peg system, in which each number is assigned an iconic object. I would heartily recommend that those interested in such methods read a book such as *Your Memory* by Kenneth Higbee.[54]

Lares and the Shrine

A shrine is a small space set aside for household or private worship. A shrine may house a cult figure just as a temple does, but it is the center of personal, not civic, devotion. Shrines in Neopaganism are popular, giving rise to the saying about a Neopagan's house: "Every wall a bookshelf, every surface an altar." These altars are really, usually, shrines, containing one or more deity figures, certain tools of religion, and perhaps an offering bowl or dish. Every Roman household had a particular shrine, some more ornate than others,

54 Kenneth Higbee. *Your Memory: How It Works and How to Improve It.* (Boston, MA: Da Capo Press, 2001).

known as the *lararium*. The lararium usually consists of a peaked roof or painting of one, supported by two pillars. In the middle of this portico is the figure of the family genius or guardian spirit flanked on either side by two lares figures. The lares were household gods, supporters and protectors of the family. Below these figures there is often the depiction of a serpent, representing the land's fertility. In addition, there may be a shrine to the penates, the guardians of the cupboard.

These shrines, the ancient lararia and the modern Neopagan altars, are collections of synthemata to achieve a particular theurgic effect. When the young Roman boy offered a lock of hair to the lares of his family, he symbolically sacrificed himself to his own duty as an adult: he became the synthema of sacrifice. And when Neopagans burn incense or make offerings to the goddesses and gods on their private altar, they are situating themselves in relationship to those deities, reenacting the establishment of divine order.

The minimum a shrine requires is an image of a deity—which can be simple or complex—and a means of offering. An incense burner and a forked twig may be enough for a witch of certain traditions, while some of us may prefer more complex arrangements. Working tools, devices of divination, and whatever other impedimenta we gather in our esoteric practices may end up on the table as well.

A shrine may also be made portable and can consist of nothing more than a drawing of the deity and a bowl or cup. The point is simply to focus one's mind on the deity; complexity isn't required.

It is useful to establish a place for theurgy in your home, so you can work with the material and intermediate synthemata while simultaneously training your mind in harmony with the noetic synthemata.

CHAPTER 4

Rituals and Tools of Theurgy

All of our preparation and work so far has been chiefly mental. And this is the method chiefly preferred by the Neoplatonist Plotinus. Iamblichus, a student of Porphyry, took it a different route, though, realizing that in the material world, the rituals and their synthemata are a sacred reenactment of actions in the Psyche and the Nous. We can learn to control the course of our minds and souls by performing rituals. He looked specifically at the rituals in common use at the time—sacrificial rituals to the gods—as a way for the common person to achieve henosis. I will describe these sacrificial rituals in depth and discuss how we might perform them ourselves even if we are not exactly Romans of Late Antiquity or ancient Greeks. But before I get to that, I imagine some readers may have an objection to the idea of ritual, an idea shared by Philanike's student Euthymios:

> **Euthymios:** A toga? Are we going to a frat party?
>
> **Philanike:** No, I'm reenacting a sacrificial ritual.
>
> Eu: And . . . why?

Ph: Partially out of the fun of it, but also because it'll help you see a particular avenue to henosis.

Eu: And this is authentic, then? Where are the cows?

Ph: By Late Antiquity, it was actually more common to sacrifice bread instead. Plus, it's hard getting the stains out of the carpet, not to mention my soft side doesn't like to watch things die, even if I am going to eat them later.

Eu: And the toga?

Ph: Highly inauthentic, actually. Togae were men's clothing; if a woman wore one, she was a prostitute. But they're comfortable.

Eu: I'm not a fan of ritual.

Ph: Oh? Really? Why not?

Eu: It just seems like empty posturing. If you were really good, you wouldn't need ritual.

Ph: Let's define our terms. What is "ritual"?

Eu: A set of actions, I guess.

Ph: All actions are rituals? If they come in a set? Is making soup a ritual?

Eu: It can be. If it's something you do at a particular time or place. Making a turkey on Thanksgiving is a ritual in America.

Ph: What makes it a ritual on Thanksgiving but not if I decide to make a turkey for dinner tonight?

Eu: I suppose it's the symbolic meaning, the community involved.

Ph: Do rituals always have a community component?

Eu: Often they seem to. So a ritual is a set of actions with symbolic meaning, often with a communal purpose.

Ph: If I, in a society where pagans are rather scarce on the ground, perform a pagan ritual, is it a ritual? What community does it serve?

Eu: It puts you in a sort of community with your gods.

Ph: Do you have to know the symbolic content for a ritual to work? There are some words, called Barbarous Words of Invocation, of which no one knows the meaning. But I use them in rituals.

Eu: That's what I'm talking about: they become empty then. It's just posturing.

Ph: But wait...do we have to know the meaning of a word to use it?

Eu: I'd say so!

Ph: What does "the" mean?

Eu: It's a word that... it's a definite article.

Ph: Meaning what?

Eu: That the word that follows it is—definite. It's a particular one of a set of things, like...

Ph: "The Romans ruled much of Europe and Africa." Is "the Romans" a particular Roman?

Eu: No.

Ph: Then that's not what "the" means. Do you know exactly how to define "the" to cover all of its uses?

Eu: Guess not.

Ph: Yet you can use it and understand it. So I can perform some actions as part of a ritual whose exact symbolic meanings I do not know, but that have an effect in creating communion with the gods: are there any parallels to things in our world that are like that?

Eu: I suppose passwords. I don't need to know what a password means to type it in and get access to a computer. So some ritual actions might be like passwords, signs of recognition to the Nous.

Ph: Exactly. Hardly wastes of time, then. What about your second objection, that one shouldn't need ritual. Why is ritual a crutch?

Eu: Well, you used the word "crutch," not me. But okay, it's a crutch because it's material.

Ph: And matter is bad? You almost sound like Plotinus.

Eu: No, I know you don't agree with him that matter is corrupt. So it's not just that it's material, it's that it's…showy. It's showing off.

Ph: You're the only one here, so who am I showing off for?

Eu: If that toga slips and the blinds are open, the neighbors. But okay, I see your point.

Ph: So in what way is this a crutch?

Eu: Well, you should be able to do everything that ritual does with your mind alone.

Ph: "Should"? Says who?

Eu: It's weak to rely on physical objects when you can just do all the work in your mind.

Ph: Did you drive here or walk?

Eu: I drove.

Ph: Why? You could have walked.

Eu: It's four miles, and it's raining. It would have taken forever, and I'd be soaked.

Ph: So why is that okay but using ritual—which can be faster and easier for some people—not?

Eu: I guess it's just that I feel ridiculous.

Ph: Does feeling ridiculous damage your soul or just your
personality?

Eu: Just my personality. My soul can't feel ridiculous.

Ph: Is your personality always right about what is good?

Eu: No, sometimes it just wants to eat or drink.

Ph: Then why trust it with this matter
until you test it out in your soul?

Eu: All right then, fix your toga and let's see how
this works with my soul. But I'm wearing pants!

Anthropologists, archeologists, social scientists, and probably a few unemployed eccentric people have all studied and written about ritual. We can dig up long, elaborate accounts of the rituals of people from diverse cultures, analyze the parts of a ritual from them, and discuss at length their social function. But while that endeavor is probably valuable, it's not going to help us understand how ritual can play a part in our theurgy.

Like Euthymios above, some people may dislike the very idea of ritual. Some of that dislike is, I think, a result of early religious training: the puritan antipathy to pomp runs deep in American culture. And some of it might also be a rejection of early religious training: for many people, being dragged to their church's religious services on Sunday is a tedious memory of childhood. But for many others it is an exciting and stirring event, and I know people—ordinary, practical people and not religious fanatics—who enjoy going to church and look forward to Mass or communion every week. What they enjoy, if you press them, is the community and the sense of spiritual calm that comes over them after having participated.

This same kind of spiritual communion is at the heart of antiquity's most important rituals. I will divide rituals into two broad classes and describe how the specific rituals in those classes were (or may have been) performed. The first is the ritual of communion, which almost always involves an exchange of offerings to create a relationship with a deity, hero, or daimon. The second is the mythic reenactment, a somewhat more freeform structure applicable to a broad range of theurgic uses.

Rituals of Communion

In ancient Greece and Rome, every ritual of communion operated on an often misunderstood principle expressed in Latin as *do ut des*, "I give, so that you may give." Now, Latin is a very concise language but unfortunately a lot of people misinterpret this principle as one of the flaws of Pagan religion: that all relationships with the gods are merely utilitarian, and that one gives offerings and worship only in return for some material benefit. This interpretation may well have been one that some people held in antiquity, but by Late Antiquity Neoplatonic philosophers had reinterpreted this phrase in a more charitable (and frankly more reasonable) way.

A gift, as Marcel Mauss informs us, requires a return gift.[55] It's a universal cultural assumption that gifts create obligations, and gift customs arise as a means of negotiating those obligations in a peaceful way. Giving a gift to a god also creates a sort of obligation, one that must be repaid with an answering gift. Obviously what the human gives to the god in offerings is of relatively little value to the god. What need does a god have for food or drink or incense? Gods are not material, so none. But the offering is a pretext for the god to offer us what the gods already offer: a pathway to henosis.

The gods already give us form: it is form that makes the wheat, eggs, butter, and whatever else turn into cakes for us to sacrifice, or the grapes to turn to wine for us to pour out. This form is imposed onto the elements by the gods of those things, and when we offer them up what we're acknowledging is that the form itself is a gift. We are paying the gods back: "I give because

55 Marcel Mauss. *The Gift: The Form and Reason for Exchange in Archaic Societies.* (New York: W. W. Norton, 2000).

you gave." At the same time, it gives the gods an excuse, a pretext, to lift us up beyond the world of matter as well.

Ultimately, offering is two polite people standing at an open door. "After you." "Oh no, after you." "No, I insist." This sort of back-and-forth exchange might be useless for entering a building, but it's how our human souls climb back up to their origin. This, I think, is something even Plotinus misses when he discusses how souls interact with bodies: the communication goes both ways, from the world of Ideas down to matter, and back from matter up to the world of Ideas. We don't change the gods by offering them gifts; we change ourselves, making ourselves receptive to the gifts they offer in return.

Obviously, the fact that the sun does not go out or that people do not spontaneously fly off the surface of the earth indicates that the gods are not capricious, despite their bad reps from mythology. People who do not respect the gods or even believe in them live perfectly content and useful and even spiritually fulfilling lives. The gods are not establishing the road of particular kinds of offering as the only road to the One, nor are they forcing or demanding anyone to take that road. Other roads are also good roads, going to good places. I rather like this one, however, and maybe you do too, since you've stuck with me for a hundred pages or so.

The Things Shown and the Things Said

The ancient Greek mystery religions divided a ceremony into three parts: the things shown, the things said, and the things done. From a theurgic perspective, each of these is a symbol of the gods. The objects shown in the ritual—that is, the ritual implements or tools—each represent a faculty of the soul. The things said—the words of the prayers and hymns and incantations—create a relationship between the theurgist and the gods. And the things done are a participation in the maintenance and harmonizing of the world; by participating in this work of the gods, the theurgist becomes divine. To participate in the work of the gods is to become godlike.

Still, one of the greatest sins of the ancient world was hubris, attempting to become what one was not. The Greek oracle at Delphi had the inscription "know thyself," something contemporary people often take to be an exhortation to contemplation. But it was also a warning: know that you are human, not divine; do not strive to be a god. At the same time, the mystery religions of Late Antiquity recognized that humans have a divine part—in one myth, we are sprung out of the ashes of the god Dionysos and the evil Titans who consume him. To reclaim and recognize that divine part is to indeed know oneself, and the theurgist must always guard against hubris.

Things Shown: The Ritual Tools

Classical sacrifice required relatively few implements: fire, water, a knife, and a basket. For some rituals in ancient Rome, the priest may have a special staff used to outline the sacred space. Other rituals may have involved other tools or embellishments, too. But for the most part these four objects are the necessities. In fact, as the basket exists mostly to transport the knife and the groats, we can reduce the typical religious ritual to three elements: fire, water, and a knife, and the knife is only used for blood sacrifices.

Fire is a symbol of divine Form and the realm thereof: it represents the Nous, the consciousness of the universe that becomes the thoughts it thinks. Of fire, Plotinus writes: "Always struggling aloft, this subtlest of elements is at the last limits of the bodily. It admits no other into itself, while all bodies else give it entry... It sparkles and glows like an Idea."[56] When the worshiper throws incense on the fire, it is a sacrifice of Form to the Nous, and a recognition of the connection between matter and Form. Fire, therefore, is ubiquitous in theurgic rituals, and a common theurgic implement is the sacred lamp. The instructions we receive for this lamp are simple. We get them chiefly from the Greek magical papyri, a collection of ritual notes from theurgists and thaumaturgists from Late Antiquity: "Put an iron lampstand in a clean house at the eastern part, and having placed on

56 Elmer O'Brien, trans. *The Essential Plotinus.* (Indianapolis: Hackett, 1975), 37.

it a lamp not colored red, light it. Let the lampwick be of new linen."[57] The requirements for this tool in modern terms are these: it is a lamp never used for anything but theurgy—hence, the new wick—and it is not colored red, a color regarded as ill-omened in Egyptian magic. These lamp spells, which are various, are almost always spells of divination or revelation: the lamp is the light of the Nous, which by perceiving we gain knowledge of the Forms.

Water, on the other hand, represents Psyche, the soul. Where the lamp is the mind—illuminating the Forms—water is the soul, taking on the forms from above and transferring them to matter. The symbolism of purification is, of course, obvious: one washes with water. But the ritual of making *chernips,* or holy water, which will be discussed more fully later, involves extinguishing a burning stick in the water to make it sacred: this is a reenactment of the descent of the Forms into the world of psyche and hence to matter. A common recipe for holy water in the Greek Magical Papyri is to mix natron with the water. Natron is a naturally occurring mixture of salt, sodium ash, and sodium bicarbonate (baking soda); it has a number of practical uses as a detergent and antiseptic, and was used as such in Egypt throughout antiquity. While the ritual of chernips is a symbol of creation, natron water is a substance of cleansing.

The knife is the tool of death that brings the sacrifice over into holiness. As such, it's hidden in the basket under the more benign sacrificial grains. But at the same time, the knife is used as a tool of demarcation. It is carried, hidden in the basket, around the sacred area to outline it before the ritual—much as ceremonial magicians or Wiccans today might inscribe their circle with the athame. As a tool of analysis and separation, it's therefore a symbol of Logos or Ratio, the fundamentally rational order of the universe.

Theurgists and thaumaturgists alike sometimes use other, secondary tools as well. A particularly important one of these is the magic wheel, a historically

---

57 Hans Dieter Betz. *The Greek Magical Papyri in Translation: Including the Demotic Spells.* (Chicago: University of Chicago Press, 1992), 133. PGM VII 540

difficult-to-identify object (or maybe variety of objects) that the theurgist used to participate in the creation of the universe as demiurge. Spinning the magic wheel apparently opens a gateway to the gods by emulating the circular motions of the heavens. Unfortunately, few such wheels have survived, and descriptions of them are sparse. In one of his poems, Theocritus describes a witch who uses a magical wheel as a tool to summon back a lost lover. This wheel is described as a "bronze rhombus" that "whirls by the power of Aphrodite."[58] Of course, Aphrodite is the goddess of the spell that Theocritus describes, so we cannot conclude that all such magic wheels were symbols of a single goddess. The word "rhombus" doesn't just mean the shape we associate with that word; it can mean anything that spins and appears to be a common word for what we would call both tops and bullroarers. The bullroarer is a prehistoric musical instrument that involves a weight on a cord that is whirled about the head to create a humming or howling noise. In fact, many scholars suggest that Theocritus is describing two different instruments, a iunx and a rhombus, and that the terms are not synonyms.[59]

The iunx (plural iunges) is named after the wryneck, a bird with an unusually flexible neck and a distinctive song. It's possible that actual wrynecks were attached to wheels, but the few specimens of magical wheels that we have have the wrynecks molded out of terra cotta. Probably, the idea that birds were tied to these wheels was merely a gruesome embellishment of popular literature. We have one particular example of a terra cotta iunx designed to be hung by cords on the circumference so that it hung horizontal to the floor. When spun, the cords along its circumference would twist it upward, and as it fell they would untwist. Inertia would then cause them to twist back up, raising the wheel, causing it to fall again and so on, until friction brought it to a halt.

58 Georg Luck. *Arcana Mundi: Magic and the Occult in the Greek and Roman Worlds.* (Baltimore: John Hopkins University Press, 1985), 69.

59 Fritz Graf. *Magic in the Ancient World.* (Cambridge, MA: Harvard University Press, 1997), 179–180.

The Chaldean oracles command the theurgist to "Operate with the magic wheel [στρόφαλον] of Hecate,"[60] which indicates clearly that a magic wheel of some kind was dedicated to this goddess. This word *strophalos*, here translated "magic wheel," appears to mean "something twisted or spun." Marinus, in his biography of the Neoplatonic theurgist Proclus, describes his use of the "supplications of the Chaldeans, together with their divine and ineffable revolutions."[61] Michael Psellus, an eleventh-century scholar, describes the use of a special bullroarer sacred to Hekate, consisting of a sapphire enclosed in a golden sphere and swung about on a rawhide string. This is puzzling, since a sphere is too aerodynamic to make a good bullroarer; it will not whistle. But it may be that Psellus is trying to describe another kind of instrument related to both tops and bullroarers, and he makes it clear that there may be some variation in the structure of these stropholoi (which he explicitly equates to iunges), saying that they may be "spherical or triangular or some other shape."[62]

It is my conjecture that all these objects—iunges, strophaloi, bulloarers—are tools similar to the prayer-wheel of Tibetan Buddhism: a mechanical object regarded as offering a prayer when spun. Psellus's description, that it is inscribed with sacred characters, is evidence that it was regarded as a sort of solid prayer. Moreover, the model he describes is a simple (although hardly simple to create) model of the universe as understood at the time: a sphere—earth—surrounded by the spheres of the planets. I doubt, however, that the actual strophalos was spherical, as the noise it made was probably part of its psychological and symbolic efficacy. In fact, several objects appear to have been called *iunges*, including sacred objects that hung from a temple of Apollo.[63] Since the word "strophalos" appears to come from the root for "to twist," it may be that this object is what is often called a

60 Ruth Majercik. *The Chaldean Oracles: Text, Translation and Commentary.* (Leiden, NL: Brill, 1989), 127.

61 Mark Edwards, trans. *Neoplatonic Saints: The Lives of Plotinus and Proclus by Their Students.* (Liverpool: Liverpool University Press, 2000), 100.

62 Sarah Iles Johnston. *Hekate Soteira.* (Atlanta, GA: Scholars Press, 1990), 90.

63 Sarah Iles Johnston. *Hekate Soteira.* (Atlanta, GA: Scholars Press, 1990).

whirligig, a disk with two holes through which a cord loops. The disk can be twisted up, then the loops pulled, which causes the disk to spin and make a whistling noise. Since the iunx is associated in magic with attraction and bringing together, this conjecture seems likely.

Making this kind of strophalos is simple. You can get a length of cord from a craft supply store, as well as a small piece of wood to shape into a disk. Drill two holes, one on each side of the center of the disk; measure them carefully so that the centers of the holes line up with the center of the disk. Run the cord through the holes into a large loop. Give it a few twists, then set it spinning by pulling and relaxing the loop.

If you wish to inscribe it with sacred symbols, we are stymied by not knowing what sorts of things might have been on the strophalos of Hekate. The best bet is to simply inscribe the wheel with an appropriate versicle. In Hesiod, for example, Hekate is granted three domains, and it is suitable to write them on the strophalos: she is said to rule in the heavens ΟΥΡΑΝΩΙ (ouranoi), in the sea ΘΑΛΑΣΣΗΙ (thalassei), and on the earth ΓΑΙΗΙ (gaiei). See the following illustration:

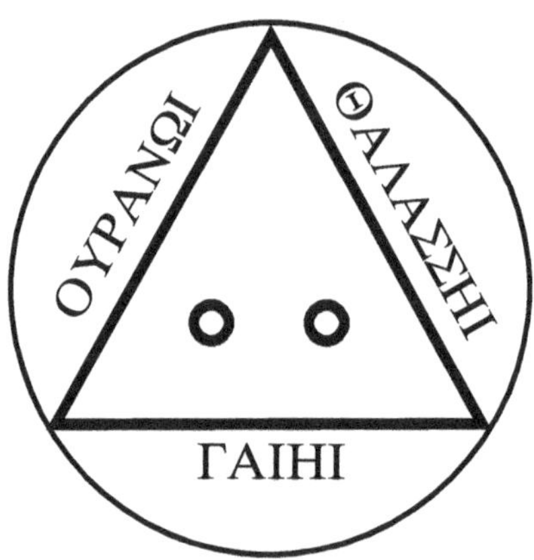

Fig. 9: Inscriptions on the Strophalos

This tool can be used at the beginnings and ends of rituals to enter into a ritual state of mind. The twisting and untwisting creates a double revolution, first inward then outward, which is worth meditating on discursively. The sound made by the wheel—which you can intensify by serrating the edges—can also induce trance and offer a sort of auditory scrying tool. Finally, the magic wheel is said to be particularly useful in summoning spiritual entities; the Chaldean oracles even call the intermediate deities between the world of matter and the highest gods *iunges*.

While probably a physical object, the strophalos also may have had a meditative analog. In other words, the external tool may have reflected an internal exercise. We cannot know for sure, but it's possible that the material strophalos was only one part of the equation. The wheel about which the theurgist is to labor may have been internal.

Exercise 4.1: The Meditation of the Strophalos of Hekate

Step 1: Sit or stand upright. Calm yourself by deliberately relaxing and begin to breathe. Inhale from the bottom of your lungs, filling them to 80 percent capacity, hold briefly, and then empty them from the top to the bottom. Do this several times.

Step 2: Imagine a small blue light in your solar plexus. As you inhale, imagine it getting brighter.

Step 3: Visualize a golden light that surrounds this blue speck in a sphere. As you inhale, let it spin clockwise, stopping while you hold your inhalation for a second, then reversing when you exhale. As it spins clockwise, let it expand outward. As it spins counter-clockwise, let it concentrate and shrink. It helps to work with an actual strophalos beforehand to get that physical sense of expansion and contraction.

Step 4: Let it spin for several breaths. With each spin, let the light concentrate on the contraction.

Step 5: Finally, exhale and imagine it fading out of your perception.

Try this exercise as a preparation for rituals that involve attracting the attention of forces or spirits. For example, you might use it as preliminary invocation. I have also experimented with placing the mental strophalos elsewhere. The third-eye area and the base of the spine seem to be particularly interesting places to imagine this spinning sphere concentrating the light.

Things Said: Prayer

In theurgy, the line between prayer, hymn, and incantation is blurred. Classical, formal prayer was rather formulaic while hymns were metrical and narrative, and incantations sometimes contained "barbarous words," which were actually occasionally "barbarous" (in the sense of "foreign") and were sometimes strings of vowels possibly meant to be sung. One quickly turned to another, however, and in various accounts we sometimes have prayers that turn to hymns, hymns that end in prayers, and incantations that bust out in the middle of either.

Prayer for the ancient Greeks and Romans was not merely communication with a deity. It was about establishing and maintaining a relationship. Valerie Warrior defines two broad categories of Roman prayer: the petitionary (asking for something) and the laudatory (offering praise).[64] In this, Roman prayer was not much different from Judeo-Christian prayer. In fact, like Christianity, Roman prayer had an actual liturgy: certain traditional prayers spoken at certain times. Because they often made use of forgotten Etruscan or archaic vocabulary, these prayers sometimes crossed the line into incantation. Greek prayer, on the other hand, followed a formula but not a particular set liturgy of the Roman complexity. At least, no such Greek liturgy has come down to us. A Greek prayer breaks down into predictable sections:

1. **Identification:** This stage involves naming the god, usually beginning "Hear, O … " For the Greeks and to some degree

64 Valerie M. Warrior. *Roman Religion: A Sourcebook.* (Newburyport, MA: Focus, 2002), 38.

for the Romans, naming a god wasn't a simple matter. A name was important; it defined a relationship. To name a god wrongly was to imply the wrong relationship and prevent communion. So both cultures erred on the side of excess, and named every name or epithet that might be relevant, often ending with "or whatever you wish to be called." Such a string of names ensures knowledge of that god's names and attributes and also exerts a somewhat hypnotic effect. The identification is sometimes followed by mention of particular locales wherein a god may dwell or come from, often the locus of that god's largest or most influential temple.

2. **Justification:** This step might seem odd to a Judeo-Christian culture steeped in the concept of a god of grace who offers favors freely but whose favors cannot be earned. The justifications offered to the gods consist of previous acts of piety: "If ever I have made sacrifice, kissed my hand to your image, set up a temple" or whatever. This isn't an attempt to wheedle or guilt the deity into listening (not to imply there probably weren't worshipers who thought of it exactly in those terms, but then there are present-day Christians who think that Jesus cares about which football team wins the Superbowl). The purpose is to remind the theurgist the nature of the relationship: again, just as the names show knowledge of the god, the justifications remind the worshiper of his or her piety.
3. **Petition or Praise:** Here, the worshiper asks for what he or she wants, or offers praise. Often in thaumaturgy and ordinary folk religion these were requests for material things, but philosophers stretching back to Socrates encourage people to ask more wisely in their prayers, and many later philosophers simply pray for the Good.
4. **Vow:** Here is the *do ut des*—"I give so that you may give"—of classical religion that is much maligned but serves a very valuable spiritual purpose. The vow is a promise to the god. This kind of

> promise is familiar to those who pray when they find themselves in trouble: "I swear, if I get out of this, I'll never go to the casino again!" That example is a negative vow, but the vows of classical prayer were positive. "I will offer you a hecatomb of cattle," for example, or "I will burn you a handful of incense." Such a vow serves again to cement the relationship between the worshiper and the god and also ensure gratitude.

I can imagine someone objecting that this formula drains all the life from prayer, but it serves a useful purpose. Probably, people still prayed in a more informal manner from time to time, and I certainly do, but following the formula allows one to hit the bases, as it were. For example, I've occasionally launched into a prayer to a god and found myself in the justification section with nothing to say. That's an indication that perhaps I need to work with that deity a bit more before I start making requests. In other words, the formula outlines the nature of the relationship itself.

The attitude and posture of prayer is also important. In praying to most gods, the Greeks and Romans stood, with hands in the air and palms facing upward. For chthonic gods or the dead, hands might not be raised and the prayer may be murmured. Finally, prayers to the gods of the sea—and perhaps to nymphs and spirits of the earth—are spoken with the arms spread wide. Kneeling is not common, although clutching the knees of sacred statues is sometimes described. These vertical postures mark the worshiper as worthy of respect: again, it is not the relationship of slave and master but a reciprocal relationship. Certainly nothing we give the gods can improve them or change them, but by standing up we acknowledge the divine inside of us.

Things Done: The Thysia or Offering

The central ritual of offering is called a *thysia* (Greek)or a *sacrificium* (Latin). Let's clear the air about what a sacrifice consists of and what it does not.

First, although there are attested instances of human sacrifice in Greek and Roman culture, the practice was entirely abhorred in most periods.

Lurid depictions of such things in myth are meant to be lurid: they are meant to shock, not be a familiar part of what one does. In the late empire, the gladiatorial games were sometimes conceived of as a kind of human sacrifice, but many philosophers spoke against those games as a repulsive failure of social virtue. So a sacrifice is not a human sacrifice, and the concept of human sacrifice is not central to the classical concept of sacrifice with which we will concern ourselves. Of course, one particular religion centered on a human sacrifice became quite popular in Late Antiquity: this cult, Christianity, spread effectively. Few people now even consider that the central organizing myth is one of human sacrifice, although of course it is.

The second delicate issue is that of blood sacrifice. While human sacrifice was abhorred, blood sacrifice of animals was not. For most citizens of Rome or any given Greek city state, the meat of sacrifice was the only available meat. Many people only ate meat at the public barbecue that was sacrifice. While authors sometimes squirm to imagine the rivers of blood involved in sacrificing a bull (let alone a hundred bulls, enough to feed a town), such rivers of blood flow in our own culture—we just keep them tidy and out of sight. Watching the bull or goat be slaughtered was one way to assure its quality, at least, without government inspectors. Our own squeamishness about the origin of our meat is a peculiarity of our culture, not a universal law or a sign of moral superiority.

That said, I do not advocate you practice blood sacrifice for a number of important practical and spiritual concerns. First, it may be illegal for you to do so in your jurisdiction, at least if you are in the United States. Some religions such as Santería that still practice animal sacrifice are allowed to do so by United States law, but you would need to prove that it is necessary and fundamental to the practice of theurgy, and I don't think it is. In addition, it often violates local husbandry laws to raise or slaughter animals within a city limit. Second, you may not have the knowledge to do so effectively and painlessly, which not only may put you up against charges of animal cruelty but may also offend the gods. According to the traditional rituals, the animal must come willingly to the slaughter and consent to its death (usually accomplished by sprinkling water on its head to make it nod). I interpret this to mean that undue pain should not be caused, and slaughtering an animal is a complicated process requiring skill and physical strength. Third, doing it wrong can kill you: if you nick the wrong part of the viscera while slaughtering some animals, you could make yourself very sick off the meat. Fourth, it's frowned on in our culture. While I'm not by any means an advocate of doing only what is socially acceptable, you will create a bad name for esoteric spirituality by making use of blood sacrifice. And finally and most importantly, it is unnecessary. We can do perfectly well with bloodless sacrifice, and since cattle no longer symbolize wealth to us, it is more or less meaningless to kill one.

If you are a farmer with a permit to slaughter meat and you intend to use it for your family *and* you have the facilities and know-how *and* are willing to undertake the research and the responsibility, *and* perhaps you already slaughter your own meat and wish to do it in a sacred manner—then by all means, look into it. Or if you are a hunter who dresses his or her own deer and wishes to make that act a sacred offering to Artemis, then be my guest. If, however, you have read a ritual in the Greek Magical Papyri or other ancient source that involves sacrificing a cat or strangling a bird and you want to do that ritual . . . then I suspect you merely selected a spell in that text of hundreds of spells that would allow you to torture an animal, and then I think very, very little of you as a person. In fact, such rituals are almost always easily and effectively adapted to remove the requirement of animal sacrifice.

It is not a cop-out to avoid animal sacrifice. Theurgists of Late Antiquity were already arguing against animal sacrifice. Porphyry wrote "On Abstinence from Animal Food," a work that makes the argument that animal sacrifices were a recent invention and that the most ancient sacrifices were of grain, fruit, and bread. Consequently, these sacrifices pleased the gods more, and were to be preferred. Porphyry also advocated for vegetarianism and laid out a thorough philosophical case against the teachings of Stoics and Epicureans in that regard.[65]

The bloodless sacrifice practiced by the ancient Greeks and Romans has much in common with similar practices throughout the area settled by the Indo-European people in about the fourth millennium BCE. The cultures descended from those Indo-European people all exhibit the ritual sharing of food, both of animals and of grain: the Norse, the Celts, and the Vedic religion of India. The thysia, to use its Greek name, is the ritual consumption of food with the gods. This ritual partakes of the powerful symbolism of the banquet: what we eat with the gods makes us companions of the gods. The etymology of words of Latin origin often reveals interesting symbolism: the word "companion" is from two words: *con*, meaning "with" and *panis*, meaning "bread." We become companions with those with whom we share bread.

The ritual of thysia had a set order.[66] I should point out here that the Roman and Greek rituals differed in details. For examples, Romans usually covered the head with a fold of the toga before offering the sacrifice. Other details may differ from festival to festival or even region to region. There was not a universal, standard missal. But from what we gather from ancient sources, these eight steps remained more or less constant throughout the Greco-Roman world.

Procession: This is a procession toward the place of sacrifice. In the home, of course, this was simply approaching the lararium or shrine, but a larger festival may have a procession with music, dancing, and so forth. We have many images from Greek vases depicting these processions featuring lines of dancing boys and girls, cattle or other animals, and at the front a basket and a jar of water. This basket contained groats and a sacrificial knife, used to slit the animal's throat. The water was for purification, the next step.

---

65 Porphyry. *On Abstinence from Animal Food.* Thomas Taylor, trans. http://www.tertullian.org/fathers/index.htm#Porphyry_Abstinence

66 Walter Burkert. *Greek Religion.* (Cambridge, MA: Harvard University Press, 1985), 54–59.

Purification: The Greeks created "lustral water" by dousing a brand into pure water. This water was used for washing the hands. The act of ritual purification is common throughout the ancient world; the idea that one must have clean hands to approach the gods is an old one. Symbolically, it is the evacuation from one's being of the extraneous, the dirty, or the day-to-day. Like the procession, it serves to mark us out as being in a different place, a new state of mind. More elaborate purifications are not unheard of for certain rituals, such as ritual baths made to expiate a flaw or crime or in preparation for magical workings.

The formula for holy water here—the quenching of a brand from the sacrificial fire into the water—is called *chernips* (literally "hand washing"). In other sources, and especially it appears in Roman rituals, the water was sacred due to its origin: particular sacred springs produced holy water.[67] Although we do not know the exact recipe, you can make chernips very easily by lighting an appropriate herb—rosemary is always appropriate and easy to come by—and extinguishing it in the water. This chernips is not only used to wash the hands, but also sprinkled over the altar, sacrifice, and so on. This, along with the circumambulation of the holy objects, creates a sacred space and is, I suspect, a precursor to the magician's circle, which later became the circle of Wicca.

The chernips is also sprinkled over the head of the sacrifice, which nods in response. This nod is important: the animal to be sacrificed had to seem willing to undergo the procedure. Sometimes modern authors sneer at this as a "trick" to get the animal to nod, as if the Greeks and Romans didn't realize that the animal was merely responding to droplets of cold water. Of course they realized this, but they wanted to make it clear that they understood the importance of this act, and this action symbolized that this was not an act of violence but an act of communion between three participants: the worshipers, the sacrifice, and the gods.

---

67 Walter Burkert. *Greek Religion.* (Cambridge, MA: Harvard University Press, 1985), 77.

These first two steps establish a typical opening ritual for all theurgic ceremonies whether of worship or more practical magic. The next steps involve sacrifice specifically, but often sacrifice is folded into the practical magic of the ancient world.

Invocation and Immolation: The next step is the invocation of the deity through an invitation and a libation of wine and an offering of barley mixed with salt. In animal sacrifices, the barley and salt were thrown on the sacrificial fire, an act referred to as *immolatio*, from which we get our word "immolation." The grain and wine are offered not by the priest in charge of the sacrifice but by the audience. In this way, everyone has a hand in preparing the offering and so they all participate in not only the eating of the meal but its creation. It's not unlike the wonderful custom in some Christian churches in America of having parishioners prepare and bake the bread to be used at communion.

No matter the sacrifice's intended recipient, it is very common that particular gateway deities are invoked first. In Roman ritual, this is Janus Pater, who is invoked before almost all sacrifices because it is he who opens the door to the gods. In Greek rituals, the deity invoked first is often Hestia, who is thought to preside over the sacred fire just as she presides over the sacred hearth, although in theurgic rituals Hekate often fulfills this role of gatekeeper.

Dedication: The priest in charge of the ritual approaches the animal to be sacrificed and produces the knife from the basket. He cuts a small lock of hair from the forehead of the animal, and throws that hair on the fire. This dedicates the animal to the god and is regarded as the first stroke of sacrifice, even though no blood has spilled.

Prayer: The priest says a prayer. Sometimes this is a formulaic prayer, and in ancient Rome the prayers that have survived sound more like legal contracts than prayers of devotion. The prayer is loud enough for the crowd to hear. This is not private or whispered or silent prayer, but prayer on behalf of the community.

Killing: The priest kills the animal according to a prescribed manner. Smaller animals have their throats slit, larger animals are killed by a blow to the head. This is actually almost exactly the procedure used to kill animals in modern slaughtering, by the way: it is efficient, quick, and minimizing suffering. Of course, there is still some suffering and in response to that the attendant participants—especially the women—raise a ritual cry variously interpreted as sympathy with the animal, "life crying over death," or an expression of grief.[68] In any event, the custom strikes me as more humane in many ways than the quiet and clandestine way we now produce our meat.

Examination: In both Greek and Roman rituals, the entrails are examined for flaws. This custom probably began as a way to ensure that the animal was healthy and the offering good. If any flaw was found in the entrails, the meat was discarded and the sacrifice redone. The result is that diseased animals were not often eaten.

It is a small step from deciding that the meat is unfit for offering to deciding that the gods have rejected the sacrifice. And it's a small step from *that* conclusion to the idea that the sacrifice becomes a place where the gods communicate: by examining the sacrifice, we can determine the future. Particular patterns of development on the liver and other organs could be read as a sign from the gods, and even variations in a healthy liver may indicate a sign. This practice was called haruspicy. More fully developed in Rome, haruspicy is the result of this chain of reasoning, which must have come about very early. The Etruscans, the inhabitants of the Italian peninsula before the arrival of the Romans, had already written handbooks and guides to the art of haruspicy, to the point where it was sometimes called the Etruscan art.

Sacrifice and meal: The animal's bones were laid out to reconstruct the original form and covered in fat, which was then lit. This, mingled with incense and fueled by strong wine, was the offering to the gods. The worshipers ate the meat, with a common prohibition that the meat must be eaten on site and not taken out of the sacred precinct described by the circumambulation. The

68 Walter Burkert. *Greek Religion.* (Cambridge, MA: Harvard University Press, 1985), 55.

reconstruction of the skeletal form can be interpreted as an acknowledgement of the underlying Form or Idea of the animal being offered. The restraint on the location of the sacred meal is a symbolic recognition that the act of sacrifice has elevated this particular earthly location above and beyond, for a moment, the rest of the earth. To take what is holy out of it would be to enact a sort of Pagan fall-of-man. To eat it in the sacred *temenos* or precinct was to commune with the gods.

At its most basic level, this ritual of thysia is a ritual of communion. To get tied up in the blood (as many modern writers do) is to miss the point. The slaughter of an animal appears to us as disturbing and barbaric, with our modern sanitized practices, so we hide it from sight. But the sacrifice rituals of ancient Greece and Rome made it a sacred thing. Far from barbaric reveling in blood, this practice underlined the human need to kill to preserve life, making of it an appropriately solemn act.

My vegetarian readers may well point out that they do not in fact need to kill to live; they get by on plant foods just fine. Interestingly, vegetarianism was not unknown in ancient times: there were those who forewent meat under much the same moral objections as those raised by contemporary vegetarians. The most famous of these ancient vegetarians was Pythagoras, who famously managed to go without both meat *and* beans, something modern vegetarians might find difficult. The rationale for his vegetarianism is spiritual: he believed in the transmigration of souls and did not wish to violate the cannibalism taboo by eating a body belonging to a once-human soul. Why he eschewed beans is another question entirely, one subject to a lot more debate and speculation than it deserves.

The thysia is not always a blood ritual, even among those who are not vegetarians. In fact, later thysias were often simply symbolic of blood rituals, and the practice of offering cakes shaped like animals began in Late Antiquity. Probably this innovation was in response to the difficulty of staging a full public sacrifice in populations that were increasingly Christian.

The choice of what to sacrifice also has symbolic significance. While certain things are always appropriate—wine, bread, grain—other things are set aside for particular deities. Dogs, for example, were offered to Hekate (don't even *think* about it), and virginal animals were given to the virgin goddesses such as Athene. The offering of the wrong sacrifice could obviate the whole ritual or even cause a rift in the relationship between the god and the theurgist.

Offerings to the Dead

Where the thysia reaches upward, the offerings to the dead reach downward. The sacrifice for the dead differs from the thysia in several points. Instead of an altar, there is a trench—a clear reflection of the symbolism of up and down. The dead were regarded as below us, even the blessed dead and heroes, and so offerings to them were placed in the earth. The Greeks referred to such daimones as *chthonic*, "of the earth." In fact, even deities like Hades were given sacrifice in this chthonic manner. The offering itself was burned completely, rather than shared out like a thysia. This offering is less a communion with the dead than a nourishment of them.

Symbolically, the theurgist stands between two extremes: the world of matter and the world of the nous. She reaches up to the world of the nous by making offering to the gods. She reaches down to pull up the world of matter by making offering to the chthonic deities and heroes. To eat the sacrifice to the dead would be to "stoop below into the dark-gleaming world beneath which an abyss is spread."[69] But there is a responsibility to go back into the dark, just as the person who escapes in Plato's allegory must return to free the others. The theurgist therefore becomes a bridge between the world of matter and the world of the nous.

The theurgist, through sacrifice, becomes a synthema of the gods. The ritual cry of the women as the throat of the sacrifice is struck identifies the worshipers with the object of sacrifice, acknowledging mortality and the necessity

69 Majercik, Ruth. *The Chaldean Oracles: Text, Translation and Commentary.* (Leiden, NL: Brill, 1989), 111.

of death-in-life. But it also is a cry of exultation, a raising up of the self beyond death. The sacrifice illustrates the process of death and offers a promise in the fire. As the fire consumes the flesh but doesn't become it, so does our soul inhabit our flesh but not become it. As it raises up, so do we. And as form is found in the midst of the ashes, so does form descend into matter from above. For the theurgist, the sacrifice is a ritual of contemplation of divine mystery, not merely an excuse for a barbecue.

Libation

A widespread Indo-European custom of pouring out drink offerings to the gods as well as the dead points to an ancient origin for the custom of libation. The Greco-Roman practice was ubiquitous. Every banquet involved a libation, as did nearly every prayer. And libations solemnized agreements. The verb for "they make a treaty" is *spendontai*, which literally means "they pour out a libation for themselves." Three particular liquids are widely offered in Greco-Roman traditions: wine, which is probably at the top of the list because of its commonness, the ordinary drink of day-to-day life; honey, often offered to the dead specifically; and oil, poured over sacred objects as an offering.

The process of offering a libation has three parts: First, a small or large portion of the liquid is poured out. To the dead, this may be the whole quantity, and if it is oil, it almost certainly will be. Second, a prayer is made. Then, finally, if wine is the libation, the remainder of the wine is drunk by the worshiper. This last stage may be done rather cavalierly, without much pomp, almost exactly as we might drink our afternoon cup of coffee. A libation, unlike a sacrifice, can be made anywhere, at any time, to any deity at all. The symposium, a formal drinking party, has a specific ritual of libation in which libations are poured for Zeus and the Olympians, the heroes, and then Zeus Teleios, Zeus the Finisher, god of endings. Alternately, the order can run Agathos Daimon (the person's personal spiritual guardian, like a guardian angel in our terms), the heroes (which may include cultural heroes as well as ancestors), and Hermes.[70] Each of these orders is significant, of course: the first addresses the heights, then the depths, and then establishes order around the two by invoking Zeus Teleios. The second order addresses the good spirit who watches over each person, the dead who came before, and the mediator between them. After this somewhat formal ritual, however, the libations may flow as individual desire, piety, or whim directs.

I used to imagine that Greek and Roman houses had floors stained a sticky purple from all the libations offered. Archeological evidence, however, has turned up many stone tables with hollows in them to receive liquid: these libation tables probably served as small altars for daily prayer, as well as a way to keep the floors clean. There's every reason to guess that dishes for the purpose may also have been used then emptied outdoors after the meal or simply allowed to evaporate over time.

The symbolic significance of the libation is in many ways more profoundly communal than that of the sacrifice itself. Where the sacrifice burns matter to reveal the form beneath, the libation takes the formless and pours it out. The libation is a reenactment of the soul's descent to trigger a corresponding ascent. The word for "treaty" is, as mentioned before, the same as that for "libation." Hence, libation makes peace with the gods.

Other Offerings

Food isn't the only thing offered to the gods; there is a long tradition of offering incense as well. The practice of offering incense is simple: a sacred fire is lit, usually with fire gathered from the temple of Hestia or by other ritualized means, and then grains of fragrant gums and bark are sprinkled on the fire. These were usually imported from the east, but Ovid waxes nostalgic, longing for the day when:

> As yet no foreign ship had brought bark-distilled myrrh cross the
> blue seas; the Euphrates had sent no incense, India no spice;

70 Walter Burkert. *Greek Religion.* (Cambridge, MA: Harvard University Press, 1985), 70–71.

> nor were the threads of red saffron then known to man. The altar would smoke, content with Sabine herbs, and the laurel would burn up, crackling loud ... And the knife that now lays bare the entrails of the stricken bull then had no work to do in sacred rites.[71]

We know now that Ovid is historically wrong in some sense: the practice of blood sacrifice is ancient. But he was already imagining that blood sacrifice might be replaced with the sacrifice of sacred herbs, not the fancy myrrh and expensive saffron of the east, but local, ordinary fragrant herbs: laurel (which we usually call bay) and the "Sabine herbs," or juniper.

Not every sacrifice or offering is poured out or burned. Archeologists have discovered pits of artifacts in the midst of sacred temple precincts. Often, these pits contain small terra cotta figures of men and women, sometimes holding animals as if for sacrifice. Sometimes, they are sculptures of body parts, chariots, ships, and various other objects. Other times they're just plaques with inscriptions. Usually the inscriptions are short: a name and the name of a god. Sometimes, they are more elaborate, offering a testimony of miracles accomplished by the god.

The practice of making a votive offering, or anathema is a symbol in honor of a vow.[72] In making the offering, the worshiper is saying not "I give so that you give," but "you gave, so I give back." These offerings could not leave the sacred precinct, as they belonged to the god after being dedicated, so they would pile up and priests would even bury them in pits for storage.

---

71 Valerie M Warrior. *Roman Religion: A Sourcebook.* (Newburyport, MA: Focus, 2002), 42. Fasti 1.337–61.

72 The contemporary meaning of the word in English comes from the fact that *anathemata* were set aside and sacred. To touch or remove them was considered very improper. Later, it was used as a word to describe those that the Catholic church wished to separate or set aside from communion—in other words, the excommunicated. In this way, the idea of sacredness was reversed and to be anathema was to be cursed rather than sanctified.

These pits are treasure troves of archeological information; hopefully the gods are not offended when we take these objects away for study.

The joke, ancient in its origin, is that although there were many votive objects of those who had been saved, there would have been many more if those who had not been saved had been displayed. This cynicism about traditional religion is very common even in the ancient world, and it's a welcome shot of critical thinking in the midst of a topic sometimes open to wishful thinking. However, the practice from a spiritual, rather than a practical, sense is a kind of thanksgiving and not necessarily evidence-gathering.

While the votive offerings filled up temple grounds, private citizens offered their own votives to the gods of the home. In Rome, for example, a young man surrendered "symbols of his boyhood" when he came of age.[73] A young girl would offer her old childhood playthings and clothing. Here, the young man or woman becomes a bloodless sacrifice to the family gods, a rite dedicating oneself to a life of piety and moral virtue.

So, what's the payoff for us, living in the twenty-first century? How can these rituals of offering help us in our new theurgy? The answer to that is obvious on one level: we can make offerings to the gods to establish a relationship with them and participate in their work. By participating in divine work, we become divine ourselves—not gods (that'd be hubris), but what we as humans already are and have forgotten: partners with the gods in the great work of creation.

Exercise 4.2: Performing a Libation to a God

Step 1: Have a glass of liquid, preferably something you like to drink.

Step 2: Pour a small amount out onto the ground or into a libation dish. Imagine the essence of this libation expanding throughout the local space, becoming available to the god.

---

73 James B. Rives. *Religion in the Roman Empire.* (Maldon, MA: Blackwell, 2007), 119.

Step 3: Pray, beginning with "To you," and the name of the god. Feel free to use this prayer of Socrates as a model:

> Beloved Pan, and all ye other gods who haunt this place, give me beauty in the inward soul; and may the outward and inward man be at one. May I reckon the wise to be the wealthy, and may I have such a quantity of gold as a temperate man and he only can bear and carry.[74]

Socrates directs this prayer to Pan, a god of nature, which is not insignificant, but you could direct the same prayer to any god of your liking.

Step 4: Drink. Moderately, please, if you are drinking alcohol.

Exercise 4.3: Performing a Sacrifice to a God

Preparation: You will need something to sacrifice, a source of fire, and a bowl of water. Tap water in a small bowl works fine. You will also need a stick or match or taper that can be lit. I find a sprig of rosemary to work well, and it also has the benefit of smelling nice.

Step 1: Kindle a fire on charcoal or a simple lamp for less elaborate rites. Make sure you know what you're doing—keep the room ventilated if using charcoal and don't burn anything on it you wouldn't want to inhale. (A single pinch of hot pepper might be very symbolically appropriate to Mars, but it's hard to complete a ritual when suffering the results of being pepper-sprayed. Trust my hard-won experience on this, and accept my plea of youthful ignorance.)

Probably you're lighting this with a match or lighter. So it goes. But it might be worthwhile to sanctify this fire with an incantation. Even if such actions were not done traditionally in sacrificial rituals,

---

74 Benjamin Jowett, trans. *Phaedrus by Plato*. Accessed 10 May 2013, http://classics.mit.edu/Plato/phaedrus.html

they were done in theurgist rituals. You can use the following, which I've stitched together from various bits of the Chaldean Oracles, or you can devise your own formula of sanctification. The goal is to identify the fire itself with the Nous so we can use it as a gateway:

> The Sun is the outpouring of Fire and the steward of Fire. For the maker of the fiery cosmos is the mind of Mind, and everything is engendered from a single fire. And when you see that most sacred holy fire leaping and shining down through the whole world, hear and know the voice of the fire. For a mortal, having drawn near this fire, will apprehend the light from god.[75]

STEP 2: Light a small stick, a sprig of rosemary, or even a match in the fire and plunge it into the water. In doing so, realize that you are mingling the water of soul with the fire of mind, and while the fire seems to be extinguished in the process, it actually infuses the water with its heat, just as the forms in the mind infuse our souls and hence matter.

STEP 3: Walk about clockwise, holding the water and—if using it—a sacred knife. If not, the water will suffice. When you return to the altar, sprinkle the altar and the ground within the circle with the water. If you like, you can say something signifying that the water is purificatory, such as this verse from the Chaldean Oracles: "Foremost, let the priest undertaking the work of fire himself be sprinkled with the icy waves of the deeply roaring sea."[76] (If that sounds familiar

75 I have modified and translated freely various fragments of the oracles, from the Greek text in Ruth Majercik's *The Chaldean Oracles: Text, Translation and Commentary.* (Leiden, NL: Brill, 1989).

76 Again, I have been very free and easy with the Greek in Ruth Majercik. *The Chaldean Oracles: Text, Translation and Commentary.*

to those inclined to ceremonial magic, it should: the same verse was cribbed for the same purpose by the Golden Dawn although with a different translation.) Pour some water on your hands to clean them.

Step 4: Offer a small amount of the offering to the fire to sanctify it. Use the sacred knife to cut it if it is a cake or piece of fruit; otherwise, just throw a pinch on the fire or begin to light the stick of incense in the lamp flame. Offer this to Janus or Hestia or some other gateway deity of your choice with a simple formula like "First, for you, Janus, this offering."

Step 5: Pray, stating the goals of the sacrifice and to whom it is directed. This may be multiple gods, of course, so this prayer could be lengthy. Pray aloud unless praying to chthonic deities or doing some form of practical magic, in which case it is appropriate to mumble or whisper.

Step 6: Sprinkle the remainder of the incense on the fire, or if offering food, cut the portion in half, leaving one half on the altar and eating the remainder, unless offering this to a chthonic deity or the dead, in which case leave it whole and on the altar. If using stick or cone incense, just place it in the holder. Again, imagine the essence and form of this sacrificing expanding out, multiplying, and becoming available to the god.

Step 7: Watch the smoke for omens, if you like. A strongly rising column is a good sign. A broken, wavy, or diffuse cloud is sometimes an omen that you have left something out of the sacrifice or are in a state of spiritual ill health, although it may also just be an omen that you need better weatherstripping.

Step 8: Clean up by putting the offering outside and putting away ritual tools. If offering incense, simply let it burn out over time.

Rituals of Reenactment

The various types of sacrifice and libation are rituals of communion, but the mystery religions, in addition, ritually reenacted particular myths. These reenactments allow the theurgist to participate in the work of the gods and thus elevate himself or herself to the nous and hence to the One.

Unfortunately, we don't know much of what went on in the mystery religions, but we do know that reenactment was a part of the initiation. For example, the initiate into the Eleusian mysteries apparently underwent certain ritual experiences including drinking *kykeon,* or water flavored with barley, something Demeter also drinks in the Homeric Hymn to Demeter.[77] The mystery at Eleusis and other mysteries elsewhere are lost, and attempting to reconstruct them is probably a fool's errand. Anything we create will not be a reconstruction but at best a new mystery.

That said, these rituals of reenactment point to a powerful theurgic technique in which the theurgist endeavors to experience the myth of a god as a mystery. However, it's hard to imagine how this might look, written in a book as a series of discrete steps. Some of the power of the mystery religions lay in their surprise, which is why they insisted on secrecy. If, as some Christian writers claim, the ultimate culmination of the cult of Eleusis was the showing of a single ear of wheat, this could be a profound symbol demanding contemplation and realization if the initiate had been prepared beforehand.[78] Merely reading about it robs it of its power.

We find public rather than secret reenactment rituals in the festival practices of Greek and Rome, such as the Lupercalia festival in which boys would whip girls with strips of hide, which was (somehow, apparently) a reenactment of Romulus and Remus's establishment of Rome.[79] These rites were public, but re-creating them now runs into the problem of cultural expectation. Lupercalia wasn't just a couple people doing a reenactment; it was a holiday like Christmas or Thanksgiving, and part of the significance was that the entire city participated. We lack this communal significance of the reen-

77 Marvin W. Meyer. *The Ancient Mysteries: A Sourcebook of Sacred Texts.* (Philadelphia: University of Pennsylvania Press, 1987), 18.

78 Meyer. *Ancient Mysteries.* 19.

79 Valerie M. Warrior. *Roman Religion: A Sourcebook.* (Newburyport, MA: Focus, 2002). 60–62.

actment ritual and thus most of its point. Re-creating such ancient festivals would not be a theurgic act but a cultural and artistic one, worthwhile in its own way but not necessarily useful for the practical purposes of theurgy.

If a theurgist should wish to make use of the power of mythic reenactment, rituals could be constructed rather than restored from the myths of antiquity. For example, we could take the hymn of Hermes described earlier and break it down into ritual actions and words. Begin, for example, with the music of stringed instruments. Then a backward circumambulation (tricky!), followed by twelve individual sacrifices to the twelve gods—I'd probably content myself with twelve grains of incense there, as twelve loaves of bread would get awkward. Next, a prayer and justification to Apollo, a prayer and confession to Zeus, and a vow of devotion to Apollo's harmony with another offering of music and the taking up of the caduceus and the responsibility of shepherding—viewed symbolically, of course.

What effect this or any other ritual would have depends entirely on the strength of the worshiper's contemplation. It loses the sense of surprise, other than that surprise that arises as a result from contemplation. Therefore, the theurgist must cultivate a ritual state of mind—and this is true of all ritual work—that is hyper-contemplative. Nothing just means one thing in ritual, and every object must be perceived not only with all the physical senses but as its ideal object in the Nous. Regular contemplative practice will help with this.

Enlivening Icons

For any ritual, it's helpful to have an image of the god or gods who are the focus of that ritual. This is especially true in ritual reenactment, because an ensouled statue of a god can stand in for that god's position and function in the original myth. For example, a statue of Zeus can be addressed directly during the Hermes reenactment mentioned above. Such enlivened statues were probably part of the "things shown" in these rituals, and I suspect that the famous "ear of wheat" the initiates beheld in the mystery of Demeter was an enlivened or ensouled image of the goddess in the shape of grain.

In chapter 3 you created a statue infused with some of the synthemata of the god. The following ritual is about animating the statue, as you now have the background and knowledge to do so. I mean the word "animation" in its original sense: to put a soul into. I am not suggesting that your statue will get up and move around physically. Although frankly, if it did, I'm not sure how surprised I'd be.

I would not undertake this ritual unless you have built up a relationship with the god in question. I'd strongly advise several libations, sacrifices, and prayers of praise in the weeks or months before attempting this ritual. And consider carefully: you will have a god in your house, and you can't exactly decide to throw it out when you move. At the very minimum, you will be responsible for dusting it and keeping it clean. Probably you will need to make libations and offerings of incense to it occasionally. It's not exactly as complicated as having a pet and certainly not as complicated as having a child, but you are inviting a powerful being into your life.

Our ancient instructions for how to complete this ceremony are limited. It's clear that the concept of the animation of statues comes from the Egyptian practice of opening the mouth, which was done to newly created mummies as well as divine images in order to enliven them. This practice involved touching the mouth with a forefinger or a special iron instrument. We have the entire ritual from ancient Egypt, but unfortunately it requires several participants and is extremely lengthy and difficult to perform without the full force of a theocracy behind you. Since we don't live in a theocracy, we need to modify our approach—and, doubtless, the Greco-Roman world modified this ritual as well, to the point where it may not have had any resemblance to the original.

Here is one ceremony I have constructed from ancient and modern sources. You can modify it as you wish. For the sake of clarity, I will give this ritual for the enlivening of a statue of Artemis, but I will place the names and incantations specific to her in italics so you can modify them to fit the god you wish to work with.

EXERCISE 4.4: RITUAL FOR THE ANIMATION OF A STATUE

STEP 1: Prepare the altar with a dish for libations, another for sacrifice, a censer with a charcoal fire, and the statue behind it. Also have a cup with wine or an appropriate beverage, a symbolically significant sacrifice (such as bread or grain), and an incense significant to the deity or otherwise appropriate (in this case, I am using myrrh). You will also need some water (about a half cup is usually more than enough unless you really get into your purifications) in a bowl, a sprig or twig to light in the fire, and a candle or lamp. You can also do this ritual with stick incense rather than charcoal, which might be more convenient for those of you with sensitive fire alarms.

STEP 2: Light the lamp, saying, as before, a prayer sanctifying the fire, such as this:

> The Sun is the outpouring of Fire, and the steward of
> Fire. For the maker of the fiery cosmos is the mind
> of Mind, and everything is engendered from a single
> fire. And when you see that most sacred holy fire
> leaping and shining down through the whole
> world, hear and know the voice of the fire.
> For a mortal, having drawn near this fire,
> will apprehend the light from god.[80]

STEP 3: Light the twig with the lamp, then use it to light the charcoal (this is easier said than done, so you may just wish to use a match or several, but the goal is to get the fire of the lamp to the charcoal; depending on your brand of charcoal, you may have to be persistent), and extinguish the twig in the water, saying the following:

80 This is, again, my own translation and free adaptation of the several Chaldean fragments. I have taken my Greek text from Ruth Majercik, *The Chaldean Oracles: Text, Translation and Commentary.* (Leiden, NL: Brill, 1989).

> Inflame the water of the soul with the light of
> Mind, to purify matter and drive out all the profane.

Pour some of the water over your hands and dry them on a clean cloth.

STEP 4: Circumambulate the altar, holding the statue in your right hand and the water in your left. When you return to the center, put down the statue and dip the three fingers of your right hand into the water, sprinkling it over the altar and then in the four directions.

STEP 5: Perform the contemplation of matter from exercise 1.1 on the statue until it is reduced to formlessness in your mind.

STEP 6: Recite the following from the Hermetica while looking upward and aspiring as much as possible to the Nous:

> Holy is God, and the parent of everything.
> Holy is God, whose will is done by his own powers.
> Holy is God, who wants to be known
> and is known by his own.
> Holy are you, having coalesced existence in a word.
> Holy are you, from whom all nature takes form.
> Holy are you, whom nature did not shape.
> Holy are you, the strongest of all powers.
> Holy are you, better than all goodness.
> Holy are you, too great for praise.

> Accept pure spoken offerings from a soul and a
> heart stretching out to you who are ineffable,
> inexpressible, named in silence.
> Give a sign to me that you will not reject my
> petition for the knowledge of our being.
> Empower me, and with this grace I will enlighten
> those of my kind who dwell in ignorance—

my siblings, your children.
Therefore, I believe and I witness:
I progress to life and light.
You are the basis of rationality,
and your people want to join with you in
the sacred work, as you provided them
with the power to do so.[81]

Step 7: Recite a prayer to the god in question, like this:

Hear me, Artemis of Ephesus, Potnia Theron, mistress of animals, Phoebe the bright, Locheia who guards the newly born, and Kourotrophos the nurse of the world, Agrotera, Cynthia, Diana, or by whatsoever name it pleases you to be called. Come from Ephesus, quickly, quickly, for you are able, goddess. If ever I have kissed my hand to the moon, burned you sweet herbs, or written poems in your honor, or offered you prayers of gratitude and praise, hear me. Come from Ephesus and dwell within this image, as a body upon the earth, which I will clean and honor and dress for you while it pleases you and while I am able. Come, goddess, and dwell herein, which I have made a fit place for your habitation.

Step 8: Build, as you pray, a phantasm of the god in question standing behind the statue. After the prayer, continue to strengthen the power of that phantasm while reciting the following words of power, taken from the Greek Magical Papyri:

81 My fairly free translation of Corpus Hermeticum I:31–32.

AEĒIOYŌ IAŌ AIŌ AŌI IŌA ŌIA ŌAI ŌYOIĒEA[82]

Allow the phantasm to give form back to the statue, in your mind reconstituting all the qualities you have taken away from it back into place, but this time, their divine counterparts.

STEP 9: Perform a libation to the deity, then recite a poem or sing a song in honor of the relevant deity. You can compose one yourself, or you can simply chant one of the shorter of the Homeric Hymns or one of the Orphic Hymns to the appropriate deity, or speak extemporaneously.

STEP 10: Burn part of the offering (a few crumbs will suffice) on the charcoal along with a few grains of incense, and say:

> O *Artemis*, I have brought this to you. I have offered
> this to you. Take of it and be glad, and enter into
> this image, to walk among the gods.

STEP 11: Touch the mouth of the figure and say three times:

> O *Artemis*, I open your mouth with the finger.
> I bring your mouth to the earth. I open
> your eyes. I bring your eyes to the earth.

STEP 12: Add more incense, then pray again:

> *Artemis of Ephesus*, who has come from your
> home to set foot in this place and join me
> in holy conviviality, be praised and thanked.

STEP 13: Contemplate the god as long as you wish. This can be a few minutes or quite a long time, depending on your personal

82 Instructions for pronunciation of Greek vowels are available in the appendix.

desire. There's no extra credit for taking longer, but also don't rush through it.

Step 14: When finished, offer a short prayer of thanksgiving such as the following:

> I give thanks to the gods, the daimones, and the ancestors who have led me to this place and who support and aid me in the great work of creation. May there be friendship between us.

Step 15: Close the ritual by placing the statue in an appropriate place (some statues you may wish to cover from prying eyes). When done, kiss your hand to it, turn around and leave the room in silence. Make sure you can easily clean and care for the statue as well as burn incense to it periodically. Pour out the libation outdoors, and let the incense burn down and cool before putting it away.

Step 16: To prevent foggy-headedness, I find it helpful to eat and do something mundane after a ritual like this one.

Don't make the mistake of thinking that this statue itself is a god; it is the dwelling of a god, and the god is not bound to it and can and will come and go as it pleases. Moreover, it may very well not be a god at all, but a daimon or messenger of the god (see chapter 6 for more on daimones). As Plutarch explains, to call the statue of Artemis "Artemis" is a convention like calling a collection of Plato's writings "Plato." When I buy a copy of Plato's dialogues, I might say "I'm buying Plato," but of course I'm doing nothing of the kind. Similarly, when I'm anointing the statue of Artemis, I am not anointing Artemis.[83]

---

83 James B. Rives. *Religion in the Roman Empire.* (Maldon, MA: Blackwell, 2007), 37.

I like to think of it as a telephone hotline to the god and an easy way to work with a deity for a long period of time without necessarily having access to a temple. You will notice that once animated, the statue does seem to take on a certain additional presence to the sensitive. It may be my imagination, but they almost seem to have facial expressions and react to events, although they do not move, of course. I suspect the mind anchors the phantasm to the statue, and what one perceives is the movement of that phantasm. You don't need to make such an object to be effective at theurgy, and while it may be tempting to fill a room with statues of gods, the cost is prohibitive and the work is considerable. Instead, carefully choose particular gods you wish to work with in this intensive way, based on your previous experiences, resonance with particular myths, and even insights gained through divination.

CHAPTER 5

Divination and Oracles

Most of what we've looked at so far has been about us talking to the divine forces of the universe, but as anyone who has ever been on a blind date knows, talking at someone isn't the same as holding a conversation. *Do ut des*—I give so that you may give—is the principle underlying the practice of making offering; the same reciprocity applies to the practice of prayer. The *des*, the giving back, of a prayer is an oracle. The word "oracle" itself (don't you love authors with a fetish for etymology?) comes from the Latin *orare*, "to speak," which is apparently cognate with the Hittite word *ariya*, "to consult an oracle." This idea of speaking to the gods, then, stretches back to the beginning of Indo-European history. Similarly, the word "divination" comes from the Latin *divinus*, meaning "pertaining to a deity." Divination was and is a sacred activity in which the gods speak back.

In my opinion, it's also the most fun of the theurgic practices. It's more common now to think of divination as an entertainment; we can visit a fortuneteller at the corner of the street and have our hands fondled, our cards read, and hear a string of pleasant and vague lies. This is, of course, nothing new. The ancient Greeks played a divination game at symposia: it evidently involved flinging the dregs of a wine cup into a brass canister and listening to the quality of the ping. It's hard to imagine that anyone took that terribly seriously.

At the same time, oracles and divination were a serious business. In the late Empire, it was a capital crime to consult an oracle or diviner of any type for the answer to any question concerning the Emperor. This act, as a threat to state security, was a crime of treason.[84] Later, Christian emperors obviously banned many of the practices, only relenting bit by bit as particular types of divination developed Christian justifications, such as astrology. Currently, in the United States, many states have a precarious and touchy relationship with "fortunetellers." As a laudable effort to crack down on fraud, some states have gone a bit far and banned any such activities, which then raises first amendment questions. For example, one could argue that divination is part of the religious practices of Neopagans, not to mention older religions such as Santería. What, then, happens to the practitioners of those arts? Are they automatically assumed fraudulent, or do they have first amendment rights to practice their religion? A long list of cases have gone to local courts, and in general the courts tend to uphold the first amendment rights of the diviners as long as no fraud is occurring. Some states and cities, in an effort to prevent fraud while honoring the right of people to believe what they like, require licenses. Others ban the practice outright. If you intend to offer divinations for money, don't trust that the courts will go your way in the case of a dispute: call your local courthouse or police station and ask about the local laws.

Fraud is a real problem now as it was in the ancient world; however, pseudoskeptics sometimes take these frauds as standard, ignoring in the process centuries of positive examples of diviners. Other skeptics, more intellectually honest, admit that people might well believe in their "woo-woo" but that it doesn't really work. Skeptics and pseudoskeptics have an arsenal of arguments for why divination doesn't really work even though it seems to. For example,

---

84 Valerie M. Warrior. *Roman Religion: A Sourcebook.* (Newburyport, MA: Focus, 2002), 150.

there is the well-known phenomenon of selection bias: we notice our successes and not our failures. This is true; it really does happen. But I don't know a single serious diviner who doesn't keep records and mark off successes and failures both. In other words, we are aware of selection bias and try to correct for it. Similarly, Barnum statements are often invoked as a common way to appear to say something serious but really say nothing at all. A Barnum statement is a description that applies to a large number of people, such as "you're a very social person sometimes." TV psychics use enough of these to fill a dumpster, which is where they belong, and skeptics are right to criticize them. But at the same time, in a real divination, I rarely run into such statements.

This criticism isn't new, by the way. Cicero, a skeptic of divination, argued in 44 BCE that divination is bunk because oracles are often vague. He cites the famous example of the oracle of Delphi, which predicted that

> When Croesus o'er the river Halys goes
> He will a mighty kingdom overthrow,[85]

Croesus did so, and lost his empire in the resulting war. Cicero argues that no matter what happened, the oracle would be right; it was a kind of Barnum statement, although Cicero didn't have that term. The Neoplatonists answered such criticisms by pointing to Heraclitus's maxim about the oracle: It communicates "neither talking nor concealing... but 'giving indications by signs.'"[86] In other words, yes, the oracle (and divination) doesn't talk to us in the language of linear logic, of true-and-false; however, it points to those things we might consider. What was the god saying to Croesus? "If you want to destroy empires, go ahead—to the gods, it's all one whether your empire or another is destroyed." Cicero ignores the important point of the oracle, which

---

85 W. A. Falconer, trans. *De Divinatione by Cicero. Loeb Classical Library, vol XX.* (Cambridge, MA: Harvard University Press, 1923). Accessed 13 May 2013, http://penelope.uchicago.edu/Thayer/E/Roman/Texts/Cicero/de_Divinatione/

86 Emma C. Clarke, John M. Dillon, and Jackson P. Hershbell, trans. *Iamblichus: On the Mysteries.* (Atlanta: Society for Biblical Literature, 2003), 157.

is the "when" statement. Croesus could have taken a moment to think about whether or not he really wanted to overthrow a kingdom or whether diplomatic means might be more appropriate. The oracle answers like a teacher: giving him an opportunity to rethink his previous ideas.

Frankly, as a skeptic, I am actually in some sympathy with Cicero, despite mostly accepting the Stoic and Neoplatonic doctrines that divination is real because the gods are real. I think it's healthy to cultivate a skeptical mind about all magic—theurgy, thaumaturgy, or divination. To accept unquestioningly is to be unthinking. As Socrates said, "life without enquiry is not worth living."[87] Similarly, the unthinking religion is not worth pursuing.

One trap I have seen in divination, in various discussion forums online as well as in conversations in person—and even in myself—is the tendency to justify. Here the skeptics are right, and we must guard against it. I see it especially in more complex systems that require interpretation, such as astrology and geomancy. If someone asks a question such as "Will I get the job?" and the chart says no, people often struggle to find some way in which to interpret it as a yes. "Sure, the moon is void of course and the signifier is square the quesited, but did you notice that Jupiter is in exaltation?" I call this tendency "obfuscation through elaboration," a desire to find some obscure detail or method that allows you to get the answer you want. It is rife in modern astrology and also common among tarot readers and other diviners.

Leaving this kind of fallacy aside, however, my anecdotal but skeptical experience of divination is that it works. Through it one can attain correct answers to questions, and not only that: one can gain insight into problems that previously might have been elusive. I also think it works best when the diviner has some connection to the divine: in other words, it is a theurgic act. This isn't to say that an atheist cannot divine effectively, but to do so he or she must be in touch with the Nous, whether or not there is belief in it.

---

87 W. H. D. Rouse, trans. *Great Dialogues of Plato.* (New York: Penguin, 2008), 526.

So how does it work? In Neoplatonic cosmology, the Nous is outside of time. Time is a form that exists in the Psyche, so if we can raise our own minds (little-n nous) up to behold the mind of the universe (big-N Nous) then we can see the timeless landscape of existence. We can use various methods to rise up and see this timeless landscape. Sometimes, special visions are created in the mind, phantasms that come not from our senses but from the Nous. At other times, we seek out inspiration in randomness, allowing us to break out of the cause-and-effect world of the physical to gain some insight into the larger picture. The ancient Romans and Greeks developed myriad methods of doing so, and we'll explore a sample of them in the remainder of the chapter.

Dreams

Plutarch calls dreams "the oldest oracle,"[88] and in the *Odyssey* Penelope describes a theory of dreams, after having what seems to her to be a prophetic one:

> Dreams are very curious and unaccountable things, and they do not by any means invariably come true. There are two gates through which these unsubstantial fancies proceed; the one is of horn, and the other ivory. Those that come through the gate of ivory are fatuous, but those from the gate of horn mean something to those that see them.[89]

The words "horn" and "ivory" are puns in Greek for words that mean, essentially, "come true" and "deceive," respectively. Virgil, imitating Homer but writing in Latin, which doesn't have the same pun, justifies it by pointing out that horn is transparent when cut thinly, while ivory is not. The art of dreaming true, called oneiromancy, consists almost entirely of determining

88 Georg Luck. *Arcana Mundi: Magic and the Occult in the Greek and Roman Worlds.* (Baltimore: John Hopkins University Press, 1985), 231.

89 Samuel Butler, trans. *The Odyssey of Homer.* Accessed 14 May 2013, http://classics.mit.edu/Homer/odyssey.mb.txt

which dreams are true and which are false, of which comes through the ivory gate, and which through the gate of horn.

To aid in this determination, lists of dream symbols were recorded in scrolls or books and probably sold as popular guides to divination, just as dream books are now. One of the oldest we have is an Egyptian papyrus that details what specific dreams mean, frequently based on a puns or transparent symbolism. For example, it tells us that "if a man sees himself in a dream with his bed catching fire, bad; it means driving away his wife."[90] Similar books also exist in ancient Greek and Latin literature.

General principles for dream interpretation, requiring more thought and less page flipping or scroll rolling, appear in more serious works. For example, Macrobius describes dreams in which a person of authority—a god or a parent for example—makes a direct prediction as a kind of prophesy.[91] In my experience, other warning signs that a dream is prophetic include not seeing the face of the person speaking, remembering the dream in unusual detail well after most dreams of the night have been forgotten, and the ability to do something in the dream that one normally cannot do in a dream, such as reading. All of these can be tip-offs that a dream is a message.

These are prophetic dreams that come without warning, but sometimes we need an immediate answer to a question. In order to trigger a dream, ancient dreamers engaged in the practice of the incubation of prophetic dreams. At the famous temples of Aesclepius, for example, the ill came to make an offering, sleep on the skin of the sacrificed animal, and dream of their cure. Sometimes these cures were miraculous, sometimes medical, and sometimes a mixture of the two (such as requiring that the worshiper take some ashes from the altar and drink them in wine). After receiving the cure, the

---

90 "The Dream Book." Accessed 14 May 2013, http://www.britishmuseum.org/explore/highlights/highlight_objects/aes/t/the_dream_book.aspx

91 Georg Luck. *Arcana Mundi: Magic and the Occult in the Greek and Roman Worlds.* (Baltimore: John Hopkins University Press, 1985), 234.

cured would make a votive offering often in the shape of the organ afflicted. Quite a lot of these votives have turned up in these temples of incubation.

Probably, private citizens—especially theurgists—performed their own incubations. In fact, certain folk magic traditions of incubation survive, such as the practice of putting a piece of leftover wedding cake under the pillow to dream of a future husband (or to dream of future ants, I'd think). I've had some luck incubating dreams with a bedtime prayer including a vow of a libation or offering if the dream comes through. The Greek Magical Papyri offer a wide selection of possible incubation spells, some simple, some complex. Most involve writing a particular incantation or the question on an object which is then slept on or near, or burned as the wick of an oil lamp. Lamps are popular devices in divination in the Greek Magical Papyri, not only as a means to incubate a dream but as a scrying medium as well.

Scrying

The Greek Magical Papyri list many means of achieving visions of gods. What these deities revealed were probably additional spells, as one occasionally finds a spell described as "god given." I don't think this was a figure of speech. The other thing probably revealed about the gods was philosophical and mystical insight into one's existence: in other words, the aim of theurgy itself. These rituals are very simple. We can divide these spells into two rough classes: lamp divination and saucer divination—or if we wish to be erudite, pyromancy and hydromancy.

In pyromancy, the focal point is a lamp. These lamps were shallow dishes with a spout into which a linen wick was laid. The lamp was filled with olive oil and the wick, once wet, was lit. Lamps as physical objects were about as ordinary as lightbulbs, and although particular spells demand particular types of wicks or mixtures of oil, in general all that is required is an ordinary, everyday lamp that is, as many of the lamp spells in the Greek Magical Papyri tell us, not painted red. Betz suggests that red was a color associated with Seth and therefore of ill-omen, but I suspect that it was an optical rather than a religious requirement. The spell works better when the flame stands out from the lamp, and a brightly colored lamp will not work as well as a dull-colored one. For that reason, a glass oil lamp doesn't work that well for scrying—too many reflections.

Hydromancy, on the other hand, calls for a shallow dish, usually specified to be silver. It is filled with spring water, and often a young boy is used as the scryer. Again, the optical effects of the water—here, the reflection—is paramount, which is why a shiny bowl works better than a dull one. Sometimes, the water is tinted with a little ink. Wine was also sometimes used, being dark enough to offer a clear reflection.

The physical effect of looking with single-focused attention at a reflection or a bright light in a dim room triggers an optical illusion called Troxler's fading, in which details in the peripheral vision, no longer being updated by the moving eye, fade out of consciousness. A secondary effect in reflections creates distortions, and while it has been known to magicians and teenage girls at sleepovers for a thousand years, Giovanni B. Caputo describes the illusion for the first time in 2010, naming it "the strange-face-in-the-mirror illusion."[92] This kind of scrying takes advantage of this optical effect, as well as a "sensation of otherness"[93] produced by it. Skeptics are welcome to say that such visions are nothing but this optical illusion, but I would counter by pointing out that the face transforms, or the visions in the lamp take shape, based on the subtle and unknown inclinations in the mind. In other words, this illusion is a means of systematically deranging the senses to produce a vision.

The magical manuals of Late Antiquity describe a third class of visions: direct vision. These are akin to what we think of as scrying in the more modern sense. Edward Kelley probably wasn't seeing his reflection in the shewstone of John Dee, but was using it as a means to arrive at a state of consciousness in which he could see and hear phantasms. These phantasms, images in the mind, are projected outward from the imagination and seem to take on a life

92 G. B. Caputo, "Strange-face-in-the-mirror illusion," *Perception* 39.7 (2010): 1007–1008

93 Caputo, "Strange," 1008.

separate from one's own will. In other words, unlike a fantasy in which the fantasizer can control what happens next ("Let's see, then I'll use the lottery winnings to buy a car, no, a boat"), a phantasm takes on autonomy. Maintaining focus on the crystal or shewstone helps the will in letting go of the image, freeing it to become the vessel for the divine or daimonic influence evoked by the ceremony. But a scrying surface isn't necessary and is often absent in these rituals, so the magician instead relies on the ritual itself to focus his will on something other than controlling the phantasm.

EXERCISE 5.1: SCRYING

This is a simple ritual outline to which you may add particular prayers or evocations or barbarous words of power. You can use the animated statue you created in exercise 4.4, but you do not need such an icon. Instead, you can focus it on one of the gateway deities such as Janus or Hekate, or you can scry Apollo for an oracle. When you become skilled at the practice, you can use scrying to devise spells and rituals and receive theurgic techniques that are particularly suited to your own particular temperament.

STEP 1: If doing a saucer divination, you will need a shallow silvery bowl that is very clean and brightly polished. If doing lamp divination, you need an oil lamp or a candle. If using a candle, brown or black is best. You'll also need a comfortable seat. Prepare by purifying yourself and the place of working with chernips or natron water.

STEP 2: Make an incense offering to the deity of whom you wish to have a vision, asking it a specific question. The only things on the working table should be the incense and the scrying object in front of the icon if you are using one.

STEP 3: Dim the lights so the flame is the brightest thing in the room, or if using hydromancy, until you can make out your reflection only dimly in the water.

STEP 4: Stare at the scrying medium while consciously relaxing your body, from the head down to the feet. Modulate your breath, perhaps using the fourfold breath in which you inhale for a count of four, hold for a count of four, exhale for a count of four, and hold for a count of four.

STEP 5: As you stare at the object of focus, you will experience optical effects, including distortion and areas of your vision blanking. These are not visions, but they are an indication that you're preparing for visions.

STEP 6: At first, you may experience visions in your imagination, and have a sense that they are internal. The more you work with scrying, the more these visions will externalize, but do not worry about whether or not the vision is in your mind or outside it. If the vision provides you useful information, it really doesn't matter.

STEP 7: Also be prepared to receive perceptions with your other senses, including hearing, smell, and even your kinesthetic sense.

STEP 8: When finished, offer your gratitude to the god you have called, then end the ceremony as you would any other ritual. It's useful to ground yourself in some mundane activity immediately afterwards.

This particular ritual of scrying with the lamp also hints at the theurgic practice of photagogia, or leading in the light. This practice is mentioned in several sources as a way of meditating or perhaps divining with light. Iamblichus describes several procedures: conducting the light through water, focusing it on a divine figure, concentrating it in one spot, and so on.[94] I suspect that he is speaking only tangentially about material light here, and is instead offering several means of meditating and concentrating the mind, through contemplation

---

94 Emma C. Clarke, John M. Dillon, and Jackson P. Hershbell, trans. *Iamblichus: On the Mysteries.* (Atlanta: Society for Biblical Literature, 2003), 155–56.

of water or of light itself. In these practices, the lamp becomes a tool of meditation.

Clairvoyance

Scrying relies on and helps develop the ability to have visions, called clairvoyance. Clairvoyance is a divine gift, a means of perceiving the invisible world and making it visible. Of course, as with most gifts, this is a gift we can develop with practice.

The mind operates by creating phantasms, sensory copies of its experiences. It constructs those phantasms out of three storehouses. First, it can take in sensory objects from the environment and construct a phantasm. This is what happens when we see an apple: we don't really see an apple. We get some sensory input and then we construct the phantasm of an apple and project it onto the place where that sensory input comes from. We never really experience anything of the world of matter: we only experiences the phantasms triggered by our sensory experiences of matter.

But then we can store those phantasms in our memory, which is the second storehouse. We can take images out of the storehouse of memory and combine them, as if we were editing a movie. Again, we are never really experiencing our memories: we are editing them. This is why memory decays over time; we have reworked the material of the storehouse to such a degree that we've eroded it. We can also take those images and combine them in ways that never existed. I can imagine flying a unicorn to Spain, while I've never seen a unicorn in the world of matter and never been to Spain. But I can use pictures I've seen of unicorns, experiences I've had that were like flying (jumping, diving, swinging), facts I know about Spain, and fill in the gaps with memories of other places I've been to. Ultimately, I can create a nice fantasy out of the phantasms stored in my memory.

The third storehouse is the one that concerns us the most, because this is the source of divine phantasms. The first storehouse of our senses exists in the world of matter. The second is locked in the lower reaches of our psyche. The third, however, is timeless, a reflection of the ideas of the Nous as well as the source of clairvoyance. These images are hard for our minds to grasp, however, and we clothe them in the phantasms of our memory and our senses, occasionally making it hard to distinguish between them.

We learn to have these clairvoyant images the same way we learn to do anything: practice. Here's a regimen of training and some tips that may help you:

EXERCISE 5.2: DEVELOPING CLAIRVOYANCE

STEP 1: Begin by learning to create phantasms as described in chapter 2.

STEP 2: Practice creating phantasms of simple geometrical figures in various colors. The pentagram is a good one, since it has a lot of magical uses anyway. For many people, simple figures like these are actually harder than more complex and detailed scenes, so if you wish, start with memories and work up to abstract geometry.

STEP 3: Exteriorize, or project, the phantasm. For example, if you are making a pentagram, project it and imagine it in the air in front of you, a few feet away. Practice this for a few minutes daily.

STEP 4: You may get to the point where you can see the pentagram as a ghostly image that is "half there." That's usually all you need for effective magic.

STEP 5: Continue to practice exteriorization. If you have a particular talent for clairvoyance, you may begin to see the phantasm as an external image.

STEP 6: Now, using a location or object you have enlivened such as the divine image you constructed earlier, look at it. Instead of constructing a phantasm, ask yourself what you see.

STEP 7: You may not see anything at first, so try these tricks:

- Close one eye so the image becomes two dimensional. Then imagine turning it like a page. What's behind it?

- Play "what if?" Ask yourself, "If I were clairvoyant, what would I see?" Then project that phantasm onto the place and let go of control of it.
- Imagine a door in the shape of the image, and then imagine opening to see what's behind it. What is it?

Step 8: The biggest part of the trick is giving up control of your imagination. Once you do that, you will discover that imagined objects can take on a reality outside of your will.

The potential for self-deception is large, of course. I can pretend to see a nymph, or I can see a nymph. How do I know the difference between a nymph I made up and a real one? One answer to that question is exteriorization. We know when a phantasm is in our mind alone, such as an imaginary nymph. We know, unless we have a psychological disorder, that our memories and fantasies are not happening currently, because we do not perceive them exterior to ourselves. If we can train ourselves to see the phantasms of clairvoyance exterior to ourselves, we can identify them as real in a way our fantasies are not.

There are those in the occult community who insist upon the exteriorization of visualization. If you cannot see the spirits you evoke, they say, you have not evoked any. They have a good point, and I admire their firmness in the face of a lot of fuzzy-wuzzy occult blatherskite. But at the same time, I have to point out that an exteriorization of a phantasm from the memory or imagination is also possible. We call this a hallucination, and it's not a guarantee of magical success. A lot of mentally ill people are exteriorizing visions all the time, and not all of them—maybe not any of them—are clairvoyant. The second objection I have is purely empirical: many people do some quite remarkable magic without exteriorizing their clairvoyance at all. Some of my most impressively successful evocations, judging by results, did not come with exteriorized visions of the spirits.

So how can we tell whether a phantasm in our imagination comes from the storehouse of our memory and imagination, or from reality? While it might be nice to have a quick touchstone, there's no substitute for careful introspection and self-honesty. In my experience, the most useful technique, which you should not neglect even if you have exteriorized your visions, is to follow the image backwards to its origin. If you find the origin of the image in the physical world (if, for example, it's retina burn, or fatigued eyes), it's clearly not clairvoyance. If, similarly, you can trace it back to your fantasies or memories, it also may not be clairvoyance. For example, if I suddenly have a vision of getting in a car accident but I watched a movie the week previous in which someone got into a car accident, that's probably just memory and imagination. A daymare, in other words, and not a vision.

Trance and Invocation

The classical practice of trance is not simple, nor was it always healthy. Descriptions of trance in ancient literature describe it as damaging to the health and dangerous to the recipient. For example, Lucan describes a Pythia overcome by the spirit of Apollo in terms that a modern reader cannot help but regard as epileptic.[95] It was a common belief that drawing a god into oneself was dangerous, because it is too much power for the body to hold. We find relatively few rituals in ancient sources for direct invocation and identification with deities in distinction to other polytheistic religions like Vodou or Candomblé. Modern magical practices such as assuming the godform were not—as far as I can tell—common in classical and late ancient magic.

---

95 Georg Luck. *Arcana Mundi: Magic and the Occult in the Greek and Roman Worlds.* (Baltimore: John Hopkins University Press, 1985), 282.

On the other hand, the act of inspiration, in which a god breathes into a person, was regarded as a kind of divine madness to be admired. Poets are called *vates* in Latin, meaning "prophets," and Plato writes about poets and other divinely inspired people being like iron rings given the power of magnetism by a lodestone.[96] In other words, the divinely inspired transmit the force of the gods downward into matter. While this is seen as a kind of madness or mania, it is not regarded, apparently, as an entirely bad kind of madness.

In contemporary magic, it seems everyone and their cousin is going about invoking gods willy-nilly. Part of this is the influence of the Golden Dawn, and part of it is—well, Aleister Crowley and his crew. Most of the advice about how to invoke a god is reflected in a single novel by Dion Fortune, *The Goat-Foot God*, a fun read if you like stuffy prose. In it, the main character, frustrated by his boring life, decides to invoke a god: Pan. He does so by buying a monastery, decorating it in what he imagines is Pan-like decor, and then breaking social mores in the most boring and stodgy way imaginable for about two hundred pages. At the end, there's a ritual. It's delightful. But it's also profoundly, deeply, almost painfully modernist in conception.[97]

It is modernist in its assumptions that the gods are signifiers for psychological states, and that we need a balance between society and "wildness." The wildness is never allowed to get even remotely out of hand (if you need to hire a landscaper to build your sacred grove, you're a modernist). And the psychological states are solidly Freudian, and to contemporary conceptions of psychology, almost smug. It's a good novel to read if you're into magic, and Dion Fortune's novels are a bit better than Crowley's. But it's still a novel.

The postmodern magicians of the late twentieth century took two avenues in regard to invocation. The chaos magicians, being materialists (as far as I know, the only strand of materialist magic ever to exist in the history of

---

96 Benjamin Jowett, trans. *Phaedrus by Plato*. Accessed 10 May 2013, http://classics.mit.edu/Plato/phaedrus.html

97 Dion Fortune. *The Goat-Foot God.* (York Beach, ME: Weiser, 1999). Originally published in 1936.

the world—go figure) argued that we could invoke any figure whatsoever as a "god" if it had enough followers.[98] Hence, Mickey Mouse is a more powerful god these days than Ereshkigal because he has more worshipers. That's good logic if you're a materialist. The other strand of postmodern magic, the semiotic approach, with no formal organization behind them and no formal orthodoxy, either adopted the methods of the Modernists with a pick-and-mix approach to deities—invoking now Hermes, now Quetzalcoatl—or they started digging through the original texts and analyzing them not as early psychology but as effective symbolism in which the symbols point to something that really exists, but with an awareness that we might not understand what it means to exist.[99]

The drawback to the modernist approach, whether we are chaos magicians, semiotic magicians, or traditionalists (whatever that means), is that it requires a time and energy commitment that can be intense. Not many of us can buy a villa, and even very few modernists ever did so. Yet the strength of this approach is also that same drawback: it does take time and energy to draw a god into oneself. But the whole operation and the intensity of it requires us to raise a single question first:

Why do we want to draw a god into ourselves?

In other words, what benefit do we gain from this kind of invocation? I'm not talking about invocations that are essentially prayers that invite the presence of the god into a ceremony: that's obviously helpful if the goal is to work with that god. But why would *uniting* with a god help us in any way?

---

98 There will, doubtless, be some chaos magicians who say they are not materialists, and they may well be right. It's a very anti-dogmatic school of magic. But many of the core writings on chaos magic are quite materialistic in their assumptions.

99 A distinction of my own making. Chaos magicians like to embrace magicians like A. O. Spare as a sort of pre-chaos magician, but his system of magic actually shares relatively little with the theories of chaos magic. It has a lot more to do with a growing understanding of symbolism and semiotics.

One answer to that question might be that it allows us to work with that god in a more direct, intimate way. Allowing the god to have the reins of our consciousness makes us a tool of the god, and it can potentially elevate us. In those living religious traditions where divine possession is common, that's what we see: people join with the gods to feel a stronger kinship with them and for a moment, take on their powers. The practice of divine possession can thus speed henosis, at least hypothetically. But there's a philosophical objection to that method, which is that you are no longer working with the god once you have given up your body and mind to it. Instead, you become merely a tool of the god and not an agent in your own right. The gods want partners, not slaves, in the great work of creation.

Another answer is that we wish to prophesy, and this answer has an ancient pedigree. The Pythia takes on the god in a manner that is not pleasant or necessarily safe in order to offer herself as a spokesperson for the deity. The metaphor for this, again and again in ancient literature, is that the Pythia is raped by the god, and later allegorical interpretations of the myths allege that a scene of "rape" in a myth is a metaphor for divine possession.

Another danger of divine possession is that a god may not leave. There are few spells to call in a god to take over your own body in the Greek Magical Papyri, but there are plenty to get one to leave. Nor is it easy to guarantee that you'll get the god you call.

The good news is that there is a method of invocation that lacks some of the dangers of the others but still maintains the benefits. New Agers call it overshadowing, and that's as good a name as any. In this method of invocation, the deity acts as a partner and together you maintain joint custody of the body and mind.

EXERCISE 5.3: OVERSHADOWING

STEP 1: While you don't need to hire a landscaper to plant you a sacred grove, you do need to have a relationship with the deity. In other words, you should have performed sacrifices and hymns of praise over a period of time before attempting this. Often, the Egyptian gods are preferred for this sort of work by contemporary magicians because they are very easy to visualize. Let's imagine that we've built up a relationship with Thoth, and we intend to ask him to overshadow us to achieve an oracle. We could also use this to get his help in empowering an object, but that will be the subject for a later chapter.

STEP 2: Part of the relationship with the deity will be researching him. What does he like, what does he dislike, and most importantly, by what names was he called. First, we learn to write his name in hieroglyphs.

Fig. 10: Thoth in Egyptian

We learn that Thoth is the Greek version of his name, which was something like Djehauti, give or take some vowels.

STEP 3: Prepare the place of working by having an image of the god, water for purification, and an incense offering. Also have some paper and a good reliable pen.

STEP 4: Purify the area by carrying around the image and the water, then sprinkling as usual.

STEP 5: Perform an offering, praying that Thoth will come and guide your hand in writing.

STEP 6: Sit in the god-posture—essentially, sitting upright in a chair with your hands on your knees. Have the pad and paper handy, because you'll need them in a moment. I use a lap desk for convenience and comfort.

STEP 7: Perform an operation called "taking on the godform." In this operation, you create a phantasm of the god in front of you in as much detail as you can. Project the phantasm and then release control of it. When you feel that it is present, ask it to join with you and guide your hand. Imagine it settling down over your body, so that the two forms—yours and its—overlap. Don't lose track of *your* form; that's important.

STEP 8: Pick up the pen and position it over the paper. Imagine the god's hand moving with you.

STEP 9: Now, release the hand by moving the image of *your* hand back to your knee. But leave your physical hand where it is, held now by the god rather than by you. In other words, the two overlapping images now no longer overlap over the hand. You imagine the god holding the pen, while you feel and imagine your hand back on your knee. This particular operation takes some practice and some getting used to; the important thing to remember is to let your kinesthetic sense believe your hand is still on your knee. It helps not to look down, but keep your gaze fixed on the icon of the god in front of you.

STEP 10: Ask your question, and let—but do not force—the hand to move. This is sometimes called automatic writing. Some people remain unconscious of what the hands write. I, however, become aware of it a word or two at a time, as if transcribing rather than writing it.

STEP 11: You'll probably find this a bit tiring, so when the hand stops or you become exhausted, move the phantasm of your hand back to overlap your physical hand and return the physical hand to the god-posture.

STEP 12: Project the phantasm of the god standing up and stepping away from you. Salute it by kissing your hand and then reassert your body once again, limb by limb. It's important to check each limb, making sure you have control over it and that it is where you think it is. It's a way of regrounding into your body.

STEP 13: Offer a prayer of gratitude and add more incense to the fire, then close the ritual as usual.

STEP 14: Interpret the writing on the pad. Those things you don't remember writing are often the most important and significant.

Of course, this ritual is just an example: you can give any part of the body temporarily over to the god, such as the mouth if you wish to speak for the god. You can also use any tool you like; for example, you can release the hand holding a pendulum if you like that tool. The point is that you don't surrender completely; you join in a mutual arrangement. Thus there's a reciprocity and mutual respect. We recognize that the god is more powerful, but we're still human and that's also an important thing to be, with its own role in creation. We don't have to denigrate ourselves or surrender to the will of another being, even a divine one. We may choose to follow that will, and that's a more meaningful choice than simply giving up our body.

Omens

Popular folk magic has reduced omens to superstition, but omens were taken seriously in antiquity. In ancient Greece, any involuntary reaction of the body such a twitch or a sneeze could be the indication of an omen. One would look to what had just been said or done to determine the meaning of the omen. Obviously, not every twitch or sneeze was the marker of an omen; if you have a cold, sneezes probably mean nothing at all. Other omens included unexpected weather events, earthquakes, and the flights of birds. The omen is marked by being unusual; it is an oddly timed sneeze, a strange formation of birds.

The ancient Greeks had a system of reading the flights of birds and flashes of lightning, but leave it to the later Romans to codify and complicate this into the system of augury. Augury, the practice of reading weather and the flights of birds, was the domain of a class of priests called augurs. An augur would define a sacred precinct in the sky with a curved wand, then watch for birds flying into and out of various areas or listen for their cries. Lightning flashes, as well, were a particularly bold statement of the gods' wills. Under the Republic, an augur's job was to determine the gods' assent before any person took office, a role that has given us our word "inaugurate."

It is hard to reconstruct augury. It may not have been a matter of augury being occult knowledge; probably it was common knowledge so no one felt the need to write it down. Or if they did, it hasn't survived. Essentially the gist of it is that certain birds were recognized by sight, and other birds were recognized by cry. Some birds fell into both classes. The flight or cry of a bird on the right was, in general, beneficial, while a cry or flight to the left was a negative answer. Individual birds were sacred to particular deities, the most obvious example being Zeus and the eagle. Birds who perched, circled, or took off from certain areas were also regarded as significant. Both the Greeks and the Romans agree with this, even though the Greek system is less codified and rigid. Augurs could also request particular signs as oracles, for example asking for an eagle if such-and-such was the case, and a different bird if otherwise.

Haruspicy

Haruspicy was the practice of examining the entrails of a slaughtered animal for omens about the future. As difficult as it is to duplicate augury in modern times, haruspicy is nearly impossible. As explained earlier, it began as a way of judging whether or not the deity found the sacrifice acceptable, but it quickly extended to more general questions. A sacrifice to Iuppiter might be made, for example, and the animal's entrails, especially the liver, studied for shape, size, and deformity. Deformity was a clear sign of a problem, but as the questions became more complex, more subtle interpretations of the shape and texture of the liver became necessary.

The liver of the sacrificed animal, like the sky, was divided into zones, again named for particular Etruscan gods. The Etruscans themselves learned it from a small man who sprang from the ground where a furrow was plowed. This small man, named Tages, taught the art of haruspicy then disappeared, or so goes the legend.[100] Not much but legends survives, sadly, although we do have brass model livers used as teaching aids with delineation of the relevant areas.

It stands to reason that in a ritual of communion like that of sacrifice, the gods might find a way to speak back in the sacrificial animal, whose death becomes the center of the communicative act. For modern practitioners, we again find ourselves stymied. We're not sure of the details of the art, but even if we were, it's problematic to dig through the entrails of a freshly slaughtered animal and start examining the liver. It simply isn't done; it tends to interfere with your guests' appetites. And, as I've said before, I don't recommend animal sacrifice anyway.

Kledon

A more popular system of divination, both in antiquity and now, kleda require no special equipment or training. Essentially, a person seeking a kledon goes to the marketplace and whispers his or her question into the ear of a statue of Hermes. While walking amid the people of the agora, the first words the inquirer overhears are the answer to the question. In modern times, a radio on scan works just as well, if not better, and in fact I learned this as a game before I knew it had ancient origins.

The kledon has a long literary pedigree. When Odysseus prays for divine guidance on how to get rid of the suitors trying to steal his wife and his lands, he hears a clap of thunder and receives a kledon from an overheard servant: "I wish the suitors would die tonight!" The kledon is so flexible even Christians make use of it: Augustine writes of an occasion in

100 Falconer, W. A., trans. *De Divinatione by Cicero. Loeb Classical Library, vol XX.* (Cambridge, MA: Harvard University Press, 1923). Accessed 13 May 2013, http://penelope.uchicago.edu/Thayer/E/Roman/Texts/Cicero/de_Divinatione/

which he found himself seeking guidance, which he receives from a young child playing outside his window:

> So was I speaking and weeping in the most bitter contrition of my heart, when, lo! I heard from a neighbouring house a voice, as of boy or girl, I know not, chanting, and oft repeating, "Take up and read; Take up and read." Instantly, my countenance altered, I began to think most intently whether children were wont in any kind of play to sing such words: nor could I remember ever to have heard the like. So checking the torrent of my tears, I arose; interpreting it to be no other than a command from God to open the book, and read the first chapter I should find.[101]

What's interesting here is that Augustine is led by this kledon to pick up the Bible and perform another kind of kledon, a bibliomantic kledon.

Bibliomancy, divination by book, does not have to involve the Bible, and in ancient times often involved Virgil or Homer instead. A person wishing to consult the book would make a prayer and ask a question, then open the book at random, pointing to a particular line. That line was the oracle, in much the manner as a random word on the street would be in an aural kledon. Obviously, the nature of the divination one receives from these texts will be colored by the nature of the text itself. The *Iliad* does not provide a lot of options for sweetness and light amid its lines, and if one is too familiar with the book, it's easy to select a section nonrandomly. My copy of the *Iliad* falls open to a few of my favorite bits, for example (like the scene when Priam comes to beg for Hector's body—gets me every time).

---

101 Augustine. *Confessions 8.12.* Edward Bouverie Pusey, Trans. Accessed 1 November 2013. http://www9.georgetown.edu/faculty/jod/augustine/Pusey/book08

Skeptics have criticized the kledon because it's easy for the inquirer to select a phrase that resonates, thus choosing his or her own answer. It is clear to me that such skeptics have never tried it; a true kledon is unmistakable in its applicability, and it raises the hairs on one's arms.

For example, some years ago, when I was finishing graduate school, I had very little money. I had no car, no job, and no real prospects for a job. I was more or less on the edge of despair, living in a small studio apartment next to the train tracks. The guy across the hall from me had a large string of suspicious visitors who stayed only a few minutes and left again, almost as if he were running a retail business of some kind. The people above me apparently did not sleep, but instead did jumping jacks every night, pausing only when the train roared by and shook everything in the room. I was nearly finished with my degree but had run out of money and was rapidly losing hope for the future. So I went to a small quiet spot near a college campus to pray and meditate, asking the gods for guidance. On the way back, I passed a young man talking into his cell phone much louder than he needed to: "You have to stop worrying," he said. "I'm going to take care of you. I'll get you a car and a house, and you'll get a job soon. Do you understand?" I couldn't help myself: "Yes," I said.

He probably thought I was a crazy man.

Yet that was an unmistakable answer to my question, as clear as I could ask for. He and I were the only people on the sidewalk, and his conversation was the very first thing I heard another person say after I finished my prayer. And, at this time, cell phones and loud conversations on them were not as ubiquitous as they are now. A skeptic is welcome to dismiss that as anecdotal evidence, confirmation bias, or any other thing, but no such explanation saps that event of this truth: it was a great, even profound, comfort to me. It gave me the confidence to proceed, and the hope to carry on. Within a month, I had a car. Within a year, I had my dream job. Within two more years, I had a house in a beautiful neighborhood. The kledon was true, but even more importantly, the kledon offered me help and friendship at a time when I sorely needed it.

Oracles

Specific locations in the ancient world were renowned for their connection to the gods, and at those places people could ask questions and be answered. These oracles were very much tied to place, and they often provided economic income to the location that housed them, just as pilgrims circulated money in the Middle Ages and tourists do now.

The most famous of these oracles is the oracle of Apollo at Delphi, wherein a priestess called the Pythia offered mantic utterances which the priests of Apollo translated into verse. This oracle served an important social function as a source of religious authority and arbiter of disputes. A trip to the oracle was expensive, and the oracle only saw querents at certain times of the year. Often, therefore, cities would gather together questions and send them in batches to be answered there. Legend had it that the priestess sat on a tripod above a chasm that exuded gases which sent her into a trance. Whether or not that chasm existed is a matter of debate, although recent geological research indicates that it may have at one time. If it did, I cannot imagine that being a Pythia was a particularly healthy occupation, a suspicion the literature confirms.

Oracles were not always permanent. Plutarch, writing in the first century CE, was a priest of Apollo at Delphi, and wrote a treatise on the decline of oracles, in which he argued that oracles were the mouthpieces not of the gods directly, but of their daimones or angels, and that those daimones were, unlike the gods, mortal and changeable. Hence, a daimon may leave an oracle, which is what he says occurred at Delphi. This explains the decline of the oracle of Delphi in this period, although other oracles were still active at this time, including the oracle at Claros, near Ephesus, and the oracle of Zeus-Ammon at Siwa in Egypt, which told Alexander the Great that he was the son of Ammon.[102]

At Dodona, an oracle of Zeus offered oracles through the sound of rustling leaves in a sacred groves of oak. This oracle was still active well into Late Antiquity; the emperor Julian, the last pagan emperor of Rome, consulted it in 362 CE.[103] In 392 CE, the Christian emperor Theodosius had the oak grove cut down and burned, implying it was still active enough to be a threat to Christianity at that time.[104]

The decline of the oracles, Plutarch explains, has less to do with the burning by Christians and more to do with the changing lifestyle of the people that consult them. Plutarch's point can be extended: we are not as tied to place as our ancestors were. It stands to reason that the gods might not be so bound to place, either. Just as we move about from place to place, living in one city for a few years, then in another, maybe they've also become unanchored. Of course, this is all speculation, and if anyone wants to take on the quixotic task of reestablishing oracles, I'll happily watch from over here. For our practical theurgic purposes, there's not much point in yearning for the lost glories of the past.

On the other hand, we may very well discover places, locales, in our own lives where we feel a stronger connection to the gods we choose to work with (or who choose to work with us). It wouldn't be out of place to develop our own personal places of power where our divinations may bear richer fruit. Putting up marble columns over a chasm is one thing; finding a grove in the nearby forest preserve where you feel a sense of the numinous and quietly and

---

102 James B. Rives. *Religion in the Roman Empire.* (Maldon, MA: Blackwell, 2007), 134; Horace Leonard Jones, trans. *The Geography of Strabo.* Loeb Classical Library Vol. VIII. Accessed 14 May 2013, http://penelope.uchicago.edu/Thayer/E/Roman/Texts/Strabo/17A3*.html.

103 Joseph Eddy Fontenrose. *Didyma: Apollo's Oracle, Cult, and Companions.* (Berkeley: University of California Press, 1988), 25.

104 Joseph Fontenrose. *The Delphic Oracle.* (Berkeley: University of California Press, 1978).

unobtrusively seeking omens there is quite another. Both have value, but from my practical bent, I find more value in the second than the first.

Sortes

So aside from kleda, which anyone with hearing can do (and, by the way, if you're hearing impaired, you can also do them with sight as well, letting your gaze fix on the first thing you see), what sorts of things can we do to consult the gods? Those familiar with more modern divination systems such as tarot cards or runes might be familiar with the concept of *sortes*. Sortes are what we sometimes translate into English as "lots." Unfortunately, "lots" has also taken on the meaning of a random way of determining who has to do some unpleasant task, so it's not always the best word for divination.

Late Antiquity's remaining literature offers us several systems of lots, which are the tips of an iceberg, I imagine, of a diversity of systems very similar to what we have now. Cards didn't yet exist, because the means of manufacturing them wasn't available. But the use of dice or chips of wood or stone on which figures had been drawn was probably very common.

Divination by Letter

John Opsopaus, writing as Apollonius Sophistes, describes and translates one such oracle, the Olympus Tablet. In this system of divination, the querent selects a letter by some method, which is unclear. It's possible that the letter was selected mathematically, through rolling dice or astragali (the knucklebones of sheep) or—and I find this most likely—by drawing a chip or piece of pottery inscribed with the letter from a jar or bowl.

Each letter is assigned a line of verse which begins with that letter. Presumably, the verse acts as an all-purpose answer, and the word beginning with the letter is given added significance. This may have been a flexible oracle, in which the diviner or interpreter might have offered the verse from the tablet, but then followed it up with additional insight on the nature of the letter, its shape, its place in the alphabet, and other significant words beginning with it.

Similar oracle-books were consulted by means of dice or astragali, the latter of which can fall in one of four ways, numbered 1, 3, 4, and 6. Five astragali were thrown and the sum calculated, which would point to one of fifty-six possible oracular verses headed with a divine name. For example, a roll of 23 was headed "Athene," and the oracle reads as follows:

A one, three sixes, and the fifth a four.
Honor Pallas Athena, and everything you want
Will be yours, and your resolves will be achieved:
She will loosen fetters and rescue you in sickness.[105]

It's clear from this that the purpose of this oracle was less fortune-telling and more theurgic. It may look quite practical, but the fact that each throw is assigned to a deity hints that this oracle was a way to check up on one's relationship to the gods. Similar oracles exist in other polytheistic religions; in Santería, for example, the oracle of Lukumi, known as Ifa in Yoruba, is an oracle in which divine and sacred oral stories are selected and retold in response to a complex ritual manipulation of various objects. A similar system of dice divination called Mo is used in Tibet to select a particular verse relating to Buddhist deities.

You can get your hands on this dice oracle in several ways. Fritz Graf reconstructs and translates the dice oracle in his article "Rolling the Dice for an Answer."[106] If you are interested in a scholarly take on this oracle, you cannot do better than Graf. If, however, you wish a more practical—and, not incidentally, less expensive—approach, Kostas Dervenis has recently published a book containing the entire dice oracle as well as instructions for using knucklebones (either real ones or the resin-cast ones available at many

105 William Hansen, ed. *Anthology of Ancient Greek Popular Literature.* (Bloomington, IN: Indiana University Press, 1998), 286.

106 Fritz Graf. "Rolling the Dice for an Answer," in Sarah Iles Johnston and Peter T. Struck, eds., *Mantike: Studies in Ancient Divination.* (Leiden, NL: Brill, 2005), 51–98.

gaming stores and online) or coins to consult it.[107] He also includes interesting background as well as illustrations of the bones themselves, which are essential if you are going to use real ones or models, since you need to distinguish one side from another. What really sells me on Dervenis's book is that he includes not just the translation but the original Greek as well. It's a nerdy thing to like about the book, I know—but there it is.

Astrology

In the nineteenth century BCE, a city named Babili was founded by the Akkadians in the area that is now southern Iraq. In the eighth century BCE, a group of people from a (literally) mushy backwater area named Kaldu came to conquer Babili. These people, the Kaldu, were later given the Greek name "Chaldeans" and their city Babili was called Babylon. Just as we have a tendency to call both continents of the far Western Hemisphere "America" as well as the country that dominates much of the northernmost of those continents, the Greeks came to call the entire region "Chaldea" even well after the Kaldu people were barely a memory. What wasn't just a memory, though, was their learning, which was remarkable.

The Babylonians cared deeply about the night sky. They made some of the first systematic measurements of it in the West, and began to name the stars themselves. They identified seven moving bodies visible to the naked eye and charted their courses with extreme accuracy. They also identified methods to measure distances across the sphere of the sky. Since they used a base 60 system, they broke the sky into 60 x 6 = 360 parts, now called "degrees." Since twelve was a nice round number for the Babylonians, they broke this into twelve chunks. They identified constellations that at that time rested in those chunks and gave names to these divisions based on those astronomical signs. They noticed that at particular points in the geography of the sky, particular events happened on earth: for example, when the sun entered the first degree

107 Kostas Dervenis. *Oracle Bones Divination: The Greek I Ching.* (Rochester, VT: Destiny Books, 2014).

of the part of the sky identified with the constellation of the Ram, the length of the day and the night were exactly equal. This, they realized, was also the first day of the spring.

It was clear and beyond doubt that what happened in the sky affected what happened on earth. After all, humans did different activities in the spring than they did in the winter, when the sun entered the part of the sky named after the constellation of Capricorn, and the days became their shortest. What, then, could this mean for the other planets? Could their placements also have an effect on the earth?

"Effect" is used loosely here. Even ancient astronomers didn't all think (although some did) that the planets had a literal causative effect on the earth. The sun entering Aries didn't make farmers plant crops. It just meant it was time to do that, and farmers could just sit on their hands and starve if they really liked. Wisdom was knowing what it was time to do, and the stars could tell us that.

They built a body of knowledge out of empirical observation and reasoning from first principles that came to be called the Chaldean knowledge, and the practitioners of this knowledge were called Chaldeans, whether or not they were really from Babylon. This body of knowledge was taken up by the Greeks, and at some point in the second century BCE it became a system very much resembling our current conception of astrology involving signs, houses, planets, and aspects. Currently, it is among the oldest and most widespread belief systems in existence.

The attitude toward astrology throughout the ancient world was often as ambivalent as it is in our culture but for different reasons. The Romans regarded it well enough to fear it: it was banned at several times in the Roman empire, and there was more than one instance of the "banishment of the Chaldeans." Even when astrology was tolerated, to cast a horoscope for the emperor was a good way to get your head removed from your body. Even the Neoplatonists and Hermeticists were not unified in their attitude toward astrology. Plotinus railed against it and refused to allow his birth information to be published. Porphyry, on the other hand, published Proclus's horoscope at the end of his short biography of him. Skeptics raised objections to it, and astrologers answered those objections. Some of the same arguments appear even today. I was amused to see such an argument on the Internet recently, where a skeptic suggested that if astrology were true, twins would all have exactly the same life. This same objection was raised over a thousand years ago. The answers now were also the same: the stars sketch out general patterns, not exact events; twins do often have very similar lives; twins aren't born at exactly the same time, so they don't have exactly the same horoscope, and small changes can mean a lot, as can later events and free will.

I can't explore all of astrology in this chapter. It is a huge and complex topic, worthy of careful study whether or not you believe in it, especially for the theurgist who can use it as a way to meditate on the gods themselves. For example, Ptolemy, the author of one of the most influential ancient astrological textbooks (the *Tetrabiblios*), has this to say about his study of astrology:

> I know that I am mortal, the creature of one day. But when I
> explore the winding course of the stars I no longer touch
> with my feet the earth: I am standing near Zeus himself,
> drinking my fill of Ambrosia, the food of the gods.[108]

Astrology, then, as more than just a system of divination, can also be an avenue to theurgy if used properly.

As a skeptic, I *admit* that astrology has no convincing scientific support published in a peer-reviewed journal. As a philosopher, I'm not sure it ever can. I think the scientific investigation of astrology might be asking the wrong questions. I know that astrology as well as other forms of divination seem to work for me. I know that this is anecdotal evidence and therefore not scientific, and that it is subject to endless "artifacts," as scientists call them, those statistical errors which lead to erroneous conclusions.

108 Georg Luck. *Arcana Mundi: Magic and the Occult in the Greek and Roman Worlds.* (Baltimore: John Hopkins University Press, 1985), 348.

So as contemporary practical theurgists rather than scientists, what are the right questions to ask? I can think of several particularly interesting questions raised by astrology and other systems of divination as well. First among these is "Why are the heavens orderly, and if we imagine they reflect events on earth, what does that say about the universe?" It implies that the universe, too, is orderly, no matter how chaotic it seems. The orderly cycles of the universe tell us something about the Nous: it, too, is orderly. The divine, in other words, is not mad, not fickle, not unpredictable. It may appear that way to us, but from the perspective of the Nous whose laws govern the movements of the stars, it is not so.

It also implies that the universe is correlated in its parts. What happens in the sky matters to what happens on earth. Any gardener will tell you that. And one hardly needs a direct causal link to find these correlations. When the sun enters Capricorn in the Northern Hemisphere, people will usually wear a lot more clothes, and when it enters Aries, people in the Northern Hemisphere start digging up their gardens. This is just another way of saying that first winter comes, and spring comes after. They are correlated to the movements of the sky and so are subtler cycles as well.

Moreover, perspective matters. We know that the math explaining planetary movement is a lot easier if we imagine the sun at the center of the solar system rather than the earth. But from earth, what we see is what we see, and we see the planets describing large circles around us. Both, we know, are true: the Hermetic philosophers could have told Einstein all about relativity long before he figured out the math of it. What we see is a function of where we stand, our context, our past and our perspective, and they thus help determine what we are. But, as Dr. Seuss tells you, you have "brains in your head. You have feet in your shoes."[109] You can change your perspective, both mentally and physically.

Discussions of astrology always seem to raise two questions: "Is everything fated?" and "Do we have free will?" At the risk of contradiction, I'd

109 Dr. Seuss. *Oh, the Places You'll Go!* (New York: Random House, 1990).

answer both questions yes. From the perspective of the Nous, the world is a landscape whose future and past and present are all universally present. From the perspective of the Psyche, we choose our actions by will. And from the perspective of matter, everything is a chaotic system of cause and effect with no consciousness or choice at all. All of these, from their perspectives, are correct. From the perspective of the One, of course, all of these viewpoints are unified in a way that's impossible to explain in words. I think of it as a song: the One hears the whole song, but when you're playing a song on an instrument, it's ongoing. It's a product of the choices you are making in the moment: play this phrase fortissimo, this piano, accent this note, pedal here. Anyone who plays an instrument knows no two performances of a song are ever the same, they're all products of our choices. But we also have the sheet music that lays out or predestines what we are to play. If we play what is written and *only* what is written, we will have a very dull little song. If we play too much what is not written—start, for example, adding notes to Beethoven—we have a mess. The difference between me and a master musician is that I play by rote with only a few little decisions here or there—or I improvise and it sounds at best okay, certainly not inspired (and often quite terrible!). A better musician, however, makes choices with every attack of every note. She uses her will to impose upon the written music without breaking it. Similarly, we have free will, but we usually don't use it. Astrology can train us to use our free will rather than be carried along by chance.

Astrology's greatest benefit to the theurgist isn't in prediction or divination at all, actually, but in systematizing and giving a grammar to human experience. The seven visible planets represent divine forces that are forms in the universe, and we can place everything that exists into one or several of those categories. Their positions and relationships to each other pick out the patterns of fate that likely befall the person. For example, if Mars is in Libra and square Venus, that may indicate a pattern: those things that Mars rules are weak and at loose ends, and they are often imposing themselves like a bad guest on those things that Venus indicates. Seeing these patterns, therefore, can act as an engine for contemplation.

To the ancient mind, the stars were a vague threat as well as a promise. The belief that the orderly movement of the stars revealed or reflected a secondary order on earth evolved into an ancient fatalism. The majority of people in the ancient world, whether they had free will or not, had few chances to exercise it. Unless you were the emperor, you had a superior who told you what to do and you could not say no. The emperor could decide to send you into exile or kill you on a whim. Moreover, a lot of people not only had superiors, they had owners, as slavery was a very much living institution. Yet at the same time, fortunes could change by no effort of your own. The emperor who sent you abroad in exile could die unexpectedly and his successor could invite you back home. Your master could free you, and freed slaves were eligible to become citizens and gain rights. All of this, however, both the fortunate and unfortunate, was mostly in the hands of others or chance.

One response to this fatalism is to embrace it, and this is the answer of Stoic philosophy, which teaches that one should act in accord with nature. If nature sends you into exile by means of a cruel emperor, go into exile gladly. If he sends you back home, go gladly. If the emperor orders your death, if your master whips you, if your master offers you freedom, if you become a citizen, if you become a slave—all of it is to be considered outside of one's control and therefore accepted. Of course, the Stoics recognized that not everything was outside of a person's control, and those things in your control you could take responsibility for: but for the Stoic, that entire list amounted to "your soul, and your response to events." Everything else was external.

The other response is to strive against fate, to fight it with magic or with mundane means. This approach appeals to Americans, certainly, with our myth of progress and our can-do attitude, but it didn't show up in the classical world very often and when it did, it was mostly regarded with horror. The witch who summons back her lover is a pathetic or terrible figure in Greek drama and Roman fiction. Moreover, the cultural heroes are not often ones who strove against unimaginable odds and beat them, like our action movie heroes. Cultural heroes were more often people who strove against unimaginable odds, fully aware that they would lose, but acted anyway because it was the right thing to do.

If both of these options seem a bit extreme to you, you're not alone. I actually have a bit more sympathy for the Stoic position as I find it more realistic, but at the same time I'm not going to roll over every time something goes wrong. To be fair, the Stoics never said you should, but it's easy to interpret them that way. I would like to find a middle ground between blindly obeying the stars and trying to wrestle them into place, and I'm not alone. The Hermetics make it very clear that we humans are not bound by the positions of the stars:

> Each of us at birth, when we receive a soul, are taken under the wings of the daimones who are assigned that sign of birth, who govern each of the stars ... So they, plunging into the two parts of the soul through the body, twist each to their particular energy; but the rational portion of the soul stands, unruled by the daimones, ready to welcome the divine.[110]

The daimon here is a spirit of a god, not evil but not always benevolent. But we are told that the rational part of the soul—our personal nous—stands unmastered by any daimon. We are not taken over by the stars or any other symbols of our fate.

In the next chapter, we will investigate the nature of these and other daimones, and later we will look at ways to change our fate when it does not match our goals. Of course, some things cannot be changed; bad things will happen. Through theurgy, one can learn to focus the rational part of the soul, the will, on the best parts of fate and cope with the worst parts with greater grace and aplomb.

---

110 Corpus Hermeticum XVI: 15. My translation.

CHAPTER 6

Daimonology

Once again, let's look in on the kitchen of Philanike, where her student Euthymios is helping her bake bread.

Euthymios: You know, there are stores that will sell you this stuff for ready money.

Philanike: What fun is that? I like making bread.

Eu: And yet here I am, kneading dough.

Ph: There's actually a lesson in this, you know.

Eu: When is there not a lesson in your kitchen?

Ph: See that notecard there?

Eu: The one stained with butter and flour? Yes.

Ph: What is it?

Eu: The recipe, I gather, for this bread. Although why you need a recipe I don't know, since you haven't looked at it once.

Ph: So tell me, Euthymios, what is a recipe?
Is it an object? If I burn this card, do I lose the recipe?

Eu: I doubt it. You probably know it by heart. So it exists in your mind as well as on that card, and probably on countless other cards.

Ph: So the recipe exists in my mind, or in any mind that peruses the recipe card, or any mind I tell it to. So what does that make it?

Eu: An idea. The recipe is the idea of bread. This sticky dough is hyle, or matter, and I guess I'm the Nous.

Ph: Actually, I'm the Nous in this allegory.

Eu: What does that make me?

Ph: Blinkered if I know. Let's try to figure it out. Reasoning by allegory isn't rigorous, but it can be instructive and creative if you do it right. So the recipe is the Idea, I'm the Nous in which the Idea dwells, and the dough is Hyle which will by the ministration of the will of the recipe become bread.

Eu: So the recipe is a god?

Ph: Just so: the god of bread. Of course, there is a god of bread who is greater than any particular recipe, but let's just take the allegory where it takes us. So if the recipe is like a god, and I am like the Nous in which the god dwells, does the recipe change?

Eu: It could, but then it'd be a different recipe, a different god.

Ph: Does the recipe make bread?

Eu: Hardly. *You* do.

Ph: Not right now I don't. I'm mixing myself a mimosa and watching you pound dough. Make sure you get the air bubbles out.

Eu: Seems a pretty meager religion, worshiping recipes.

Ph: Who said theurgy was a religion? Didn't you read the first chapter? Anyway, you're right, it seems to me. Recipes aren't very tasty, even if you have a pretty good culinary imagination.

Eu: So the recipe is the god, you are the Nous, the bread is the Hyle, and I am the agent of change in the world. I'm some sort of hand of the gods, then? Is that your point?

Ph: Exactly. You're a daimon of the recipe of bread.

Eu: Whoa. A demon, eh? I hope this particular loaf of bread doesn't come out of the oven speaking in Latin obscenities.

Ph: I didn't develop a sudden British accent there: I said "daimon," not "demon." *Dye*, not *dee*. Some daimones are good, some "evil" to our eyes, but they're all agents of the ideas in the world of the Nous.

Eu: Ahh, cosmology. Why don't the gods make bread themselves, then? Why do they need me?

Ph: You said if the recipe changed, it'd become a different recipe. Growing hands would certainly be a change in the recipe, and we need those big strong man-thumbs to make proper bread.

Eu: You've got stronger hands than I do!

Ph: That's 'cause I work for a living. Knead, knave. Don't make me get out my thwacking stick.

Eu: So daimones exist as an intermediate between the unchanging Ideas and the world of matter. Are they spirits, then?

Ph: If you wish. But I wasn't really being completely allegorical when I said that you were acting as the daimon of bread right now. You're carrying the message from the recipe to the dough: the Greek word for that role, the role of messenger, is *angelos*.

Eu: From demon to angel in just a few minutes. I'm doing well tonight, eh?

Ph: Passably well. That's enough, throw a towel over it and let it rise for a bit.

Eu: So how many daimones are there?

Ph: How many messages do you imagine must come from the Nous to the world of matter?

Eu: Probably quite a few. Let's say pretty much infinite. And do messages go the other way?

Ph: From matter to the gods? What happens if you revise the recipe after having made bread? Perhaps you decide, "Holy cow, that's too much yeast, let's cut that back." What then?

Eu: We already decided: it becomes a new recipe. So I make a new god?

Ph: Well, remember that the realm of the Nous, unlike my own personal mind, has no time. So "new" means nothing there. But if you change an idea, it's a different idea.

Eu: So a daimon can carry messages back to the Nous, but doesn't really change the Ideas there, just selects among them? Like if I flip open a cookbook and decide instead of bread to make cupcakes.

Ph: So it would seem. And if our neighbor stops by and says, "Hey, Euthymios, bake me a loaf, would you?" you could choose a recipe and begin work.

Eu: So I'd be carrying a message from your neighbor, to the cookbook, to the bread, then back to the neighbor when I deliver it. But I'd tell your neighbor to go find a baker.

Ph: Perhaps he'd pay you for the bread.

Eu: That'd be something, I suppose, although I don't know how much he'd have to pay me. I really prefer eating to baking.

Ph: Then perhaps he would bat his eyes at you and win your love.

Eu: Not since that experimental couple of weeks in college, he wouldn't. But I see your point: there're ways to encourage me to carry certain messages. Just as there are with daimones.

Ph: Exactly.

In the *Symposium*, Plato wrote of a dinner party Socrates attended where the topic of conversation was love, or eros. Each of the guests had a story or theory of love, and, typical of Plato's early (and, in my opinion, best) dialogues, no one came to a clear conclusion. But Socrates offered an account of Eros, Love, arguing—in the words of Diotima, a holy woman well-skilled in the arts of desire—that he was not a god but a daimon, an intermediate being. Diotima argued that Eros grew out of lack: that we want what we do not have. Since Eros is therefore lacking, it could not be a god, who lacks for nothing. Hence, it must be an intermediate spirit: a daimon. Socrates recounted his conversation with Diotima:

> "What then is Love?" I asked; "Is he mortal?" "No." "What then?" "As in the former instance, he is neither mortal nor immortal, but in a mean between the two." "What is he, Diotima?" "He is a great spirit (daimon), and like all spirits he is intermediate between the divine and the mortal." "And what," I said, "is his power?" "He interprets," she replied, "between gods and men, conveying and taking across to the gods the prayers and sacrifices of men, and to men the commands and replies of the gods; he is the mediator who spans the chasm which divides them, and therefore in him all is bound together, and through him the arts of the prophet and the priest, their sacrifices and mysteries and charms, and all, prophecy and incantation, find their way. For God mingles not with man; but through Love all the intercourse and converse of god with man, whether awake or asleep, is carried on. The

> wisdom which understands this is spiritual; all other wisdom, such as that of arts and handicrafts, is mean and vulgar. Now these spirits or intermediate powers are many and diverse, and one of them is Love."[111]

These intermediate powers, or daimones, have the characteristic of leading the way to god. Eros is one daimon out of many, one intermediate spirit, albeit an important one. Others also exist.

The earliest mentions of the word *daimon* are in Homer and Hesiod. Homer uses the word more or less interchangeably with *theos*, or "god," but Hesiod recounts how two earlier ages of humanity became daimones: The golden age of humans who lived in peace and plenty with the gods under the rulership of Kronos became good daimones; the silver age that followed became daimones of the earth.[112] Both good and evil needed to be propitiated, the good for their blessings and the evil to avert their ire.

The Genius and the Paredros

It's nearly a cultural universal that magicians, shamans, or witches have spiritual helpers and allies: invisible friends who work for the benefit of the magician. These invisible friends, their natures and names, vary from culture to culture. Sometimes these helpers perform a theurgic purpose and bring the practitioner closer to the divine. Other times the helpers serve a more thaumaturgical purpose, helping to achieve particular material goals. The beliefs of Late Antiquity Pagans describe both types of spiritual helpers.

This particular concept is a good example of how Paganism's spiritual ideas filtered through the Middle Ages and arrive in our own time. Two concepts of these helper spirits survive, one popular and one more esoteric. For the popular opinion, one need only search the internet for the phrase

---

111 Benjamin Jowett, trans. *The Symposium by Plato.* Accessed 15 May 2013. http://classics.mit.edu/Plato/symposium.html

112 Hugh G. Evelyn-White, trans. *The Theogony of Hesiod.* Accessed 14 May 2013. http://www.sacred-texts.com/cla/hesiod/theogony.htm

"guardian angel" to buy cheap ceramic figures of winged humans standing guard over wide-eyed children. The esoteric doctrine is a bit more sophisticated and slightly less decorative. It's distinguished by the addition of "Holy" to the phrase "Guardian Angel." Often it comes in the phrase "Knowledge and Conversation of the Holy Guardian Angel." It's easy to trace this back to Aleister Crowley, who himself got it from a fifteenth-century grimoire called the Book of the Sacred Magic of Abramelin the Mage.

This particular concept of the spiritual guide is ill-defined. Crowley himself argues in one place that he chose the name "guardian angel" because it was "patently absurd" to imagine such an angel standing watch, and so it wouldn't lead to complex doctrines because no thinking person could build such a doctrine on such an absurd and silly term.[113] Of course, people did just that. Elsewhere, Crowley argues that the Holy Guardian Angel is of a class of beings similar to that of a god or a human:

> Now, on the other hand, there is an entirely different type of angel; and here we must be especially careful to remember that we include gods and devils, for there are such beings who are not by any means dependent on one particular element for their existence. They are microcosms in exactly the same sense as men and women are ... I believe that the Holy Guardian Angel is a Being of this order. He is something more than a man, possibly a being who has already passed through the stage of humanity, and his peculiarly intimate relationship with his client is that of friendship, of community, of brotherhood, or Fatherhood. He is not, let me say with emphasis, a mere abstraction from yourself; and that is

113 Aleister Crowley. *Magick in Theory and Practice.* Chapter Two. Accessed 15 May 2013, http://www.sacred-texts.com/oto/aba/chap2.htm

> why I have insisted rather heavily that the term "Higher Self" implies a damnable heresy and a dangerous delusion.[114]

In fact, Crowley is convinced that the magician's main goal should be to achieve "knowledge and conversation" of this being: to know who and what it is and be able to talk to it and have it talk back. He gets this notion from Abramelin, who sets communion with this angel, "the chosen Angel of Adonai, a delightful, good Angel," as the first task of the aspiring magician.[115]

The method of achieving Knowledge and Conversation of the HGA is actually one of the few esoteric concepts laid out clearly in a grimoire (in distinction to the typical recipes and incantations that most grimoires include). Abramelin recommends an eighteen-month period in which the mage engages in prayer and a regimen of purity and abstention. This period culminates finally in a vision of the angel and the reception of its name and seal, by which it can be contacted. Following this, in the Abramelin system, the mage must bind the demons to the will of his or her angel, and then employ those demons for the work of magic. Thus, the theurgic HGA works hand-in-hand with the magician to bind the thaumaturgical demons.

There is a continuous debate in occult circles on the issue of whether or not the HGA was invented by Crowley and how much credence we should give it. One side argues that the HGA was invented from just a few sources (chief among them Abramelin) and that one should not put much credence in the concept. The other side argues, as I do, that in fact this concept has a much longer pedigree. Abramelin wrote at a high point in the knowledge of

---

114 Aleister Crowley. *Magick Without Tears.* (Scottsdale, AZ: New Falcon, 1991), 281–282.

115 Abraham von Worms. *The Book of Abramelin.* Steven Guth, trans. (Lake Worth, FL: Nicolas-Hays, 2006), 107. Crowley would have had access to an earlier, far inferior translation by Mathers, but I have chosen to cite this text because it is a superior translation. A more rigorous tracing of Crowley's ideas would require comparison with the Mathers translation, but that project is outside of the scope of this book.

theurgy. And the concept of a guardian angel who serves a theurgic purpose not only extends back to Antiquity, it was also a *sine qua non* of ancient Roman religion and present in earlier Greek religion as well.

Socrates described the experience of having "something divine," a "daimonion," watching over him and giving him signs when he was about to do something wrong. In the *Apology*, he said: "This sign, which is a kind of voice, first began to come to me when I was a child; it always forbids but never commands me to do anything which I am going to do."[116] Then, in the Phaedrus, when giving a sarcastically sophistic argument about love, he stopped and said his daimonion told him not to go on uttering such falsehoods.[117] Clearly, Socrates believed that some divine force existed to warn him away from evil. The idea that daimones existed and that each human had a good spirit, an Agathos Daimon, appears to stretch back very far indeed in Greek religion.[118] The role of the daimon is as an intermediary to the gods, and it is the root of our modern concept of the guardian angel.

While the Greeks listened quietly to their Agathos Daimon and the Abramelin operation plunged the magician into a regimen of intensive prayer, the Romans had made the concept of a guardian spirit part of their day-to-day religion. This spirit, called a *genius*, is the source of our word for a person who is exceptionally intelligent or creative. Romans believed that everyone had a genius, given to them at the moment of birth. Romans sacrificed to their genii (no relation to the word genie, by the way), as well as to the emperor's genius. Christians got themselves in trouble with the Roman empire by refusing to sacrifice incense to the genius of the emperor (or, perhaps more accurately, the empire engineered such a requirement to get Christians in trouble). A genius

---

116 Benjamin Jowett. *The Apology by Plato.* Accessed 15 May 2013, http://www.gutenberg.org/files/1656/1656–h/1656–h.htm#link2H_4_0002

117 Benjamin Jowett, trans. *Phaedrus by Plato.* Accessed 15 May 2013, http://classics.mit.edu/Plato/phaedrus.html

118 Walter Burkert. *Greek Religion.* (Cambridge, MA: Harvard University Press, 1985), 180–181.

was occasionally called a person's Iove or Iuno—a Iove for a man, Iuno for a woman—identifying it with the supreme pair of gods, Jupiter and Juno.

The Roman genius was not limited to people: every locale had its own genius, and particularly sacred or interesting places had especially powerful ones. In this, they are like nature spirits or *kami* in Shinto. Since the names of such genii are not recorded in any myths, the Romans developed a formula for prayer to a particular genius of unknown name: *si deus si dea*, "whether god or goddess." A prayer recorded by Cato for divine permission to clear a grove illustrates how such unknown deities were approached:

> The following is the Roman formula to be observed in thinning a grove: A pig is to be sacrificed, and the following prayer uttered: "Whether thou be god or goddess to whom this grove is dedicated, as it is thy right to receive a sacrifice of a pig for the thinning of this sacred grove, and to this intent, whether I or one at my bidding do it, may it be rightly done. To this end, in offering this pig to thee I humbly beg that thou wilt be gracious and merciful to me, to my house and household, and to my children. Wilt thou deign to receive this pig which I offer thee to this end."[119]

Obviously, it is essential to recognize the spiritual reality of the location before doing violence to its physical reality.

What is the role of this angel, daimon, or genius in the practice of theurgy? As a personal god, it is a patron for our spiritual development. Each person gets his or her own, and each one is intimately concerned with that person. As a guardian of place, it is a way of grounding spirituality to location. It acts as a conduit between the lower and upper world, between the nous and the world

119 W. D. Hooper and H. B. Ash, trans. *Cato: De Agricultura.* Loeb Classical Library, 1939. 139. Accessed 15 May 2013, http://penelope.uchicago.edu/Thayer/E/Roman/Texts/Cato/De_Agricultura/I*.html

of matter. In sum, the genius acts as a translator between worlds, a personal daimon.

The worship of the genius of the emperor is a good example of this translation: the ordinary citizen could participate in the religion of the state through making offering to the emperor's own genius, which became at the same time associated with the genius of Rome. The government had a spiritual double with the genius of Rome presiding with the genius of the emperor. The genius stood as an intermediary between the people and their emperor. Pouring libations and offering incense to these genii allowed the citizens to participate in this spiritual government, even as it paved the way for the late imperial tradition of apotheosis of the emperor.

But most of the worship of the genius was a personal religion conducted in the home and not in the street. Because everyone learned this worship at home from word of mouth, we have relatively few inscriptions or written accounts regarding this tradition. But we do have mentions in Late Antiquity of the genius or daimon's role in the life of the philosopher or theurgist. Plotinus participates in a ritual to achieve knowledge and conversation of his genius or daimon, led by an Egyptian priest who it is hinted may be a charlatan. The results, however, are startlingly real to all involved. Instead of a lesser daimon, a god shows up and claims to be Plotinus's genius. Startled by this revelation (or perhaps envious), one of the magician's assistants prematurely ends the ritual by killing a sacrificial bird.[120] The race of daimones, as lesser beings between the gods and humans, usually provide the genius, but for Plotinus, at least according to his biographer Porphyry, he had a being of much greater quality: a god.

Another Neoplatonic theurgist, Proclus, mentions the role of the daimon in Socrates's original sense as a being who warns away from danger. Proclus's biography recounts his fleeing from Athens when "critically harassed by certain giant birds of prey…":

---

120 Mark Edwards, trans. *Neoplatonic Saints: The Lives of Plotinus and Proclus by their Students.* (Liverpool: Liverpool University Press, 2000), 9–10.

> For it was in order to prevent his being uninitiated into the more ancient rites still practiced there that his personal daemon contrived this pretext for his departure. For he himself acquired clear knowledge of their customs, and for their part, if through length of time they had neglected any of the practices, they learned from the philosopher's directions to serve the gods more perfectly.[121]

This particular account illustrates that the daimon or genius is often seen as performing a negative action: preventing error rather than leading one into correct action. Here, the error would have been staying in one location and thus not having a particular mystery initiation.

Similarly, in the *Apology*, Socrates makes this same point that his daimon never tells him what to do but only warns him when he is about to make an error. The genius or daimon therefore preserves the free will of the person it guides by allowing him or her to choose goals and how to pursue them without interference, but warning when those goals are not spiritually healthy. This trait of the daimon has led some to suggest that the daimon is merely a personification of the personal conscience.

As a being worthy of worship, the image of the genius appears in various murals and statues in the homes of ordinary Romans. The genius of a place is often depicted as a serpent, while the genius of a person is usually a human figure without wings, and not hovering over a ruddy-cheeked child as we tend to think of it. Instead, the figure is usually holding a cornucopia and offering one hand as if to make a gift or offer a sacrifice. Often, genii are depicted pouring libations, an action that underlines their intermediate nature, who are offering worship to the gods on behalf of the person they patronize. One also sees images of gods themselves making such libations, a symbol I believe indicates that the figure depicted isn't a god but a daimon.

---

121 Edwards, *Neoplatonic Saints,* 79–80.

Iamblichus argues that there can be multiple genii for each person: a genius at birth may in some cases turn over the guardianship of the theurgist to a god or higher daimon. Thus, Iamblichus reconciles the legend that Plotinus had a god for his genius. This idea of a multiple genius shows up again much later in the Renaissance, when the Neoplatonic practice of theurgy enjoyed a sudden rebirth. Henry Cornelius Agrippa, whose work is responsible for nearly all contemporary occultism, writes that the genius has three parts. First is a holy angel, responsible for the spiritual growth and development, given directly by the gods and not controlled by the stars (and hence, not subject to fate). Then there's the daimon of the nativity or the genius, which is determined astrologically. Finally, Agrippa speculates that each person has a daimon of profession, determined by one's work which changes when one changes occupations.

Others, among them Agrippa himself, argue that in addition to a good genius there is an evil genius. This opinion was evidently ancient, as the playwright Menander argues against it, writing that "Every god must be good. But those who are bad themselves, who have bad characters and make a muddle out of their lives, managing everything badly through their foolishness . . . they make a divine being responsible and call it 'bad,' while they are actually bad themselves."[122] I am inclined to agree with this opinion, as is Iamblichus, but the impetus to create an equal and opposite evil being is probably the result of the influence of Manichean dualism (possibly through early versions of Christianity) on late Neoplatonism.

Identifying the Genius

The Greek and Roman concept of the genius has its reflection in late Neoplatonic practice as well, where the genius is identified as a being determined by the influence of the seven planetary gods on one's birth: in other words, the genius is a personification of the horoscope itself. It was a common astrological practice to identify the planet of one's genius, and several methods for

122 Gregory Shaw. *Theurgy and the Soul: The Neoplatonism of Iamblichus.* (University Park, PA: University of Pennsylvania Press, 1995), 172.

doing so existed, from the complex to the very simple. For example, one could simply find the planet ruled by the sign of the ascendent and declare that to be the planet of the genius if it is well-dignified. Of course, if it isn't well-dignified, that may present problems. One could also do the same with the ruler of the eleventh house, as the house of friends and allies. More complex methods determine the relative strength of each of the planets, or the relative power of each of particular points in the chart, and determine the planets from that.

Iamblichus argues against this urge to identify a ruling planet for the genius: "He is not distributed to us from one part of the heavens nor from any of the visible planets but from the entire cosmos—its multi-faced life and its multi-form body—through which the soul descends into generation."[123] For Iamblichus, the genius was not the influence of a particular planet, no matter how strong, but the influence of the entire cosmos on the person in question. We can think, then, of the genius as a personification of the horoscope or spirit inhabiting the moment of birth. This concept isn't simple astrology: rather than saying that some planets are well-dignified and others debilitated, this interpretation implies that all of the planets work in order to guide and warn the person whose nativity is represented.

This interpretation of the nature and role of the genius led to a system for determining the name of that genius through astrology. Agrippa, clearly influenced by this Neoplatonic doctrine, explains the procedure for determining the name, which is to assign a letter (Hebrew, naturally) to each of the degrees of the zodiac starting with alef at the first degree of Aries, starting over again and again until each degree is given a letter. Then, identify the location of each of the Hylegian points, which are the locations of the sun, moon, ascendent, part of fortune, and syzygy (the location of the nearest full or new moon). The letters associated with those five points are the name of the genius, or so he says.[124]

---

123 Shaw. *Theurgy,* 217.

124 Agrippa. *Three Books of Occult Philosophy.* Ed. Donald Tyson. (Woodbury, MN: Llewellyn, 2007), 527.

Agrippa's astrological formula only determines the name of the genius of the nativity, not the holy genius or the genius of profession, but perhaps he intended that one could find out those names simply by asking the genius. I, personally, am not yet convinced of this three-fold system of genii, nor do I find the astrological method particularly appealing.

Fortunately, we have another set of instructions, relying not on the mathematical operations and manipulations of the astrological chart but on ritual and clairvoyance. Iamblichus explains the procedure thus:

> [T]he invocation of daemons is made in the name of the single god who is their ruler, who from the beginning has apportioned a personal daemon to each individual, and who in the theurgic rites reveals, according to his good pleasure, their personal daemon to each ... [W]hen the personal daemon comes to be with each person, then he reveals the mode of worship proper to him and his name, and imparts the particular manner in which he should be summoned.[125]

From this we can construct a ritual devised to invoke the daimon, and in fact we needn't do much in the way of construction, because such rituals are not difficult to find. Aleister Crowley used a ritual he called the Bornless Ritual, which he devised from a ritual in the Greek Magical Papyri, officially designated PGM V. 96–172. There, in the original text, it is designated "Stele of Jeu the hieroglyphist in his letter."[126] He could have chosen any number of other, more appropriate rituals, as the Stele of Jeu is actually pretty clearly an exorcism, not an invocation. Nevertheless, I know many people who have used this ritual or variations of it to good effect.

---

125 Emma C. Clarke, John M. Dillon, and Jackson P. Hershbell, trans. *Iamblichus: On the Mysteries.* (Atlanta: Society for Biblical Literature, 2003), 341.

126 Hans Dieter Betz. *The Greek Magical Papyri in Translation: Including the Demotic Spells.* (Chicago: University of Chicago Press, 1992), 103. PGM V. 96–172.

The procedure of Abramelin is, of course, very much along the lines of Iamblichus. It gains its power not from any particular magical names—in fact, Abramelin suggests that one pray extemporaneously—but from the repetition of the prayers over time. As magical rituals go, it's rather simple: it requires almost no equipment and very little in the way of magical knowledge. It's designed to work as an initiation for those new to magic. This makes sense: for Abramelin, connecting with the genius was the first step of all magic. I obviously don't think that's the case, and I don't think the ancients did either. Instead, the relationship with the genius, like one's relationships with the gods, was an ongoing, lifelong endeavor.

I am of the opinion that the cultivation of the genius should be as simple as possible (not to imply that it is, necessarily, also easy), leaving more complex and arduous rituals to more elaborate tasks. One of the things that makes contacting your genius easy is that your genius wants to be in contact with you. You're not pulling the whole load here: there's an intelligence meeting you halfway. What makes it harder than contacting a known god or daimon is that you have no name, no form, and no symbols with which to make a connection. Instead of a statue filled with a deity's synthemata, you have only the vague and nebulous notion that your genius is out there waiting for you. You need the synthemata to contact the daimon; you need to contact the daimon to find the synthemata! It's almost a catch-22, although not quite: while you don't have your genius's synthemata, he or she has yours.

This paradox is why I described animating statutes first: in many ways, it's good practice for the invocation of the genius, because you have the synthemata as a tool. Here, you do not: at first you have only your own intuition to guide you. Your previous work in developing relationships with deities, animating statues, making offerings, divination, and so on can all be used to help you in connecting to the genius. Once you do so, the genius itself will give you simple techniques for maintaining communication including synthemata, names, and so on.

Another advantage of beginning with connecting to patron gods is laid out in the Iamblichus quotation earlier: namely, that there is a deity ruling over your genius, whose synthemata you may indeed know. This deity may be one you have had a particular relationship with or connection to. For me, this is Apollo: by praying and making offerings to Apollo, I can begin to make a connection to the genius he sends me. Knowing which deity or deities can help connect you to your genius requires some experience in prayer and offering and meditation, but you can also rest assured that any god or goddess to whom you feel a connection can help you achieve a relationship with your genius even if that deity did not, in so many words, "send" the genius to you. To put it metaphorically, Olympus is like a small town: everyone knows everyone.

It is best to begin simply, with offerings to make initial contact. In its simplicity, the supplication of the genius can be a daily act, or in times of spiritual retreat or special occasions, done several times throughout the day. Once you do this for a while, you will begin to get some intimations of your genius's nature and symbols. You can slowly incorporate those as you see fit. For example, my genius has given me a sigil and a sequence of musical notes I can use to call on him as well as a ritual meditation, a particular scent, and a form that he takes. Some of these I received in ritual contemplation, some in dreams. I add these to the following exercise when I call on my genius. Yours may offer other suggestions, like particular incense, offerings, and so on.

EXERCISE 6.1: CULTIVATION OF THE GENIUS

You will need incense, cone or stick is fine, and a burner. You may wish to have chernips or natron water, a lamp, and various other items, but in a pinch you could perform this ritual empty-handed.

STEP 1: Purify yourself by washing, either a full-fledged shower or, at the minimum, washing your hands. You may prefer to wash your hands in chernips or natron water, but I've used tap water and still had good results.

STEP 2: Invoke the One by aspiring worldlessly to beauty. Imagine something beautiful in the world and, as you have done before, try to abstract its beauty away from its material manifestation. Try to hold whatever apprehension you have of the Idea of Beauty in your mind as you continue the rest of the ritual.

STEP 3: Construct a phantasm of the genius. Depending on your conception of the being, you may construct a number of images. If you think of it as a traditional Judeo-Christian angel, it may be a winged anthropomorphic being. If you imagine it as a more ancient type of angel, it may be a winged creature of another kind, or even a winged sun-disk or orb. If you prefer the classical Roman image of the genius, you may think of it as a person dressed in a toga with one hand pouring a libation. Or, if you prefer the abstract, you may imagine it as a flame or shining ray of light. Eventually, the phantasm you create will change to fit the preferences of the being itself, and may even change over time to reflect a changing relationship.

STEP 4: Raising your arms, say a prayer to the genius like this one, substituting the name of your genius for N., or leaving that part out if you don't know it yet:

> Hear me, Agathodaimon, called N., or by whatever name you may be called and whether god or goddess, and come from your abodes in the empyrean to receive my praise. If ever I have burned sweet scents to you, spoken words of praise, or made offering in your name, come and hear me, as you have done before. Give me guidance to the One, true knowledge of the hidden things, and authority over the lesser daimones of the world, so I may fulfill my purpose which is to join the gods in the great work of creation. Accept this offering,

and by it may you be propitiated and increased,
and may it turn your face toward me.

Step 5: Offer the incense by lighting it, holding it aloft momentarily, and letting it burn down. If you're using a censer instead of a stick or cone and it doesn't have a chain or handle, don't hold it aloft or you'll burn your fingers. If you are doing this ritual empty-handed, you can rub your hands together and offer the heat to the genius by holding your palms up and imagining it rising upward like smoke; you can imagine this smoke taking on the forms of the preferred sacrifices and expanding to fill the available space.[127] This technique isn't necessarily original to ancient magical practices, but I find it useful.

Step 6: Spend some time in the contemplation of the genius, remaining receptive to any answer it may offer you.

Agrippa's description of the three types of genius can be interpreted as three different roles of the genius in our lives: as spiritual advisers, as agents of fate, and as professional patrons. From one perspective, these three roles are the same act in three different domains. In the world of matter, the genius concerns itself with our material actions, our professions and avocations. In the world of the Psyche, it helps us understand the working of fate in our own lives. And in the world of the Nous, it helps us understand the timeless pattern of our lives and engage in the great work itself by seeking henosis.

Our professions are more than what we do to make money, of course: they are the way our ethics play out in our lives. If we find ourselves making money by causing suffering to others or diminishing them, we are clearly not living up to worthwhile values. It's easy to justify such a life—after all, we have to live, we have to

127 I got this technique from Jason Miller. *The Sorcerer's Secrets: Strategies in Practical Magic.* (Franklin Lanes, NJ: New Page, 2009), 41.

feed ourselves, those we oppress deserve it, and so forth—but the genius will not allow us to do so. At the same time, the genius can help us find a profession that is coherent with our natural talents and skills and values: that is, in other words, suitable to our fate.

As already discussed, fate is not so much the unalterable track of our lives as it is the circumstances we create and dwell in because of the moment of history in which we find ourselves. Here, the genius can act as a guide to that moment of history, and thus in this role is not only the genius of our fate but the genius of the times we live in. In this role, the genius acts as a doctor who teaches us how to develop our natural strengths and overcome our native weaknesses. In this, it acts as the conduit of what Crowley called the "true will," the task for which we were made, which manifests in the world of matter as our professions, and is a manifestation of the timeless idea of ourselves in the world of the Nous.

Finally, the spiritual world of the Nous, wherein dwell the Ideas that underlay reality, is opened up by the genius, who acts like the personal Janus to this realm of the gods. The genius reaches down from the heights to lift us up and is the personal angel or messenger in response to our prayers. In this role, the genius is hierophant of our personal initiation. It can offer us the methods of its own invocation, as Iamblichus tells us, as well as means of theurgic and thaumaturgic ritual that will work best for us alone. It is difficult to speak more plainly about anything that has its roots in the world of the Nous.

The Paredros or Assistant

The genius, then, can guide you spiritually, morally, and ethically—but you can't send it out on errands. And while some theurgists might sniff at the idea of conducting errands, I am not one of them: I think that thaumaturgy, or practical magic, has its place in theurgy as well. So we may want something or someone who will help us with our practical goals. For that, we need a different kind of spiritual being, sometimes called a "familiar spirit," or a "familiar" for short. The witch trials of the fifteenth through eighteenth centuries often included "testimony" of witches having particular animal or spirit helpers. These helpers lived with them and were thus, in the vernacular of the time, familiar or family-like. The instigators of these atrocities were relatively learned men and therefore knew that such spirits have a long tradition in esoteric practice, although depraved imaginings like the suckling of animals at a witch's teat are of course simply the projected perversions of sadistic minds.

There are several rituals for summoning and binding a paredros, or magical assistant, in the Greek Magical Papyri. One of these, PGM I 42–195, can be found in Stephen Flowers's book on hermetic magic, where he has adapted it somewhat for modern practice.[128] I will present a different ritual, designated as PGM I 1–42, and described in the text as "A Technique to Attach a Familiar Daimon, so that he will reveal everything to you distinctly, and sit in conversation and conviviality with you, as well as in sleep."[129] The original ritual requires several sacrifices, some of which will be challenging to modern readers, and one of which I strongly suggest against. I have therefore made a few concessions to modernity. You may wish to consult the Appendix for hints on pronouncing ancient Greek words of power. Here is my revised version of this ritual:

EXERCISE 6.2: A TECHNIQUE TO ATTACH A FAMILIAR DAIMON

STEP 0: This is a bit of a complex ritual, so to aid in planning here is a shopping list to get your *mise en place* prepared:

1. A three-dimensional image of a falcon carved out of some nontoxic material or made of clay. Try *not* to get one that is clearly meant to be Horus; this is a ritual to summon a solar daimon but not necessarily the god Horus himself.

---

128 Stephen Edred Flowers. *Hermetic Magic: The Postmodern Magical Papyrus of Abaris.* (York Beach, ME: Weiser, 1995).

129 This ritual is my own translation of the Greek. An alternate translation is available in Hans Dieter Betz. *The Greek Magical Papyri in Translation: Including the Demotic Spells.* (Chicago: University of Chicago Press, 1992), 3–4.

The original text required the use of a live falcon to be drowned and mummified. Do not do this.

2. Frankincense, ground fine.
3. Red wine. Two-Buck Chuck works just fine.
4. Myrrh ink. I just mix some myrrh tincture into some ink. To make myrrh tincture, soak some fine ground myrrh in pure alcohol like everclear for a few days. Shake well to suspend the gum in the alcohol and then add a few drops to ink.
5. A small piece of parchment or papyrus. Paper will work in a pinch.
6. Your own fingernails and hair. The original text specifies "all the hairs of your head," but that may be impractical for many practitioners. If you can shave your head and keep your job, by all means, go for it. I didn't.
7. Milk mixed with honey. The original specifies that the milk should come "from a black cow," but that may not be easily arranged unless you have access to a dairy farm with a very understanding farmer.
8. Some fruit and vegetables for offering. You will partake of some of these as part of the final offering, so don't include anything you don't care to eat or are allergic to.
9. Juniper sprigs, if you can get them. If not, substitute other evergreens.
10. A small shrine in which to house your falcon. I modified mine out of a front-opening jewelry box.
11. Strips of cloth or ace bandages if you wish to mummify the falcon. I'm of two minds on the necessity of this part, because I'm convinced that the mummification step was

merely for preservation, and a statue doesn't need to be preserved. Mine is not mummified and works just fine.

STEP 1: Purify yourself by abstaining from sexual contact for a week before doing this ritual. The original specifies contact with a woman, but I'm assuming some ancient sexism here. Best skip all sex of whatever configuration.

STEP 2: Set up the ritual to take place just before sunrise, ideally on a Sunday, although the original ritual does not specify the day of the week.

STEP 3: After cleaning the image of the falcon well, immerse it in milk and honey. Say something like the following:

> "Image of a falcon, you are not an image. You are a falcon, giving your spirit to this milk. Image of a falcon, you are a falcon, drowning in this milk. Breathe your spirit into this milk, falcon, and be deified."[130]

STEP 4: On a small piece of parchment or papyrus, write the Greek vowels as below in myrrh ink:

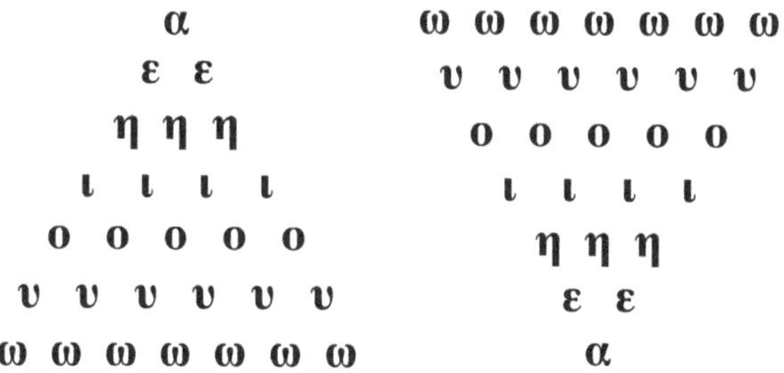

Fig. 11: Greek Vowels in Double Wing Formation

130 This is not in the original. I have added it in order to compensate for the fact that we are not, in fact, drowning a living falcon.

STEP 5: Place your hair and nails on that piece of parchment. Fold it up and smear it with a paste of frankincense and wine. This mixture will harden into a kind of sticky pink glue. This bundle is a sort of sacrificial object, an anathema, that links you to the spirit who will inhabit your falcon.

STEP 6: Set up the falcon in a small shrine, which can be a simple shelf or a cabinet with a door. Make sure there is room for a small glass of wine and some offering dishes with fruit. Place the juniper sprigs over the shrine.

STEP 7: Add the bundle to the shrine, and begin the ritual by drinking the milk and honey just before sunrise. The text says at this point you will feel "some inward divinity in your heart."

STEP 8: Make a sacrifice of the wine and fruit as you normally would, and address the falcon with this incantation:

A EE ĒĒĒ IIII OOOOO UUUUUU ŌŌŌŌŌŌŌ
Come to me, good gardener, good Daimon,

HARPON KNOUPHI BRINTATĒN SIPHRI
BRISKULMA AROUAZAR BAMESEN
KRIPHI NIPTOUMICHMOUMAŌPH.
Come to me, holy Orion, who sits up in the
north and pours out the flow of the Nile to
mingle with the sea, bringing forth life
like the seed of man in sexual union.
You have set the world on a firm
foundation.
You are young in the morning,
and old in the evening.
You descend below the earth,
and rise up breathing fire.
You part the seas in the first month,

Sending seeds into the sacred figs
of Heliopolis, unceasingly.

This is your authentic name:
ARBATH ABAŌTH BAKCHABRĒ

Step 9: When finished, step away from the shrine backwards, then sit and eat your breakfast before it. Your breakfast should be strictly vegetarian, as should any offerings you make to the shrine.

So that's a bit of work. For one thing, you've got to memorize some words of power, prepare some offerings, and so on. I would recommend memorizing all of the words of power. Memorizing such words changes your consciousness in mysterious ways.

The fact that this ritual is more work intensive than the summoning of the genius is evidence, I believe, that this spirit is a different kind of spirit from that of the genius. The genius comes to us without much effort; it's already here. This ritual asks for a particular companion, who can serve not only as the intermediate between us and the gods, but also a magical companion in the practice of thaumaturgy. In fact, while this ritual specifies that the paredros is of the divine order of daimones, Damon Zacharias Lycourinos points out that the various rituals and texts mentioning paredroi are as diverse as one could wish: sometimes it is a god, sometimes the spirit of a dead hero, and sometimes—as here—a daimon bound to a particular object like the image of a falcon.[131] I regard this as an important insight, because it underlines that the role of the paredros is less about identity and more about use. In

131 Damon Zacharias Lycrouinos. "Conjuring Magical Assistants in the Greek Magical Papyri" in *Occult Traditions*, ed. Damon Zacharias Lycourinos. (Melbourne, Australia: Numen, 2012).

some sense, you are what your genius is; the paredros is a paredros not because of what it is but because of what it does. A paredros walks beside the thaumaturgist, an assistant and helper.

The falcon here is very much a solar symbol, and the sacrifice of the hair and nails connects the theurgist to the spirit, creating a bond. It is set up as a votive offering in the shrine of the spirit, enticing the spirit to enter into the falcon statue. Eating together is also an important symbolic act, as we know from the sacrifice ritual. Finally, the essence of the falcon is added to the milk and honey, which is consumed by the worshiper. This act creates another bond: where the essence of the theurgist is giving over to the spirit, the essence of the spirit is given over to the theurgist. The image of the falcon is a physical link to the spirit.

As Fritz Graf points out, sacrificing a falcon, a sacred animal, would have been considered an act of pollution and separation.[132] It would have made the theurgist anathema in the modern sense of the word: set aside from the rest of the world that respects such creatures and does not murder them. It would have also made the falcon anathema in the original sense: a votive offering. He regards that separation as an important part of the ritual, but I respectfully disagree. The ritual of mummification described in the text is short and succinct, clearly meant merely to preserve the form of the falcon. There is no hint of opening its mouth ritually as one might do with a human mummy. Moreover, the later emphasis on vegetarian food seems to weigh against the sacrifice of animals in this sort of ritual. As an occultist familiar with obscure and often misleading accounts of rituals, I am inclined to treat this instruction as a blind. In any event, I have not found it necessary and do not suggest it (if nothing else, drinking milk in

132 Fritz Graf. *Magic in the Ancient World.* (Cambridge, MA: Harvard University Press, 1997), 114.

which you have killed a bird is a very good way to end up flat on your back with a bacterial infection or worse).

The paredros may be evoked for later use by making an offering of fruit, vegetables, or wine and speaking the spirit's name ARBATH ABAŌTH BAKCHABRĒ. Then you can tell the spirit what you desire. The spirit is useful for relatively ordinary tasks you may not have the time or inclination to perform a full magical ritual for: finding a particular book, getting somewhere on time, meeting up with someone you want to see, and so on. Another ritual for summoning a paredros, the ritual in PGM I 42–195, promises that he "carries gold, silver, bronze, and he gives them to you whenever the need arises," and "he brings women, men without the use of magical material."[133] He also is said to open doors, release from prison, bring all sorts of food (but not pork—evidently he keeps kosher), cause invisibility... in other words, anything ascribed to any magical operation whatsoever can be accomplished by means of the assistant. Sometimes, it's clear that these are metaphoric aims; other times, it might be that he can attain seemingly miraculous effects. I have found him very helpful and effective in my own work.

Genii Loci

Some daimones or genii are connected to particular locations. One can always detect a place where a daimon dwells, because it is in some way separated out from the rest of the world. It is unusual in some way. Perhaps there is a large or strangely shaped tree in a glade of small trees, or perhaps it is a locale that is often struck by lightning. Natural springs often have daimones, as do impressive rock formations, as well as rivers (Achilles famously wrestles with a river daimon in the *Iliad*). Essentially, the tipoff of a daimonic presence

---

133 Hans Dieter Betz. *The Greek Magical Papyri in Translation: Including the Demotic Spells.* (Chicago: University of Chicago Press, 1992), 5.

is a sense of the sublime. As Longinus, writing about the sublime in rhetoric, states: "sublimity is, so to say, the image of greatness of soul."[134] He is speaking of the great soul of the author of a piece of sublime rhetoric, but in nature we see the natural sublime in the great soul of a daimon. Sometimes, nothing marks a particular location as the domain of a daimon other than a felt sense of presence. We find such places nearly anywhere, and not necessarily only in untrammeled nature; there's an overpass in Chicago that I'm certain has a daimon.

The Greeks occasionally called nature daimones "nymphs" or "satyrs" and assigned them an anthropomorphic form suitable for mythology. However, the original daimonic presence is abstract and divine in nature, even if intermediate between the world of matter and the world of the gods. Later Roman writers identified satyrs with fauni, similar nature spirits with animal-like characteristics. Occasionally writers make connections between these nymphs and English fairies, arguing that they are similar in function, nature, or origin. I'm not sure that's the case, however, as whether or not fairies are divine (historically or metaphysically) is a matter of argument while the nymphs are certainly divine in some sense; they partake of the power of a particular god.

The means of propitiating such a daimon is clearly laid out by custom: an offering of livestock, fruit, drink, or even coins is often made to such spirits. The rule appeared to be that one propitiated the daimones of the location before doing anything with or to it. It was merely polite to introduce yourself and make friends, in other words, when moving to a new place. This establishment of relationship served a practical purpose: it ensured cooperation from local spirits and gods. But it also served a theurgic purpose as well.

The theurgist who makes such a connection with the genii loci of his or her home makes a link between geography and the divine. After leaving an offering and making a prayer at the banks of a river, for example, he or she

---

134 H. L. Havell, trans. *Longinus: On the Sublime.* (London: Macmillon, 1890). IX.2 Accessed 15 May 2013, http://www.gutenberg.org/files/17957/17957–h/17957–h.htm

will never pass that river again without thinking of its god. The thoughts of the theurgist are elevated by the surrounding landscape, and the beauty of nature has an additional layer of meaning as a reminder of the divine goal of henosis. Nature becomes a temple.

As an American, I find myself in a problematic position when it comes to working with spirits of place. While the idea that place has spirits is almost universal, the nature of those spirits and the means of contacting and relating to them is different from place to place. In the American continents, and especially in North America, the original inhabitants of these regions had their own means of relating to the spirits of the land. This includes their own names, rituals, offerings, and so on. And as the descendent of Europeans, I face a problem in dealing with those same spirits.

Take the river that flows through my suburb. The Potawatomi who lived in this area before European settlement probably had a name for its spirit, but I don't know it. They may have offered it particular things, or perhaps they ignored it. Maybe they had legends and myths about it. All of that may be lost. And, of course, the Potawatomi were themselves immigrants to this area having been driven south by the Iroquois, so perhaps they themselves displaced older legends, all beyond the possibility of recovery.

More fundamentally, if the Potawatomi did have a relationship with that river and I approach it as an outsider, how will I be received? I lived in a town not far from here for several years and when looking into its history, discovered that it was the site of a massacre of Potawatomi who refused to leave when they were to be forcibly relocated. So you had not just the spirits of all those violently dead, but you also had the genii loci of that place, perhaps feeling rancor over the murder of people with whom it had a relationship. As an American theurgist, I try not to forget that at any time, there may be the bones of the dead underneath my feet.

My point is, if I'm going to approach a genius loci in the United States, I'm going to try first to find out its history. Often, that's impossible: there are even place names in the United States whose original meanings are lost because all those who spoke that language died, and the language with them. But insofar as it is possible, we make an effort. Then I need to approach it with humility.

Another problem arises in what ritual actions to take. Even if I knew them, it would be a mistake for me to try to perform the original ceremonies of those who first created a relationship with these genii. It would be disrespectful to those beliefs, perhaps inconsistent with my own, and probably offensive if not to the genius loci then surely to the spirits of the dead. By the same token, it might seem incoherent or even insulting to import the rituals of Rome or Greece here. What must be found is a neutral, simple way of making offerings to these spirits without offending them.

The choice of offering is also a matter of some concern. Alcohol as a libation is problematic; strong liquor wasn't introduced until European settlement (although other, weaker fermented drinks may have already existed), and it has a bad history as a means of exploitation and enslavement of the indigenous population. Similarly, wheat may be alien, although perhaps a bit more acceptable because it lacks negative association. Maize, or what we call "corn" in the United States, is appropriate as is tobacco, but it's important to recognize that we're not trying to create an ersatz "Indian" ritual here. I'm not Native American, and I won't disrespect Native American cultures by pretending to smoke a peace pipe or engage in a sweat lodge.

Of course, I eschew blood sacrifice entirely and urge you to as well, and it would be especially inappropriate here. As I said, there is a history of oppression and murder—not just of Native Americans but also of African slaves, Chinese indentured servants, and a large number of other ethnic groups. Inflaming the angry dead with blood is a bad idea.

And not just America has such a history. Parts of Europe are also graveyards. The World Wars turned much of Europe into a battlefield soaked with the blood of the violently slain; the atrocities of the Nazis, not to mention other genocides elsewhere, stain the land with angry spirits. Any effort to speak to those spirits must include humility and care and compassion for those who died there in those or other conflagrations.

I recommend stripping down the ritual to its core: a simple offering. In fact, this offering ritual can be used as a quick offering to any spiritual being. Just modify accordingly.

Exercise 6.3: Offering for a Genius Loci

Step 1: Select an offering, such as local fruit (apples, for my area), grain (maize), or just water or honey. A coin may work in a pinch, or you can use the offering gesture of rubbing your hands together and letting the heat rise.

Step 2: Find a location that seems to form a natural altar: a stump near the river, a stone, or just a natural swelling of the ground. Aim your hands outward with palms up and toward the most striking feature of the landscape.

Step 3: Say something like the following:

Spirit of this place, whether god or goddess,
 by whatever name it pleases you to be called,
 hear my prayer. I come in humility and friendship.
Accept this offering of friendship, and may you be
 increased by it, strengthened, cleansed, healed,
 and made strong. Accept also this speech offering,
 and be praised.

Step 4: You may wish to speak extemporaneously about what feature particularly attracts you.

Step 5: Lay the offering on the altar or pour out the libation. Imagine the form of the offering expanding out, multiplying, and filling the space with abundance.

STEP 6: Say something like "May our friendship grow" to end. Only when you and the location have made a strong relationship should you try to ask for favors.

Other Daimones and the Dead

Daimones can come from any realm: there are daimones of the air, earth, water, fire, each of the planets, and even of human activities like agriculture. Each of these activities is governed by a god, and each daimon acts as an intermediary between the god and the practitioner in an unbroken chain of divine influence that, because of the graces of the daimones, flows both ways. So in regard to agriculture, for example, Ceres or Demeter rules over the grain. She is the goddess of fecundity in the world of matter. Beyond the world of matter, above the world of Psyche where time exists, she is outside of time and influence and thus changeless and perfect. But she governs daimones, who are reflections of her in the world of Psyche: souls, in other words, existing in time. It's as if Ceres in the Nous is the shoulder, and the daimones are the hands and fingers. Thus we have daimones of farming, who do the work of Ceres. At the same time, we have daimones like Pomona, the daimon of fruit, and Dysaules, who rules the plow.[135]

There are daimones that govern every activity of the universe, and only some of them have names. The Romans simply gave many nouns a daimon to govern them, so there are Roman deities of luck (Fortuna), of virtue (Virtus), and even of sewers (Cloaca). These names are simply the common, day-to-day words for those things. Modern writers sometimes refer to them as "personifications" and even doubt that they were really gods with their own cults—which misses the point. These daimones were intermediaries between worshipers and gods and a recognition of the divine power, the numen, in everyday reality.

---

135 "Theoi Greek Mythology." Accessed 14 May 2013. http://www.theoi.com/greek-mythology/agricultural-gods.html

The dead, too, may leave behind daimones. The cult of the heroes became ubiquitous by the Hellenic period, and Romans went so far as to deify their emperors as a matter of course in the late Empire. This practice became so expected and so pro-forma that Vespasian was able to quip on his deathbed, "O dear! I think I'm becoming a god."[136] Whether or not anyone really believed that the emperors were divine is a matter of debate; perhaps some did, but for the most part philosophers seemed to regard the practice with only civil respect…and sometimes not even that. Seneca the Younger ridicules the ascension of Claudius by imagining the introduction of this widely disliked emperor to Olympus:

> The news was brought to Jupiter that somebody had come,
> a rather tall man, quite gray-headed; that he was threatening
> something or other, for he kept shaking his head; and that he
> limped with his right foot. The messenger said he had asked
> of what nation he was, but his answer was mumbled in
> some kind of an incoherent noise; he didn't recognize
> the man's language, but he wasn't either Greek or
> Roman or of any known race.[137]

Yet other cults of the dead were active and respected. The cult of Hercules, for example, was widespread well into the late Empire, and Seneca the Younger uses Hercules as a character in his satire to question the new "god" Claudius, as a way of pointing up the absurdity of comparing the two. Similarly, the cult of the Dioscuri was important right until the end of Late Antiquity.

---

136 Valerie M. Warrior. *Roman Religion: A Sourcebook.* (Newburyport, MA: Focus, 2002), 138.

137 Allan Perley Ball, trans. Seneca the Younger, *Apocolocyntosis.* (West Sussex, Columbia Univ. Press, 1902) Accessed 14 May 2013, http://en.wikisource.org/wiki/Apocolocyntosis

Individuals also honored particular ancestral spirits in their home. In Rome, these were called *manes*, and they were regarded as chthonic daimones deriving from ancestors. If one had good ancestors, and propitiated them appropriately, there would be good fortune, so often the manes were worshiped together with the lares at the family's lararium. The manes of the city were offered games in their honor, a tradition stretching back to Homeric times when games and competitions were part of the funereal rites. These games later devolved into bloodsports in the late empire, an unusual example of state-sanctioned human sacrifice.

The worship of the dead was similar but not identical to the worship of the gods, and from a theurgic perspective the differences in the ritual are significant. The gods of the underworld are seen as below, dwelling in the realm of Hades, which in Neoplatonic writings is sometimes associated with hyle or matter itself. Thus, the theurgist did not aspire to join with these gods as he or she does with the Olympic deities of the Nous. Instead, these gods are honored and worshiped to elevate matter, and the manes and heroes, as their intermediaries, are similarly honored. Stories of heroes such as the Dioscuri rising to dwell in the stars are examples of this elevation of matter from death to eternity.

Yet there are similarities in the ritual of offering. First, libations are offered, then a sacrifice might be performed. Rather than an elevated altar there is often a trench into which the blood is spilled. The body of the animal is burned *in toto* rather than slaughtered and shared out in a sacrificial meal. To eat the food of the gods is to join them in society; to eat food given over to the dead is ill-omened. The offering given to the dead is given completely over to them and not shared. Similarly, the libation is poured out completely. Honey is a common libation to the dead, as it is a preservative and was used as an embalming fluid in ancient times. Similarly, oil is offered to the dead, sometimes poured on their grave markers as a means of making it glisten, thus recalling the goal of rising upward into the light of the Nous.

While eating food specifically dedicated to the dead was seen as improper, one could eat in their presence. Picnics at gravesites were common throughout antiquity, and the family would bring its own food as well as a share for the dead, which was left whole for them at the gravesite. The distinction between food for the dead and food for the living was maintained by keeping the sacrifice separate from the picnic. In this way, the manes could rejoin society for a moment, and the living and dead could join forces in the project of elevation.

As the blood sacrifices of the gladiatorial games illustrate, not all was sweetness and light when it came to the cult of the dead. In fact, necromancy—divination by means of the manes—was common in Rome, although legally proscribed. One could not only divine by summoning the dead, but one could curse by them, and we have a large number of lead tablets buried in graves or thrown into wells that were meant to curse individuals or sports teams (some things never change, it seems), sometimes for revenge and sometimes for love. A common love spell in ancient Rome takes the form of a curse: the soul of the object of love is given to the dead to torment if she will not come to the person writing the spell. Reading such tablets is a shuddery business at least for modern sensibilities, and since it was illegal to do these curses even in ancient times, probably no one regarded it as a respectable use of the manes. Nevertheless, respectable or not, legal or not, people in desperate times will take desperate measures.

We find a similar set of difficulties in dealing with the dead to when we try to work with genii loci: namely, that most of our beloved dead weren't Pagan, may not have supported the practice of theurgy or thaumaturgy, or may have been downright hostile to it. My ancestral tree is filled with Catholics, Protestants of many kinds, and a few Mormons. So what am I to do? Not work with them because they weren't my religion? Or recruit them from beyond the grave to the practice of theurgy? Neither seems respectful. Again, it helps to pare down the ritual as much as possible of any cultural elements that might be alien. Reducing it to a gift, rather than a "Ritual of High Magick," satisfies both me as the theurgist and my ancestors as

Christians. Also, it's possible they may have changed their view of religion after death and now do not look on the practices I undertake with as much suspicion as they may have when alive. I can hope so, anyway.

Exercise 6.4: An Offering to the Dead

Step 1: Again, select an offering. This time, you may tailor the offering to the person: a person particularly fond of candy may prefer sweets, while one who liked wine might like a glass of chardonnay. A hero from legend or myth may have preferred offerings, or you can fall back on the all-purpose bread, honey, oil, or incense. I would suggest avoiding blood and meat, although historically animals might well be offered in such a ritual.

Step 2: Make a prayer to the dead, usually something simple like, "Hear me, N., my [relationship], and accept this offering of friendship. May you be increased by it, made strong and healthy and well in the world in which you now dwell, and may you look kindly on me."

Step 3: Cut or break the offering and leave it in a shallow trench, offering dish, or on the grave. Do not eat any of it. Pour out the libation entirely. Again, imagine the form of that substance expanding out to fill the available space.

Step 4: If you like, make a petition. Ideally, this is connected to the person: "May I be as strong in dealing with such-and-such as you were when you did such-and-such." Alternately, you can just praise the person's virtues while they were alive, as a way of remembering their contribution to your own life.

Kakodaimones

Just as the daimones of everyday activity act as intermediaries to the gods, so do the so-called kakodaimones, or "bad daimones." These daimones are the prototype for the Christian demons, and here the comparison is justified. Just as the good daimones govern every activity of life, the kakodaimones govern the miseries and misfortunes of humankind. We have long lists of such daimones from Hesiod, who seemed to take great pleasure in naming them. For example, we have the account of the children of Nyx or Night:

> And Night bare hateful Doom and black Fate and Death,
> and she bare Sleep and the tribe of Dreams. And again
> the goddess murky Night, though she lay with none,
> bare Blame and painful Woe . . . [138]

Sleep (Hypnos) and the Dreams or Oneiroi (including Morpheus, their leader; Phantasos, the daimon of fantasy and hallucination; and Phobetor, the daimon of nightmares) are of course daimones, often helpful spirits who act as intermediaries between the god—Nyx—and humans. But at the same time Hesiod describes other daimones who are less pleasant: Blame, Woe, Doom, Fate, Death. These are kakodaimones, "bad" daimones.

The Wiccans in my readership well-versed in the lore of the dark goddess might be raising a finger to object, so let me head them off: Death or Thanatos is certainly not evil. Without Thanatos, the world might very well be an unpleasant place or at the very least, quite crowded. But the kakodaimones are evil in the relative sense: from our human perspective, death is a source of sorrow and pain. Blame is painful to us—but at the same time, without understanding blame we have no sense of responsibility. Our doom and our fate are hard concepts to wrestle—to the point where we pretend that we have no fate at all, but pure free will. But in the wrestling, we learn and grow. And woe is synonymous with sorrow—but then, there are times when sorrow or woe is a very good thing to feel, because it heals us and ties us back to the community of humanity.

The thing to remember about the daimones, all of them, good or bad, is that they answer to a god. There is no figure of evil in Pagan religion because evil is a matter of human perspective. Yes, evil exists: people do

---

138 Hugh G. Evelyn-White, trans. *The Theogony of Hesiod.* II 211–225. Accessed 14 May 2013. http://www.sacred-texts.com/cla/hesiod/theogony.htm

horrible things, and they do them for stupid, horrible reasons. Without getting into the very complex and sticky swamp of the problem of evil, and resisting strenuously the urge to quote Plotinus on the subject, let me just say that from the Neoplatonic perspective, evil is the absence of good. It does not exist in the Nous, or in the underlying pattern of the universe. It exists only in the farthest, dimmest reaches of matter, when our eyes are blinded by the fog and cannot see the underlying goodness any more. The kakodaimones are the shadows cast by the gods on the world of matter.

When in their proper place and role, their work *can* be good. A nightmare or two is a good way for the mind to blow off stress, and Phobetor is a good daimon when he brings such dreams. But if all Phobetor brings is nightmares, and you can no longer sleep, he has become a kakodaimon, a daimon of chaos and destruction, and he must be stopped. It's all very well to say, "Well, so it goes, that's the way the gods must want it." But as theurgists, we have the power and the responsibility to talk back to the gods—or at least their daimonic representatives in our world.

Even after the kakodaimones got demoted to "demons" and all shoved under the awning of the one Big Bad Guy of the Devil, Christian Neoplatonists still argued that we had a responsibility to tame these demons and perhaps even redeem them. The second magical operation of the Sacred Magic of Abramelin the Mage, after the contact with the Holy Guardian Angel, is the summoning and binding of the demons. Ironically, many of the demons in these grimoires have names clearly derived from the names of gods (which is not to imply that the beings those names refer to are gods; far from it).

This sort of summoning and binding of kakodaimones was a common practice even in antiquity, even before the advent of Christianity. It was never approved of, however, more perhaps for the reason that it required unsavory and illegal ingredients, and was akin to necromancy in the popular imagination. The term for this kind of thaumaturgy, *goetia*, from which the Lesser Key of Solomon takes its name, may come from a root meaning "howling" or "groan." Again, to the reserved Greeks and even more reserved

Romans, any activity involving shrieking was a bit suspect. Even those reveries involving divine figures—Bacchus, for example—were frowned on when they got out of hand. How much more so an operation to summon a daimon with a name like Doom? Goetia disturbed the peace.

I personally don't recommend the practice of goetia. There are so many beneficial daimones to call upon for thaumaturgy, it puzzles me why anyone would risk the very real dangers of dealing with goetic demons. Even the best intentioned kakodaimon thinks hurting people is its mission in existence. Using Goetic demons for magical tasks is like asking the nice tattooed young men and women hanging out downtown if they'd like to watch your house for a weekend while you go out of town.[139] Kakodaimones are certainly no more powerful, and absolutely much more difficult to work with, than other spiritual entities. But there is one particular magical operation we can perform with kakodaimones that is quite worthwhile: that of protection from them.

Rituals like the lesser banishing ritual of the pentagrams were unknown in the ancient world. You banished an area by cleaning it—literally. The literal cleaning also cleaned away spirits who might be there. When, for example, Odysseus kills the men occupying his house (and trying to occupy his wife), his next step is to clean away the blood with water and sulfur. Disinfecting the house also rid it of the angry ghosts. Chernips is a wonderful means of clearing away kakodaimones. But I may surprise you by pointing out that clearing out kakodaimones is not always the goal. Take the example of Phobetor, who becomes a kakodaimon of nightmares for the person whom he relentlessly visits. Sending him away is a solution, of course, but it doesn't get at the cause. Why is the person suffering such nightmares?

Perhaps she has had a traumatic experience, in which case Phobetor may well be doing his usual office right but at the wrong time. Instead of dealing with this stress during sleep, the victim may need to start working through

---

139 Which isn't to imply that *all* young men and women covered in tattoos are bad folks. I've known more than a few examples of stellar humanity and questionable ink in my time.

such issues during the day. But how do you get Phobetor to stop long enough to get enough sleep to cope? By making it clear to him that you understand his message. In other words, by "propitiating" him.

The propitiating of a kakodaimon is not sucking up to, paying off (they're not the mafia), or worshiping them. Instead, it's acknowledging them with respect but taking on your own role as an intermediary between the gods. Remember, we too are a kind of daimon—we are "mortal gods," as the Hermetica puts it—and it would be a mistake to think that we have nothing to say or share with even the fiercest of kakodaimones.[140] Moreover, if you've been following up on the exercises and making regular offerings to the gods, you have powerful allies among the greater good daimones and divinities.

Propitiating a kakodaimon is not the same as entering a contract, negotiating, or begging. It's a way of establishing power using the universal obligation created by a gift. By making an offering to a kakodaimon, you obligate it to you and thus can direct it in healthier and more beneficial ways. In other words, you use beneficence and grace to reconstitute order, which is exactly what the One is doing all the time. If one finds oneself in a state in which the influence of a kakodaimon is evident either supernaturally or naturally and you have achieved some measure of success with working with other daimones, especially the genius, then this ritual of placation might be beneficial.

This ritual can also be a means of self-improvement: every character flaw you have has a daimon who governs it, just as every virtue does. By propitiating those kakodaimones, you take away some of their sting and can begin to work at changing that flaw. Mental and physical illness, of course, should be treated by a professional in addition to any magical work you do. But even our ordinary jealousy, pettiness, fear, or lusts can be tamed with this ritual.

Identifying the kakodaimon that is involved is a simple matter: the ancients rarely bothered to give them names other than the name of the thing they governed. Phobetor, for example, just means "frightener." You can name these kakodaimones in English, or look up the equivalent word

140 Corpus Hermeticum XII:1

in Latin or Greek. You could also comb Hesiod for the names of such daimones as he lists and see if any of them are relevant.

EXERCISE 6.5: PROPITIATING A KAKODAIMON

The proper offerings for a daimon include wine, bread, and fruit. For this ritual, a libation dish and a cup of wine is sufficient. You will also need two kinds of incense. One should be appropriate to your genius, which you may have learned directly from it, but if in doubt you can always use frankincense. The other is a lunar incense—myrrh or storax being most common, unless you have a particular lunar scent you like. You will also want your wand, which can be your usual wand or a sprig of yew if you can get it. You will also need a iunx (see chapter 4). Of course, you will prepare the fire and chernips according to the methods already explained in that chapter; I'm not going to cut and paste them, as I don't get paid by the word.

Determine the superior god of the daimon you are propitiating, either by looking for clues in Hesiod or through reason. For example, if Hesiod tells us that a particular daimon is the child of another god or attends to that god, then use that as its superior. Hesiod tells us that Phobetor is the child of Nyx, so we can call on her as his superior. If in doubt, you can use Hekate, whom you will call upon anyway, as queen of all daimones.

STEP 1: Purity is always important, but here it is doubly important. In addition to purifying yourself with water and natron, or chernips, you may also want to have a phylactery that protects you from evil influences. A little bit of sulfur in a gold locket or box around your neck is a traditional and simple amulet you could use, or you could draw an ouroboros—a serpent eating its own tail—on a piece of parchment with a prayer for protection inside it. Magical protection circles do not often appear in ancient magic, but if you wish to use one it's not necessarily a bad idea. Carry the dish of chernips around the circle, sprinkling as you go.

STEP 2: Begin by picking up your wand as a symbol of authority and stating, in a loud voice, "*Hekas, hekas, este bebeloi,*" which simply means "begone, begone, profane things." It's a traditional signal that a ritual is about to begin.

STEP 3: Light incense or add it to the censer and say something like:

> May my Genius hear my prayer and stand beside me in this working. If ever I make an error, by omission or commission, leave out a word or speak awry, or in any way fail in my ritual obligations, let it be as if I had performed the ritual correctly. Accept this offering, Agathodaimon, and deliver me from any evil.

STEP 4: Add some myrrh or appropriate lunar incense and speak the following prayer to the Phantasm of Hekate:

> Hear me, Hekate, Goddess of Daimones, Threefold goddess of the gate, Apotropaia[141], Soteira[142], and by whatsoever name it pleases you to be called. If ever I have kissed my hand to the moon, made offering, or pleased you in any way, come and stand over me in this working.[143] Protect and guard me from evil, and speak with me when

---

141 "turning away harm"

142 "savior"

143 If you have not done any of these things, do not undertake this ritual, as you have not built up a relationship with Hekate.

I speak. Accept this offering and be kindly to
me, for I know your secret words:

STEP 5: Recite the following words of power, a phylactery against daimones:

ACHTHIŌPHIPH ERESCHIGAL
NEBOUTOSOUALĒTH SATHŌTH
SABAŌTH SABRŌTH[144]

STEP 6: Imagine a phantasm of the daimon standing just outside of the circle around which you circumambulated, while you spin your iunx and repeat this phrase every time it changes direction: "Magic wheel, bring N. to me," N. being the name of the daimon. Spin the iunx and repeat the formula until it becomes clear. If the phantasm attempts to become grotesque, point your wand at it until it assumes a more pleasing form. Try not to allow it to become zoomorphic or monstrous, even if you're a fan of Dürer.

STEP 7: Address it thus:

Hear me, N., daimon of [Superior god], by whatever
name you are called in the heavens or under the
earth, and from whatever abode you come, for
I am [your name] whom [your mother's name]
bore, and I stand in the presence of Hekate your
Queen, to whom you must bow.

144 Hans Dieter Betz. *The Greek Magical Papyri in Translation: Including the Demotic Spells.* (Chicago: University of Chicago Press, 1992), 126. PGM VII 317–18. I have, with Betz, read a tau for the gamma in NEBOUTOSOUALĒTH, a name commonly associated with ERESCHIGAL and thence Hekate.

STEP 8: The phantasm should bow. If it does not do so without you forcing it, again point your wand at it and place the fingertips of your other hand on the altar until it does.

STEP 9: Continue:

> Accept this drink offering, and let it mark friendship between us, that you work for my good and under the instructions of the goddess Hekate and my genius, for I know the secret words of Ephesus which are ASKION KATASKION LIX TETRAX DAMNAMENEUS AISIA to which your kind is bound to answer. Let therefore enmity be done, friendship begun, and may you submit to the authority of the gods.

STEP 10: Pour the libation completely into the libation dish. Kiss your fingers in friendship to the phantasm, then to the phantasm of Hekate.

STEP 11: Say the following:

> I offer you, Hekate, this speech offering in gratitude for your aid. Continue, O Goddess of the Ways, to keep and guide me, and protect me from evil. Accept these sweet scents, and may it be acceptable unto you.

STEP 12: Add more lunar incense.

STEP 13: Step away from the altar, kiss your hand, turn around, and leave the room in silence to end the ritual. You can of course come right back again if you do most of your magic in the living room. But don't put things away until the incense has all burned down and cooled. Then, dispose of the ashes of the incense and the wine outside, ideally at a crossroad or junction or, failing that, a liminal space like the side of a road. Don't put it in your own yard or near your own house. At least cross a street to dispose of it.

The results of this ritual should be a marked improvement. For example, you may use it to propitiate Lytta, the kakodaimon of rage and madness, to control your anger. You should see that your anger is directed in healthier directions, less out of your control and less overwhelming. If you don't, try to create a stronger relationship with Hekate by making offerings to her, and then try the ritual again when the moon is just past full.

Of course, if your rage is out of control and you're hurting people, one effect of this ritual might be the quite practical effect of getting you arrested, charged, and sentenced to anger management training. So—handle kakodaimones carefully, and handle the gods even more carefully. The kakodaimones might hurt you and those around you; however, the gods will help and love you, and sometimes that's not pretty either.

We are not, however, helpless pawns of the daimones: we have the flip side of theurgy, thaumaturgy, as a tool in our belt. In the next chapter, we will look at some ancient and more contemporary methods of practicing thaumaturgy as well as how theurgy can empower and inform that practice.

CHAPTER 7

Thaumaturgy

I'm laying waste to a lot of etymology in this book, but let me explain why I'm using the $25 word "thaumaturgy" rather than the more economical "magic." Historically, a thaumaturgist meant a miracle worker, often carrying with it the idea of being an engineer—a person skilled with manipulating matter in order to create wondrous effects. By this definition, my Mac is a thaumaturgic device: a bit of clever engineering that works wonders. I'm not using the word in that sense. I'm using it to mean what many authors, myself included, usually mean by the word "magic" (or, if you're trying to use up some spare k's, "magick"). Why not simply use the word "magic"? Because I want to make a clear parallel between theurgy and thaumaturgy, both types of magic.

Theurgy, as you know, is literally "god work." It's the practice of magic that looks upwards in order to unify the human mind with the divine. It's magic with an upward arrow: I am sending my will upward. "Thaumaturgy" comes from similar roots but means "wonder work," or "miracle work." It's also magic in that it uses the same symbolic techniques and the same manipulation of our consciousness. But it's downward-pointing magic: I send my will downward into the world upon which I stand. Thaumaturgy is magic that affects the world of matter, in one way or another, to achieve a desired effect.

This doesn't mean it's diabolical or any such nonsense. But it's the magic of the hyle (world of matter) rather than the magic of the Nous (world of Ideas).

The distinction is a minor one, perhaps, but I want to emphasize these two terms are both kinds of magic, which is a word much abused by history. The word originally comes from the Persian *maguš*, transliterated into Greek as *μάγος*. The word meant "priest" in Persian and so the Greek word took on the connotation of "foreign priest"; in other words, "priest who believed and did some unusual things." The general appeal of the foreign, as well as a bit of fear of Persia, led to the notion that the foreign priest, the magus, might have powers and knowledge beyond those of Greek priests. Moreover, just as the Babylonian "Chaldeans" became the term for astrologers because of their development of that art, so did the magoi became magicians due to the development of that art in Persia.

Magic in this sense is both theurgic and thaumaturgic. It is priestly work, but it's also wonder working. It is ultimately a gathering together of wisdom and knowledge, a kind of science in the very loosest sense: a body of knowledge and a method for gaining that knowledge. Of course, it bears no resemblance to our scientific method, but neither is it a rival. It's an alternate form of knowledge, and we in the contemporary West lose a lot by paying it little heed. But that's a rant for another place. This is why I use those two terms: to place theurgy and thaumaturgy under the general umbrella of magic.

The ancients did not, contrary to the common Neopagan impression, universally applaud the virtues of thaumaturgy. In fact, most of them excoriated it: those who didn't made a sharp distinction between magic used to achieve union with the gods—theurgy—which was all right, and magic used to get material benefit—thaumaturgy—of which only some wasn't questionable. Healing magic had a fairly acceptable reception and was often shuffled off into the domain of theurgy or systematized away from magic in order to insulate it from the general unsavoriness. But most other thaumaturgy was treated with suspicion or downright disdain, even by theurgists. In fact, through antiquity, the practice of thaumaturgy was mostly illegal in the Roman Empire.

This general distrust of thaumaturgy did not hold in Egypt, however, where magic was not only legal but institutionalized. We have a very large number of talismans used quite openly by people of all socioeconomic positions. We also know that there were a large selection of particular, either professional or part-time magic workers ranging from those who specialized in the curing of scorpion stings (a very practical concern in the desert) to healers and thaumaturgists of a general kind. This open acceptance of magic led to Egypt becoming a location of highly advanced thaumaturgic arts.

Even in the Roman empire, some spells were safe enough to be recorded in places like Cato's *On Agriculture*, where he gives a spell for setting a bone. Similar medical spells occur elsewhere and don't seem to rouse suspicion. But most of the spells we have from Late Antiquity are in the Magical Papyri, that collection of fragmentary magical books found in various places. Rather than publicly published, these were probably copied and handed around privately, and indeed they often have the form of a letter from one magician to another (perhaps because they were or perhaps to give the audience a little illicit thrill at having intercepted a private and forbidden communication). It's not hard to see why many people regarded the practice of thaumaturgy as recorded in these texts with a bit of a jaundiced eye: There is no shortage of curses, maledictions, and love spells that would probably more accurately be called rape spells. There are also grotesque ingredients, weird instructions, and an absolute pot-au-feu of religious references, throwing in Moses, Isis, Jesus, and Apollo all together and stirring vigorously.

So what place could thaumaturgy possibly have in the high-minded endeavor of theurgy? There are certainly mystics and magicians who turn up their nose at thaumaturgy or "practical magic" in favor of pure theurgy, and who refuse to do a spell for a clear, practical purpose, but I'm not sure that's more a function of high-mindedness or self-doubt. Perhaps we should look at how Philanike breaks this down for Euthymios:

Euthymios: Every time I walk in the door, you're doing something weird. Do you time it for my arrival, or are you always just doing something weird?

Philanike: I'm half-tempted to ask you to define "weird," but I need to finish this engraving before the moon slides off the midheaven.

Eu: Well, when you have a moment and can put down the goggles, I'll ask you what you're doing.

Ph: Protecting my eyes. This rotary tool can make sparks as it engraves the copper, and if one gets in my eye, that could—

Eu: Not with the goggles. I understand *their* purpose. I was wondering about the plate of copper.

Ph: Oh, this? Hold on, almost done. ...there we go. Now if you'll kindly hand me that jar of camphor, it's time to make it stinky in here.

Eu: That's an understatement. Whew! So—the point?

Ph: Let me just... there we go. The point of what?

Eu: Of the plate you're waving through the smoke, that's what.

Ph: It's a prosperity spell, for you.

Eu: Isn't that a little—I don't know, earthy?

Ph: I should hope so. That's where I live.

Eu: I'm just not sure we should be worrying about material things like money.

Ph: Ah, you've been reading Plotinus. What should we be worrying about, then?

Eu: Theurgy. Union with the divine. Henosis.

Ph: We should worry about all those things? Why? Does worrying help us achieve them?

Eu: Well, no. I don't mean "worry," I guess. We shouldn't worry. I mean "focus on."

Ph: Why shouldn't we worry?

Eu: It does no good to worry. It doesn't change anything.

Ph: But you have been worried about your finances lately. I've noticed.

Eu: Yes, but I shouldn't.

Ph: What *should* you do?

Eu: Not worry.

Ph: That's a negative. I didn't ask what should you not do.

Eu: I should put my finances out of my mind.

Ph: Noble! You could join the swelling ranks of homeless theurgists. Tell me, is it easier to learn to play music if you are struggling for survival on the streets, or living comfortably?

Eu: Comfortably, I suppose. What does that have to do with anything?

Ph: And other arts, such as, say, dancing. Is it easier to learn to dance if you eat enough or if you are starving?

Eu: It's hard to do anything physical if you're starving.

Ph: Would you say most arts are easier if you have enough money to cover the expenses of living?

Eu: I suppose so.

Ph: So why would theurgy be different?

Eu: Well, it's an art not concerned with material benefit.

Ph: Do most musicians and writers get rich?

Eu: Okay, no. I see your point. So I do need to pay some attention to money, just so I can have enough to practice theurgy. Although I maintain that isn't a huge amount of money; I can get by on very little without worrying. So what should I do?

Ph: You could focus just on getting enough money that you aren't worried.

Eu: There's not a lot more I could do. I've applied for jobs everywhere. I just don't get a second interview.

Ph: If there were something you could do, let's say a special tie that you knew the interviewer would love, or you discover in your research that they're looking for a particular skill that you have, would you make use of that—wear that tie, mention that skill?

Eu: Absolutely.

Ph: So it's not a distraction to employ your talents and skills and make choices based on knowledge in order to achieve a goal.

Eu: I guess not.

Ph: So why is thaumaturgy bad, then?

Eu: I suppose it's not. Not inherently.

My endorsement of thaumaturgy isn't to say that the ancients didn't have a point. There are dangers involved in the practice. I don't want to overstate the case and suggest that mispronouncing a barbarous word of invocation will call down the wrath of the gods, but neither do I wish to understate it and suggest that you can't hurt yourself or others with thaumaturgy. The truth is, magic is real and has real effects, and just like anything else that is real, you can use it for good or bad. In my opinion, one of the worst things that could happen to a young magician is having a love spell work. "Make her my slave!" sounds great, but it isn't. Similarly, throwing around curses when you wouldn't have the courage to throw a punch is a good way to get yourself hurt, not so much your target.

The single biggest danger of thaumaturgy is turning yourself into a credulous twit but that has nothing to do with the magic itself. I'll address how to stay sane (well, sane-*ish*) while studying the occult in a later chapter. But if you walk around telling yourself—or, gods forbid, others—that you are a sorcerer of unmitigated power or call yourself by some awful name like "Archwyzard Snakebacon" or something... well, do what you like, but you won't be invited to my dinner parties. Portentous announcements or intimations of occult power ("*Sigh.* No one understands what a burden it is to be a priest of the Old Gods!") will not impress the plumber. I can't really imagine that someone who has made it this far through the book is likely to do such stuff, but even hanging around with such people is worse than being alone.

Besides looking like a dork, there is a real occult danger in ignorance. I have met people who have claimed to have Nemesis as a patron. Really? Are you sure you want to do that? Really? I mean, as a daimon of justice, I suppose... but *really*? Sure, she's the daimon of righteous indignation, and that be an emotion you feel a lot, but that's not a sign that she should be your patron. That's a sign you should get some help coping with your emotions. Covering up moral flaws behind a curtain of magic—oh, gosh, I know I don't have money for baby formula, but I just absolutely need that new crystal ball!—is not only pathetic, it's dangerous. If you call on Nemesis long enough, she will answer you. Have you never done anything unjust, and are you *sure* about that?

The gods in the Nous are pure and unchanging; you can no more offend them than you can mark the sun. But you can turn away from them, cut the holy part of you that they represent out of your psyche, and throw it away. You can become stunted and wilted because you have chosen to be so.

You can also damage yourself in other ways. Make sure you want what you say you want. If you don't really want it, you still might get it. Now, it's hard to do magic for something you're torn about—we'll talk about that in a moment. But sometimes self-loathing, self-destruction, and a perverse desire come together in just the right way to get you hurt. For example, perhaps you think you need a job, so you do magic to get a specific job in a specific place—a job that makes you miserable but is inescapable because you've done magic to force yourself back into it. Usually, these sorts of errors, of the "I didn't really want that after all"-type, are fixable, but not all are. Be especially careful with love spells.

Some areas of the occult are not for beginners. As I said before, stay away from goetia or summoning kakodaimones, and give necromancy a wide berth, not because they're inherently bad things to do but because they're dangerous. When it comes to working with the dead, how much do you like being dragged out of bed at all hours of the morning by strangers demanding favors? There are ways to deal with these things safely and productively, but you won't learn them from this book and experimentation is expensive.

Thaumaturgy is also not a panacea. It can't fix everything. Bad things still happen to very good magicians. "Cattle die, kinsmen die," as the Havamal tells us. If you're looking to fix all of your problems, there isn't a single thing that will do it all. Magic can help with that project, but it can no more fix it instantly and completely than it can whip you up a grilled cheese and a glass of tomato juice. You've got to get in the kitchen. Moreover, sometimes, no matter how good a magician you are, stuff happens. You are still subject to chance, and for that you need philosophy to teach you to deal with it, not thaumaturgy.

Just as thaumaturgy isn't a panacea, it's not an excuse, either. Unless you've traveled in some specific countries recently and were spectacularly rude to the wrong people or you happened to seriously offend a root doctor or the priest of particular religions, you're not under magical attack. The odds are slim to none that your neighbor with the loud dog on whom you called the cops knows enough magic to curse you. Even if they think they do, they probably don't. Curses aren't the easiest magic to pull off. Don't get caught up in paranoia, and don't start assuming that you're in debt because of a curse on your money. You're in debt because the economy is terrible, you may not have a firm understanding of finances, or you were forced to make some bad decisions by circumstances arising from either of the other two. The dead squirrel on your driveway is roadkill, not a curse.

With all these dire warnings and tsk-tsks, it might seem that thaumaturgy has no purpose at all and one is better off just steering clear of it. You could get by just fine in theurgy without ever touching a bit of thaumaturgy or "practical magic." After all, Plotinus probably did, and quite a lot of contemporary Pagans do currently. But there is a value to thaumaturgy beyond the "cor blimey, let's get laid" attitude of the 1990s. It's this: It's hard to focus on the gods when you're worried about whether you'll eat.

A wonderful tool for magic is the pyramid. Not the Egyptian pyramids or those cheesy plastic pyramids they sell in occult bookstores, but a particular pyramid named after a humanistic psychologist named Abraham Maslow. Maslow's pyramid, also called Maslow's hierarchy of needs, illustrates what benefit thaumaturgy can be to the theurgist.

Maslow argued that all human needs and desires were not only organized into particular categories, but that those categories could be ranked in a hierarchy. All things being equal, people would strive to fulfill those lower, more basic or foundational needs before the higher ones. Of course, individuals may vary, and various refinements to this hierarchy exist, but as a rough guide it's illustrative of why thaumaturgy can be of value for the theurgist.

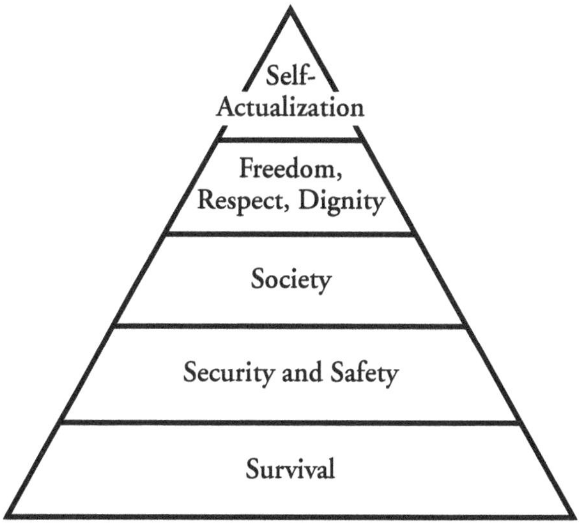

Fig. 12: Maslow's Hierarchy of Needs

In his original paper, Maslow identified five basic needs. The first and most fundamental of these needs is survival: if we are not alive, the rest doesn't matter. So we have a set of subneeds that are survival needs, which he calls physiological. They are biological necessities: if we are starving, dying of thirst, exposed to the elements, or suffocating we will do whatever we can to achieve those needs, even if it means letting other needs slide. It is hard to concentrate on the higher things in life when struggling for air or trying to stay warm enough in a Chicago winter.

Once we achieve our basic, immediate survival needs, we begin to look toward the future and consider long-term security and safety. If I'm starving, I try to find food for tonight. Once full, I try to figure out how I'm going to eat tomorrow. The struggle to meet this need can manifest as seeking a job, finding a place to live, and so on. Once a place to live and the means to pay for it is found, we seek out other kinds of security, such as insurance, investments, and so on. Here, a person with a job that keeps him or her alive starts looking for a better one or planning on a raise or working toward promotion. Again, these needs are material but they're a bit more abstract than the purely physiological because they deal with the future.

Once those needs are met, we have time to consider the next need, which Maslow calls "love." But really it could be called "society." We want friends, partners, lovers, and association with others. This need can become so strong that we'd rather have terrible friends than none, or bad relationships than be single. Criticism of Maslow often points out that even those dwelling on the level of safety, seeking shelter and sufficient food, often have friends and associations with others. Others point out that people will actively surrender their safety needs in order to feel the sense of being loved, seeking out for example destructive or abusive partners. Maslow, in his original paper, concedes that not all of these needs are met in the strict fixed order above, but in general people seek to fulfill their needs for safety before they seek out partners.

Once love is achieved, Maslow states, many people then seek to achieve esteem, either of others or of themselves. We seek freedom, respect, and dignity. People will abase themselves to fulfill the needs of safety and survival, and even for the sense of belonging that comes from association, but eventually—when those lower needs are fulfilled—they will strive to gain respect and learn to respect themselves. One of the reasons I think Maslow is so useful for the magician is the optimistic understanding of human nature: for Maslow, health is the normal state, and there is a drive and a force in each person that strives for health and goodness, which when thwarted leads to disease, but when nurtured can overcome weaknesses both mental and moral. When nurtured in the right way, the desire for respect can lead a person to make healthy choices all the way down the line.

Finally, after achieving a measure of esteem, Maslow says that a person seeks self-actualization. He defines self-actualization in a phrase that is almost theurgic in its gnomic conciseness: "What a man *can* be, he *must* be."[145] He uses the example of a poet, who to be truly happy must write. Those of us with artistic tendencies know this well: it might be pleasant to play video games (which, by the way, satisfy our esteem needs by allowing us to display mastery), but after some time without writing, I know I start to feel grumpy and anxious and even physically sore. The drive to health pushes us to achieve what we can, including achievements in the spiritual sense.

Viktor Frankl, in *Man's Search for Meaning*, adds a level beyond self-actualization called "self-transcendence," which is the drive to achieve transcendent meaning in our lives.[146] But from the Hermetic perspective, self-actualization naturally leads to self-transcendence for at least some people. Most people will self-actualize by achieving their goals in this life, but some few will not be satisfied with that and will seek beyond their material experience. They will not only want to develop their talents and take joy in learning and creating, but they also want to strive for something holy in the world. This holiness need not be transcendent; it can be the holiness of matter. This ultimate desire is what Crowley calls "the True Will."

---

145 Abraham Maslow. *Motivation and Personality.* (New York: Harper, 1954), 91.

146 Victor Frankl. *Man's Search for Meaning.* (Boston: Beacon, 1957).

To achieve this true will, the thing we really want to do, the thing we've decided we're born to do, we need to climb the pyramid by meeting our lower needs first. Maybe we can withdraw from the world and starve ourselves to enlightenment, but this practice builds unnecessary roadblocks, from the theurgic perspective. Instead, we can use the tools of thaumaturgy to build a foundation of safety, emotional security, and nurturance so that we can achieve esteem and have a full toolbox when we approach that great work of our true will.

Wealth itself is no sign of virtue or even magical ability, and some may indeed choose a life of modest means. But that's the key: they choose it. Thaumaturgy is the occult art of choice.

Theory

So if thaumaturgy is so very nifty, how does it work?

I am not fond of the dominant theory of how magic works in contemporary occult studies. Explanations of magic involving mystical energies and the like are filled with enough bombast to pass the bar exam. Some of the things people say about "energy" and magic would make Plotinus's beard curl in their philosophical fuzziness. Briefly, because I've covered it enough elsewhere, "energy" is a physical, material thing. Magic is metaphysical, beyond the physical. The use of matter to explain something that is beyond matter can only be useful as a metaphor.

As a metaphor the explanation of "energy" has its uses, but it's important to underline that it *is* metaphor. I know not everyone agrees with me, even quite a few magicians I respect as well as some of my teachers. That's fine. Let me simply point out that as far as magical theory goes, none of our ancient predecessors thought it came from an invisible and quirky "magical energy," because they had no such concept as "energy."

They had the word, or the root word, for energy. In fact, we see it in the word "theurgy": it's the last bit, that "-rgy" bit, which in Greek is *ourgia*, meaning "work." Theurgy is "god-work," and energy is "the work within." This word, however, did not have the scientific denotation it does now, because they only dimly recognized that light, heat, and other kinds of "work-stuff" were related. Nor did they understand the relationship between that "work-stuff" and matter; no one understood that until the twentieth century. Now, we can reclaim the word but we don't need to because we have a Latin word that works just fine and, unlike "energy," has connotations that actually help us rather than deceive us. That word is "virtue."

"Virtue" comes from root words meaning "power," ultimately. It's the capability to do something, and later, the capacity to do something good. Objects do not have magical energy: they have virtues. Some virtues are exoteric or clear and reliable: salt has the virtue of drying things, of preserving. A large metal ball rolled down the hill has several virtues, one of them being motion. Notice this isn't energy, which a scientist would say that ball is shedding as it rolls downhill. When the ball reaches the bottom it still has various exoteric virtues, such as its weight, shape, size, and other qualities.

It also has esoteric, or inner, virtues (sometimes called "occult virtues" meaning "hidden powers"). These esoteric virtues are what interest us as thaumaturgists, because they allow us to use objects and symbols as means of communication with the Nous. We already know about *synthemata*, and this is just an extension and application of that understanding.

Using the occult virtues of matter is not a mechanical process. One doesn't find the right correspondences and the right objects with the right esoteric virtues, apply them in the right way, and get results. Making a talisman of, say, prosperity without having a relationship with the gods of prosperity will be about as effective as cold-calling a movie star and asking for a date. This mechanical view of magic is materialistic; it implies that magic is a technology, not an art. In some sense, it is a technology, just as writing is a technology, but communication is an art and cannot be reduced to mechanical instructions.

This power to speak to the Nous was called *hkaw* (usually pronounced "hekau") in ancient Egyptian. It is personified in the god Heka, the son of Atum, the god who is the demiurge of this universe and a personification of the Nous. Hence, he's a channel of communication. The role of words in Egyptian magic is evidence from the inscriptions in tombs, wherein the words for "beer" and "bread" act as offerings of those objects. To write a thing is to bring it into being, and to speak it is to make it happen. *Heka* represents the power of words, and his power is manifested in two ways: *sia* and *hu*. *Sia* is the power of intent, and *hu* is the power of effective speech. If you have *sia* and you have *hu*, then you can make *heka*: or, in English, if you have effective intent, and you have effective speech, then you can make magic.

Words are the ground of thaumaturgy, but words aren't just made of sound. There are divine words, in the forms of geometrical arrangements, sigils, and signs that are not only unspeakable but also perhaps unknowable. These are noetic synthemata, whereas the material objects manipulated in magic are the material synthemata.

The application of synthemata from all three levels of existence helps to unite the will. The great secret of all magic is to acquire a united will. The more united the will, the easier the magic will be because your voice in speaking to the Nous will be louder and clearer. Take an example of a person who wants to make more money at work. She wants a raise and does a spell to get a raise, and it doesn't work. Why not? If she had spent some time considering her goal, she may have discovered that while most of her wants the money, some of her is intimidated by the idea of making more money, some of her is afraid of dealing with investments and the like, and some of her feels a moral qualm about being too wealthy. All of these contrary wills can be enough to drown out a spell.

To achieve clarity of heka, then, we need to unite the parts of our mind and the parts of the world. The hieroglyph for the god Heka is:

Fig. 13: Heka in Egyptian

The twisted rope in the middle of the two arms is the sound *heh*. The breast and two arms is the symbol for *ka*, the soul. While I wouldn't read a lot into the arrangement of this hieroglyph from a linguistic perspective, the graphic is representative of how we must unite our minds to achieve our goals. We have to bind our soul to the goal.

Later Neoplatonists writing in the Renaissance called these bindings *vincula*, the Latin word for "chains" or "bindings." Giordano Bruno, one of my favorite Renaissance magicians and (in my opinion) an underrated genius, suggests that we create these vincula through the agency of Eros, on attraction. We are attracted not to things in the world, as people think, but to phantasms we construct about those things. The vincula connect us to phantasms. And we create these phantasms and evoke the power of Eros through the application of principles of sympathy.[147]

Since the time of Pythagoras, the ancients were well aware of the phenomenon of entrainment. If you have a piano you can see it for yourself: open the lid of the piano and strike middle C. You'll see the C strings vibrating, but you'll also see other strings, in a regular pattern down the line, vibrating in response. These are entrained with the vibration of C because they are in harmony with it. If you look closely, you'll see that they're strings in the harmonic proportions we discussed when looking at geometry. An analogous process takes place when we construct a phantasm or work with a synthema. It begins to pluck the relevant strings in our minds, in the minds of others around us, and in the Nous itself.

The vibrations I'm talking about here are analogies, not literal realities. The principle of universal harmony that causes strings to vibrate in sympathy is the same principle that makes magic possible, but that doesn't mean that crystals "vibrate." The statement "everything vibrates" sounds true and profound, but it doesn't mean much. Instead, I'd say everything is in harmony

147 Giordano Bruno. *Cause, Principle and Unity: An Essay on Magic.* Trans. Richard J. Blackwell. (Cambridge: Cambridge University Press, 1998).

with some things, and not in harmony with other things, and together the entire universe is in harmony with the One.

Achieving Unity of Will

The first step to truly effective thaumaturgy is to unify the will, which works best by following the dictum of Apollo: Know thyself. You have to figure out what and who you are, what you want, and why you want it. And it helps to develop the habit of never taking anything for granted.

We'd have no problem unifying some things toward our will, it seems. Who doesn't want health? Everyone wants it, so shouldn't everyone be healthy all the time by magical law? And yet they aren't. Why not?

Because of course not everyone wants health, not with their whole being. You may want to be healthy, but you also want to get drunk or smoke or you want to sit around and write long occult books while your belly just gets bigger and bigger. Maybe you want to exercise but a tiny part of you doesn't want to get up in the morning so early, or a tiny part of you doesn't want to dress in ridiculous clothing because it doesn't want to be embarrassed by accidentally wearing unfashionable jogging pants. The neurotic crowd of voices that fill the average head is deafening, and we're not exempt just because we're theurgists.

And also, not everything is possible. You may be very ill and want to be better with your whole being, but perhaps it is necessary that you be ill. I'm not suggesting that you're ill for some cosmic reason, or—gods forbid—because you deserve it due to some karmic faux pas in a past life. It's just that bad things happen sometimes, and even the best theurgist can't avoid fate any more than the finest guitar player in the world can avoid breaking a string once in a while. It won't wash to run around telling everyone that they create their own reality, because theurgy teaches us that we don't. We are subject to *Ananke*, to necessity, and the fates determine a lot of our lives. That's okay. Actually, it's better than okay: it's a good thing, because it means we don't have to plan out every single thing that we do or that is done to us. Moreover, we're not to blame for every single thing that occurs in the universe, which is awfully nice. What I've always wondered about the New Age movement is this: if we create our reality, what kind of sick buggers must humans be to create the reality of natural disasters, plague, and human suffering year after year? One of the most infuriating things I run into in magic is the tendency to blame people for their own illnesses, especially cancer. No. People do not have cancer because they are suppressing emotion or because they're bad people. They have cancer because our bodies are composed of matter and matter is always in a state of constant and not always beneficial change. Even the greatest of magicians must die someday.

Nevertheless, much is possible if you are willing to look deeply into your passions and desires and sort them out. So the question is, how do you do this? Begin by taking an inventory—and I mean that literally, with pen and paper—of your values. What are the ideals you hold as valuable, that you think are precious and good? For example, perhaps you will list freedom, your family, money, love, life, and pleasure. Be honest: don't leave off "money" just because you feel like you shouldn't value it. For that matter, if some of your values are not so good, it's a good idea to get them on the page. If heroin or booze are your values, stick them on there.

The second step is to rank these values. Take any two of them and compare them. It helps to do this on notecards so you can easily shuffle them around. For example, if I have the list above, I might say "freedom" and "pleasure": which of these would I sacrifice for the sake of the other? I would sacrifice my own pleasure for my freedom. I'd rather be uncomfortable and free than comfy and a slave. So put freedom above pleasure on the list. Now take the higher of the two and grab another random value. Would you rather do without money for the sake of your freedom, or do without your freedom for the sake of money? If you decide that freedom is a higher rank, then compare money to the next lowest: would I rather have money and do without pleasure, or pleasure and do without money? For me, the purpose of extra money is to gratify pleasures, so I put money under pleasure. Now another one compared to my top value: life. Would I sacrifice my life for freedom? Yes, I would: so I put freedom above life. Eventually, you will systematically create a list ranking each of your values.

The usefulness of this analysis isn't that it'll help you make prettier talismans but that you'll learn what to make talismans for. If I make a talisman for extra money because it'd be fun to go to the Bahamas, it'll be less likely to work than if I make a talisman for money because I feel trapped at my job. The first isn't consistent with my values; I may as well just make a talisman to go to the Bahamas. The second talisman, though, is consistent with my worldview; it'll work in harmony with my own system of values.

Some values are almost universal and usually unconscious. For example, people generally value stability. But consider: would you rather make more money and work a happier job that isn't so stable, or be stable in your unpleasant and poorly paying job? Be honest! Many people would choose stability, even if they claim otherwise. People often find it hard to lose weight not because they don't desire being thin, but because they desire indulgence more (and a lot of people find it hard to lose weight because they are already a healthy weight for themselves, or because of genetics, but those are other matters entirely—see the discussion on Ananke above). For years I found it hard to find a good relationship through magic until I finally recognized that I needed one that respected my values of freedom and intellectual stimulation.

The other complication, and it is rather large, is that our values are not consistent. Get hungry enough, horny enough, or tired enough and before you know it pleasure starts racing up that tree until you'll happily surrender yourself to imprisonment for a couple good hours of sleep or a nice steak. Doing magic at such times might work, but you might find yourself no longer wanting the thing when it comes. The goal is to surf the general average of what it is you value and not obsess over what you should value at any given time.

The exception to this rule, of course, is when the value is self-destructive, such as drugs or alcohol. These sorts of values are harmful to all other values below them—and for the most part, they find their way to the top of the list pretty quickly, even if people holding them refuse to admit it. You can tell a healthy value because it actually supports you in the lesser values. Freedom, for example, helps me have a more meaningful life, a wider range of pleasures, and even make and keep my money for my own purposes. Similarly, a lesser value can offer support to higher values: money helps me secure freedom. It's when one value takes over all others that you start to undermine all your other values.

Once you figure out what you value, the next step is to create a set of goals. This in itself is the single most powerful magical act one can do, because it can literally begin to change your life. Here, divination can come into play as well as introspection and your inventory of values. Goals should be simple, objective, and time-bound. A simple goal is one that you can state in one single sentence, with an action verb and "I" as the subject: "I will go to Spain." An objective goal is one for which you can say what it will look like when you've achieved it. "I want to be thinner" is not objective: thinner than what? "I need to exercise more," again, is not objective. "I will be able to run two miles without stopping" is a bit better. "I will lose twenty pounds" is also a bit more objective: a scientist with a scale could confirm whether or not you achieved it by mere observation. Finally, it should be time-bound. The examples above are weak in that regard: better would be "I will be able to run two miles without stopping by the end of the year." "I will lose ten pounds by March" is also a better goal, because you give yourself a deadline. The time-frame needs to be realistic; losing ten pounds by March is a better time-frame if you make the goal in December than if you make it in the middle of February.

Goals also need to be *goals*, not methods. "I will work out three times a week for twenty minutes each time" is not a goal; it's a method. It's a pretty good method to achieve both goals from the last paragraph, but it's not a goal in itself. If you miss a day, the goal isn't ruined: only the method isn't working. You can always modify methods; you can't modify goals until you achieve them or don't. Goals are commitments; methods carry out that commitment. Once you have a goal, you need to start laying out methods.

I am a firm believer in what the author, teacher, and professional sorcerer Jason Miller calls "strategic sorcery." If you cannot contribute material effort toward a goal, magical methods will not suffice. This makes perfect sense from a theurgic perspective: if your soul wants the goal enough to do magic for it but your body refuses to commit, then you don't completely want it. By all means, make a talisman for better health and fitness, but you've got to strap on the shoes and hit the sidewalks if you're going to meet that goal to run two miles.

Methods—magical or material—are not exclusive. You should be able to come up with four or five good material methods for every one of your goals. For example, "I will go to Greece the summer after next" is a good, objective goal. Methods might include "I will eat out one day a week less than I do now, putting that money in my saving's account. I will automatically deduct twenty dollars every month to put into that account. I will contact a travel agent and get an estimate, as well as recommendations about economical places to stay. I will talk to my boss about taking some overtime this summer and some time off next summer." And so on. In addition, of course, you also begin to apply magically for this goal by following various methods such as the ones in this book and elsewhere. The best approach is to grab a goal and run toward it with all barrels blasting. If you find you can't do that, then you need to consider which of your values the goal is acting against and either interrogate that value or abandon the goal.

From a theurgic perspective, the power of thaumaturgy is that it not only establishes our foundation in Maslow's pyramid, it also helps us learn who we are by setting and achieving goals to get what we want.

Exercise 7.1: Set Goals

Using your magical diary if you keep one (I recommend it for this kind of work) or just a notebook or computer file you can find easily, write out a set of goals. If you're having a hard time finding inspiration, you can organize goals in three general areas:

- **Financial/Material goals:** get a raise, get a better job, buy a house, get a specific kind of car
- **Relationship/Social goals:** make a new friend, find a lover, get married, find a gaming group
- **Spiritual/Wellness goals:** acquire a specific level of physical fitness, have a particular mystical experience, perform a demanding ritual with its desired effect

Each of these areas can be subdivided further and so on, but you can spend your whole week making goals and not doing anything. It's a good idea to set three goals at a time with time limits. You can do more if you want, but three is a manageable number.

For each goal, lay out a multilevel plan of attack. List physical and mundane methods as well as magical methods, in order of difficulty, hardest first.

Your aim now is to try each strategy for a goal and fail as efficiently as possible. What I mean by this is find what doesn't work by trying the hardest stuff first. If you cannot make the hard stuff work, go on and try easier stuff. Cultivate an attitude of "Well, that was hard and didn't work, so good—I don't have to do that anymore." Later you can come back and try the harder stuff again. Don't allow yourself to be discouraged.

For example, if I wish to write a book, I try writing ten pages a day. That's way too much, I quickly discover. Rather than give up, I consult my list. The next hardest thing is five pages a day. Still too much. The next is two pages. That's doable. Almost too doable, so I go up to three. That seems to be the sweet spot, and by writing three pages a day I can finish the first draft of a novel in about three or four months. Every time I find something easy, I make it harder; every time something is too hard, I drop back to the next easier level. What I don't do is give up.

We've got an advantage in magic, of course, so let's move our focus to thaumaturgy, keeping in mind that the two must work in harmony as a concerted effort.

As it turns out, the word "harmony" is a watchword in our thaumaturgical practice. We aim always to act in harmony with the universe, even as we try to change it. Ancient writers often excoriate supposed witches for breaking the laws of nature, but thaumaturgical magic is really in harmony with nature: it's just that nature is a mind, not entirely unlike ours, with which we can communicate. Hence, Hekate, regarded as the goddess of the world's soul in the Chaldean Oracles, is also described as the patron of witches.[148] She is a personification of the psyche to which we speak, and in the highest thaumaturgy which blends intimately with theurgy, we speak even to the Nous beyond her.

The Material Synthemata, or Materials

You are already aware of the Neoplatonic theory of how magic works with materials. Each object in the physical universe is an instantiation of Ideas in the Nous. Gathering these various objects that instantiate a particular Idea concentrates and focuses that Idea in a single place. We did this when we made an animated statue of a god. We can also do it to make a talisman.

Selecting the materials themselves is sometimes a bit of a challenge. There are numerous lists and encyclopedias of various magical correspondences between objects and Ideas, but often these seem arbitrary. In fact, we can look to the nature of the object itself to determine its signature and thus its correspondences. We can also make use of legends and myths about the relevant deities.

148 Sarah Iles Johnston. *Hekate Soteira.* (Atlanta, GA: Scholars Press, 1990), 49–59.

Gathering and selecting materials is itself part of the magic. Our old friend, the Greek Magical Papyri, contains a spell for gathering materials for magic. PGM IV 286–95 recounts a spell that the magician says while picking a plant for magic, in which the person curses the ground the plant grows on if it does not work for him. I'm not such a fan of curses in general, and while such manipulative exhortations were commonplace in ancient magic, I avoid them. However, the principle is sound, namely that one should select the objects of magic (whether theurgic or thaumaturgic) in a magical way.

The Noetic Synthemata, or Timing

One of the ways we can act in harmony magically is by attending to the rhythms and patterns of the universe. The ratio of the universe, its logos, is the consistent cycling and infinite combination of elements. If we can jump into that stream when it is flowing our way, our magic is nearly done for us. If we try to subvert the stream, we won't get far. The ancients detected the nature of those eddies and flows by observing the movements of the natural world, especially as reflected in the stars. To be most effective, what is below needs to work together with what is above, in the celestial realm.

Obviously, my manipulation of stones and herbs or talismanic images does not affect the movements of the stars. But together, the significance of our joint action—mine and the planets'—works to create a *vinculum*, a binding, in the Psyche of the World. Hence, what is above affects the Psyche's mind the same way what is below does: she is the union of the two. Doing thaumaturgy without considering the harmony of the outside world is like trying to lift a foldout couch by yourself. It'd be awfully nice to get some help moving the other side of that couch, and that's where finding harmony in the timing of the spell comes in.

So I as the magician exist as a force, a small-n nous or consciousness, pushing toward a particular goal. For the sake of this discussion, let's imagine I am trying to get enough money so I can pay off my mortgage early. Aside from the manifold practical, physical considerations I undertake—not buying on credit, saving money by skipping my cappuccino once a week, and so on—I also decide to do some thaumaturgy. I want some way to draw in a steady stream of money I can divert to my mortgage. By means of my physical efforts, I've already achieved several possible avenues of manifestation. If I approach this like a lot of contemporary magicians, I might create a sigil and "charge" it by one of several means that alter my consciousness to implant the sigil in my nous or "deep mind." That's fine and might even work, but it's lifting the couch myself and dragging two legs on the rug. I might get it moved, but not without some divots in the carpet.

If I approach this from a Neoplatonic, theurgic perspective, I look to the timing of the act for confirmation that the big-N Nous is working along with me, is lifting its end of the couch. Here we have several methods. We can do some divination and probably should anyway, just to find out if the spell is worth doing or will have unforeseen effects. The traditional method, however, is to look at the relevant cycles in nature.

The first cycle we consider is that of the moon, and for many daily patterns this cycle is adequate consideration. When the moon is waxing, we do work to increase; when waning, to decrease. This rule is almost universal and is a reflection of the "as above, so below" Hermetic maxim. But there's more: the moon's cycle around the sky is divided into twenty-eight mansions, and each of these mansions has a character and a significance. We can also look at where the moon is located, or plan our work for when it rests in a mansion suitable for the goal.

We can go even further and select an hour during whatever time is consistent with the planet involved. In this case, I am seeking to increase and expand my influence in the form of financial security: a Jupiterian concern. So I time the working for the time of Jupiter, a particular sidereal hour determined according to a simple formula—say, the hour of sunrise on a Thursday. One can look these planetary hours up online, so the days of shuffling almanacs are gone.

Both of these cycles are probably familiar to most magicians trained in modern magic. It's a broad-stroke, bang-about approach to getting that couch across the floor. It'll work. But there are more subtle and refined methods of enlisting the help of the celestial Nous in your work. For example, rather than waiting for the hour of Jupiter, I might time the working so that Jupiter is in conjunction with the midheaven, the highest point in the sky. I might also look to other planets and their relationship to Jupiter: I probably wouldn't want to do this operation when Mars is ninety degrees away from Jupiter, especially if Mars is astrologically weak by being in, for example, Libra, where it is in detriment or in Cancer, where it is in fall. And, the same goes for Jupiter: we want it as strong as possible, either in one of the signs it rules—which are Pisces and Sagittarius—or in the sign where it is exalted—Cancer. In fact, we might even try to time it, if we can, for when Jupiter is at its strongest point in Cancer: the fifteenth degree.

All of this is in an ideal world, since Jupiter creeps across the zodiac at a steady but slow pace. Ultimately, when we end up looking for is some indication that the universe has agreed to help us push if we time the act to coincide with a particular configuration. In practice, we look for the best time we can find in the timespan that makes sense. If the best possible configuration doesn't happen for twenty-five years, I'll have the mortgage paid off by then anyway, so what good is it? On the contrary, I want to find something I can do within the next month or two.

Traditional Renaissance magic, of which the church sometimes approved or at least didn't disapprove of strongly, involved a set of images associated with particular planets or fixed stars. Talismans were made by inscribing the required image onto a piece of metal or even paper during the appropriate time. When used for healing or beneficial magic, such thaumaturgy was winked at, but the sky is not filled just with sweetness and light, of course. The Nous loves life, but life includes death. And so some grimoires or collections of images and astrological elections involved harmful as well as beneficial magic. One of these, the Picatrix, was passed around in manuscript form and regarded as dangerous to own. In fact, it was interdicted by the Catholic church. But other authors got away with publishing images and their astrological use, without *too* much problem.

One of these authors was Cornelius Agrippa, whose three books of occult philosophy are an incredibly rich compendium of Renaissance Neoplatonic theurgy. For the workings of Jupiter, Agrippa gives an election and some traditional images, such as:

> From the operations of Jupiter, they made for prolongation of life, an image, in the hour of Jupiter, Jupiter being in his exaltation fortunately ascending, in a clear and white stone, whose figure was a man crowned, clothed with garments of a saffron color, riding upon an eagle or dragon, having in his right hand a dart, about as it were to strike it into the head of the same eagle or dragon.[149]

If we wished to make this image, we would wait until Jupiter enters Cancer, which happened on June 26, 2013. Then we would wait for the hour of Jupiter, which we can calculate online. June 27 is a Thursday, so that's convenient, and we find that Jupiter's hours are from 5:19–6:35, 14:09–15:25, 21:12–21:56, and on the 28th (which astrologically is the same day), 3:06–3:51. Now, we have to ask ourselves which of those hours is closest to the rising of Jupiter. We can do this by plugging these times one by one into an astrology program, since we need to take into account our location as well. If we find the ascendent near Jupiter, we're in good shape—and, in fact, the first time, 5:19, puts the ascendent quite close to Jupiter for my location.

Of course, astrologers will point out that the sun is rather close to Jupiter here too, and that's not a good thing at all. It means Jupiter is combust and therefore—even though beneficially placed—is not very strong. So it's back to the drawing board to find another time that'll work. We need to

149 Agrippa. *Three Books of Occult Philosophy*. Ed. Donald Tyson. (Woodbury, MN: Llewellyn, 2007), 383.

wait either until the sun gets out of the way, or better yet, until Jupiter is cazimi, which is to say, in a very tight conjunction with the sun. Sadly, that's a pretty fiddly moment to calculate, so forget it, let's just get the sun away from Jupiter so it can shine on its own. The sun enters Leo on July 23 as usual, and since Jupiter is a slowpoke in the sky it'll be happy in Cancer for a long time. So let's see what our hours look like on the 25th, which is the Thursday after. Gah! It's getting hard to find a time when Jupiter is rising during the hour of Jupiter, and moreover, now that I look at that chart, I see that Mars is just leaving conjunction with Jupiter, which wouldn't be a problem except Mars hates being in Cancer and has been knocking over all the furniture and this is why we can't have nice things...

So you can see the whole process requires quite a lot of planning. You might despair of ever finding a time. And I've gone the long way around here, because there are some tricks in the patterns of planetary hours that will give you a few helpful clues when you develop more experience. And once we get a sense of how fast planets move in relation to each other, it's pretty easy to predict how many days to skip ahead before, for example, that pesky Mars has jumped ship into Leo, where it's not *so* destructive.

The point is, finding the time is part of the magic. By making such an effort, we're sending a message that we take this work seriously enough to accommodate it into our schedule. It's like when you're in your office with a client and the phone rings, which you let go to voicemail: you're saying "you're important enough to get my full attention" to the person in your office. That's the same message we send to the planetary gods by watching their motions with some care.

And let me annoy the traditional astrologers out there by pointing out that the planetary hour is much, much less important than the planet's dignity, and if you have to sacrifice something from Agrippa's elections, you can usually most safely disregard the hour and day restrictions and just aim for Jupiter to rise, unaffected by other nastiness, while it's in Cancer. For my location, that would be September 7, 2013, at 1:25 AM.

There is a rough-and-ready method of election, as well, which simply waits until the planet is rising in order to time the magic, paying little or no attention to its dignity by sign or aspect to other planets. For a lot of the day-to-day, quick magic I do, that's my bow to timing: I wait until Mars, or Venus, or Mercury, or whatever is rising or directly overhead, and call it good. In a perfect world, I'd do the whole election process above for everything, but that's not always practical. Sometimes, you need a protective talisman when Mars is retrograde in Libra. So I shrug, wait until Mars is rising, and do what I can when I can. But that's no excuse for abandoning timing altogether; it's a powerful way to link thaumaturgy with theurgy.

Intermediate Synthemata, or Images and Words

The intermediate synthemata connecting humanity to the divine, as you probably recall, are the conventionalized images and words we use to communicate not only to ourselves but to the divine. Magic, as Graf points out, is an act of communication; however, he points out that the sender and the recipient of the message seem to be the same person, which appears to "short-circuit the communication."[150] Of course, the missing receiver of that communicative act is the divine Psyche itself, who selects forms from the Nous to instantiate into the world in accordance with your unified will. We need to find images and words that will react most effectively with that Psyche.

I've already described some of the images Renaissance magicians used in making planetary talismans. Other, older images include the drawings of gods or representations of the desired outcome. Seemingly abstract designs also show up in ancient talismans, possibly derived through some sort of cipher or monogram system (like modern-day sigils) or received in vision or through automatic writing.

In Egyptian talismans we often find the representations of particular hieroglyphic words as talismans in their own right. For example, writing

150 Fritz Graf. *Magic in the Ancient World.* (Cambridge: Harvard University Press, 1997), 210.

the words "bread" and "beer" were equivalent to making that offering, and there are quite a few examples of Egyptian talismans and amulets in the form of hieroglyphs serving as words. For example, Geraldine Pinch depicts an image of a selection of talismans surviving from ancient Egypt.[151] One of these is a head that looks strikingly like the hieroglyph for the word *hr*, which means "over." It doesn't beggar my imagination to think that this might have been a talisman for social promotion and achievement. We also see alphabetic characters, such as a foot (the glyph for the sound *b*) and a hand (the glyph for *d*). Could these have been strung together or collected to create a word? I think the possibility is there. Alternately, they could have been charms for the healing of those body parts.

Words and incantations can be as simple as a prayer or as complex as some of the spells you have seen in earlier parts of this book. The rituals in the Greek Magical Papyri contain a representative sample of the sort of utterances used in magic: repetitive, highly metaphorical, emotionally charged, and interspersed with names and words in other languages.

In fact, the best example of an intermediate synthema is a name, whether it be the name of a deity or the name of the person whom you wish to affect. In the beliefs of the ancient Egyptians, such names had power: Isis revived her husband Osiris only by finding the true name of the god Re. On the other side, one way to threaten or harm a person was to efface their name. Knowing the name of a god is particularly powerful, because it assures you an attentive ear in a powerful place.

Making a Talisman with Theurgy

A theurgic talisman is the physical manifestation of a union of the individual nous with the cosmic celestial Nous. Like a contract with another human being, it's a "meeting of minds," but in this case quite literally. It becomes, if made correctly, the locus where mind and Mind unite, and

151 Geraldine Pinch. *Magic in Ancient Egypt.* (Austin: University of Texas Press, 2010), 119.

a frozen record of that particular place and time. As such, to talk about talismans as if they're batteries that need to be "charged" is a misuse of metaphor; this is the metaphor as magic as a mechanical act and the physical manifestations of magic as machines. A talisman is not a machine any more than a marriage is a machine. It's a contract where *I* meets *Thou* and the two work together to lift whatever couch needs lifting.

Ideally, a talisman is a union of all three worlds: it is a material object in harmony with the goal, it is timed to fit into the noetic tides that govern the world, and it is inscribed with the images and symbols of the intermediate synthemata. But putting all these things together alone isn't quite enough: you also need to bring down these divine forces so they can see what you've done and make their own agreement with it. The myth of contracts with demons has a grain of truth: these talismans are contracts (although with divine forces), and just as writing a contract doesn't finalize it until all parties have signed, so making the talisman isn't quite enough. You need to bring down the god.

You already know how to do this: You simply perform an offering rite. In this case, you want something you can use to mark the talisman: a drink offering or, more common in the Renaissance since it didn't smack of blasphemy to Christian sensibilities, an incense offering. In ancient times, sacrificial animals might be used for particular acts, but again, the symbolism of such acts was different in those cultures than it is in ours, and I don't recommend it. You're likely to end up with something you didn't intend.

The main point here, applicable not just to talismans but to any magical operation, is the idea that a theurgic approach to magic informs and powers your thaumaturgic efforts. A lot of times you'll hear people make the claim that theurgy isn't practical, testable, or useful. But when you use it to increase the efficacy of your practical magic, you can see just how practical it is. Let me give you an example of how this might look. There are countless other kinds of talismans, including simple images, found objects, and written spells. This is just one way that theurgy might inform thaumaturgy.

EXERCISE 7.2: MAKING A TALISMAN

STEP 1: Select a goal.

EXAMPLE: It currently takes me several weeks to learn a song at the piano. I want to be able to learn a song of intermediate difficulty in less than two weeks. To this end, I'll make a talisman to keep near my piano.

STEP 2: Select materials consistent with a divine force relevant to that goal. You want several different kinds of items, each consistent with the god ruling the goal. In addition, you want an object to wrap them in, such as a bag or cloth.

EXAMPLE: Apollo is the god of music, so I will gather materials related to him. Solar objects are particularly sacred to Apollo, so stones of solar nature are relevant: I have some citrine lying about. So are herbs of solar nature, such as frankincense. At the same time, bay laurel is traditionally associated with him. So are animals such as the crow, whose feathers are plentiful on the ground where I live. The cow is also relevant, so a piece of cow leather might be appropriate to wrap the whole talisman in.

STEP 3: Design an inscription. This can just be your desire written out, a collection of appropriate magical symbols, a graphic drawing of the desired goal, or a traditional image from one of the astrological magical grimoires like the Picatrix. This image should be simple enough that you can visualize it and hold it in your memory, because you'll need to call up its phantasm later in the ritual without looking at it.

STEP 4: Elect a time. You can do this astrologically, waiting until the planet is in an appropriate place, or by day of the week, waiting for sunrise on the day related to that planet.

Step 5: At the appropriate time, open the ritual by purifying yourself, the area, and the objects for the talisman. Inscribe the image onto the surface of the material you've chosen to bind up all the other items or on a piece of paper or parchment you will include in the bag. Artistic perfection counts for almost nothing here, so don't worry if you can't draw.

Step 6: Once engraved, turn to your altar and pray to the god for what it is you want. As you pray, acknowledge each object in turn and place it in the bag on the cloth to be wrapped into a bundle.

Example: Hear me, Apollo Phanaeus, Phoebus, Delius, Delphinius, Pythius, Mousagetes, and by whatever name it pleases you to be called. If ever I have made offering to your image, touch these items that carry your signature. Bless this bay leaf with glory and beauty. Give this citrine the brightness of your eyes. Grant dexterity and wit to this crow's feather …

Step 7: Bind the objects together by drawing together the bag into a bundle. Hold up the talisman briefly and project the phantasm of the image you inscribed within it onto the talisman. Don't cheat: you need to have the image clearly in your memory without having to consult a drawing or a book.

Step 8: Pour a libation into your libation dish and touch the talisman with a bit of the remaining wine, then drink. By all three sharing the same drink offering, you have linked yourself, the talisman, and the god. Immediately thereafter, pass the talisman through the incense offering so the smoke fumigates it.

Step 9: Thank the god for aiding you.

Step 10: Close the rite as usual.

Carry the talisman with you or set it in a place that makes sense. For example, I would probably put the talisman on or near the piano. You do not have to recharge a talisman, but it can help to renew the contract whenever the relevant planet is in a good position or well-aspected.

Defixiones

Not every magical effect is worthy of a talisman. Some things we want to happen once and then never consider again. If I make a talisman to get a raise, it's like building an addition onto the house because a friend is coming to visit for a weekend. It's a permanent change for a temporary goal. Instead, there are ways to connect to the Nous to express a single goal. I've written extensively about the most common ancient method of doing so, the defixio, and I'll point out a simple method of making use of them here. Those who wish to know more can read my book *Magic Power Language Symbol*, where I discuss defixiones at length.

A defixio is a lead tablet inscribed with a particular desire that is deposited in a magical place. In this it is like a talisman, but unlike a talisman, it is meant to be temporary. Thin lead tablets were the Post-it notes of the ancient world; they were essentially scratch paper, meant to be written on and discarded. Paper was expensive and difficult to come by, so lead was the medium of choice for letters and short messages. This is convenient for archeologists, since lead lasted where paper would have quickly rotted away. We can read what exactly our precursors asked the chthonic deities for:

> "... bring him to a bed of punishment, to be punished with an evil death, and to die within five days. Quickly! Quickly!"[152]
>
> "... render him without feeling, without memory, without the ability to perform rites, without marrow ..."[153]

Clearly, these defixiones were not the sweet light of modern spells, but the grimy curses of unsavory people. We might say, well, perhaps they had

152 Daniel Ogden. *Magic, Witchcraft, and Ghosts in the Greek and Roman Worlds: A Sourcebook.* (Oxford: Oxford University Press, 2002), 212.

153 Ogden. *Magic,* 218.

provocation, and indeed we find defixio tablets to avert banishment, to restrain the sale of someone into slavery, and other goals we might find acceptable in our modern sensibilities. But the two listed above fall into the largest category of curse tablets: to curse one side of a race or sporting event so the other side wins, and to curse a prospective lover so that she—almost always she—is compelled to come and have sex with the magician or waste away and die.

If you share my sensibilities and morality, you won't regard these as worthy magical goals, nor will you probably want anything whatsoever to do with curse tablets. And that would be a good decision: cursing probably isn't what you want to be doing with your time, especially if it's a curse to kill one side of a chariot race so you can win some money betting on the other side.

However, stepping back from the cursing element of the defixio, we can see what it is on its face: a letter to a divine or daimonic force for a petition. Was there a reflection of these to the noetic rather than chthonic gods? Perhaps on a more perishable substance? Indeed, we do see occasional reference to leaving prayers to the gods in their temples. A defixio is a written prayer, albeit mostly for unpleasant aims. But one may write anything one likes into a letter.

Defixiones contained four basic elements. The first is the text itself, usually an impassioned prayer identifying the target by name and the name of his or her mother. This prayer is often repetitive (even to the point of obsessive) and sometimes written in an unusual fashion, such as backwards or in boustrophedon, where each line reverses direction from the previous. It also usually contained, as a second element, *charactres* or symbols representing unspeakable words—these were probably conventionalized, but we have no idea what they might have meant. They have quite a lot of resemblance in shape and style to the figures of the fixed stars used in later astrological magic. Third, the text often includes an illustration usually of the daimon to be evoked by the spell, or sometimes perhaps of the victim with an appropriate modification, such as bound hands or the like. Finally, the entire thing is folded up and a nail driven through it—hence the name, *defixio*—to fix it together into a packet.

The defixio is delivered to a significant location, usually a well or a grave. Probably there was a ritual to enliven the text, as authors occasionally criticize the use of sacrifices to curse others. The whole thing was probably a bloody and unpleasant affair conducted in the dark of night, as being caught doing such things would have been a serious crime at any point in antiquity.

For those hypothetical prayers left at the shrines of the gods, however, all could have been done aboveboard. A theurgist could even use the public sacrifice to the deity as the enlivening ritual. Alternately, prayers could be left at private home shrines or at the sacred wells and caves. If such things were written on skin, paper, or bark, few would have survived. In fact, the defixiones, as numerous as they are, may have been a pollution and aberration of these more acceptable and presumably beneficial prayer petitions.

Historically accurate or not, there's nothing that stops us from using the same sort of technology to create more beneficial spells. The procedure is similar to that of making a talisman, although in this case the petition is written out, sometimes with *voces magicae* and *charactres*, along with a significant drawing of the deity in question. The whole thing is fixed together. A nail was probably an aggressive symbol; we may prefer to tie it in a scroll or bundle. Then the whole thing is deposited in a sacred area, a grove, spring, temple space, and so on. Petitions to noetic gods may also be burned on the sacrificial fire, which might explain why none remain. Just as the chthonic gods are gods of deep water and earth, the noetic gods are symbolically gods of fire and air.

What we get out of this, or indeed any, ritual of thaumaturgy is not absolute power over our lives. We will not become despots over fate or break the laws of nature. But we will gain a set of tools to improve and guide our lives, make the best of fate that we can, and steer the laws of nature to our wills. If we have been diligent in our practice of theurgy, our wills will become consistent with the will of the gods, communicated by our genius. When you have climbed toward henosis, your will and the will of the gods become congruent. This view of thaumaturgy reminds me a bit of an aikido throw; you move with the impulses of fate, not against them, just as in aikido you move with the strength of your opponent, not against it. Often I will find myself thinking, "I should do magic for that," and then experience the unlikely coincidence that is the signature of well-done thaumaturgy without ever getting around to doing the spell.

The overall theme of this chapter is that theurgy informs thaumaturgy. The more of a relationship you have with these powers—gods, spirits, heroes, and ancestors—the more those relationships can empower your magic. Theurgy also teaches us to think vertically as well as horizontally. If we can unify all levels of our will and make use of synthemata from all three words, we can have a much greater effect on the world. Finally, theurgy gives us a reason to do magic: to build a strong foundation for further theurgy by taking care of our day-to-day needs.

Magic is not a panacea. You will still suffer setbacks, bad fortune, even tragedies. Those cannot be cured with magic, and not all of them can be averted. That's why we still need philosophy. But we can also get a lot done with thaumaturgy, more than most people realize, because through it we can build a foundation toward henosis. The tower of henosis cannot sit on sand alone; it must have its foundation in matter.

So thaumaturgy is not a panacea but it is a medicine, and it can help us with what ails us.

CHAPTER 8

Know Thyself

Philanike: So who are you?

Euthymios: Sorry, I got a haircut. It must make me look pretty different. It's Euthymios, your student.

Ph: That's your name, what the Egyptians would call your *rn*, but that's not who you are. Who are you?

Eu: *Rn*, huh? Easy for you to say. Okay, so this is one of the little interrogation things—

Ph: *Elenchos*.

Eu: Which must be Greek for "interrogation." Fine. I'm a guy, uh, I work at a garage as a mechanic; I guess I'm Pagan, um…

Ph: Each of those is a label, a name, another *rn*. But what are you?

Eu: A human being.

Ph: Nice. To define a thing, we determine its class—its *gens*— and its difference from other items in that class—its *differens*. So what's the *gens* and *differens* of humans?

Eu: Humans are thinking animals.

Ph: Dolphins probably do something a bit like thinking. For all we know, squirrels think. So they're human?

Eu: Okay, then, we're thinking animals who are—self-aware. And use language. And tools—I know, I know, some animals use tools too—and we are rational.

Ph: Quite a list, and as you point out, mostly also applicable to animals with the possible exception of using language, and for me the jury is out on that one. How will I know a human if I see one?

Eu: Featherless biped.

Ph: You've been reading your Plato. I often think he came up with that definition to shut people like me up.

Eu: Will it please you if I just confess that I have no clear, unambiguous answer to your question?

Ph: Truth always pleases me. So if we don't even know what a human is, how can we pretend to know anything about divine beings?

Eu: I guess we can't.

Ph: We just spent an awful lot of words and quite a bit of time pretending to do just that, though, and it'd be sad if we had to throw it all away because we're essentially ignorant.

Eu: Well, maybe it has some value to think and do these things even though we are essentially ignorant.

Ph: We do have some ideas, though, that might help us. Let's see what we think of these notions and what we can do with them, and maybe we'll come to a clearer understanding of what it is to be human—and divine.

Plotinus, in the first section of the first tractate of the fifth Ennead, lays out two ways back to the One:

> A double discipline must be applied if human beings in this pass are to be reclaimed, and brought back to their origins, lifted once more towards the Supreme and One and First. There is the method, which we amply exhibit elsewhere, declaring the dishonour of the objects which the Soul holds here in honour; the second teaches or recalls to the soul its race and worth; this latter is the leading truth, and, clearly brought out, is the evidence of the other.[154]

Understanding matter and the things we strive for in our lives as unimportant can lead us to seek other things, but it can also lead us into despair and stagnation. So Plotinus points out that a second discipline exists, another way to get there that encompasses and surpasses the first: to help the soul remember "its race and worth." The original Greek for this is:

> ἀναμιμνήσκων τὴν ψυχὴν οἷον τοῦ γένους καὶ τῆς ἀξίας

Which means "remind the soul of the quality of its *γένους* and its *ἀξίας*." These two words have a range of meaning. A *genos* was a person's tribe, not just their race. It came with implications of heritage, of descent, of the past. An *axia*, on the other hand, was value, worth, and due: it looked to the future. The soul already knows both of these: it knows where it came from and where it's going, because the logos itself partakes of the nous. But we are reminding it—*anamimneskon*—because in the push and pull of guiding the chariot of the self through matter, it forgets.

So what are your *genos* and your *axia*?

---

154 Stephen MacKenna and B. S. Page, trans. *The Six Enneads by Plotinus.* (London: P. L. Warner, 1930) Accessed from http://www.sacred-texts.com/cla/plotenn/enn416.htm

As far as *genos*, your species, the *Corpus Hermeticum* takes a clear stand, in the "Dialogue of Hermes Trismegistus: Regarding the common mind, to Tat." Here we have a dialogue, much like my little dialogues throughout this book, between Hermes and his student Tat; although unlike Euthymios, Tat doesn't say much—he's not terribly spirited. But the point is, Hermes begins this discourse by defining his terms, borrowing authority from a "good demon," the agathodaimon: "For truly, the Good Daimon called the gods immortal humans; and humans, mortal gods."[155]

Consider the rather startling implications of that statement, which perhaps don't seem to startling to you. It means that our *genos*, our tribe, is of the gods. This is hubris, or at least looks like it; to aspire to be a god is a sort of sin in classical religion. But it's not really hubris, because Hermes makes it clear what gives us that power: our share of the divine mind. In another startling twist, Hermes tells Tat that not everyone has the same share of mind: some people are more conscious than others. While I find this a doctrine that rankles my democratic nerves, it's undeniably true. Not everyone takes pleasure in contemplating abstract ideas, and some people—while certainly conscious and deserving of respect and kindness and so forth—aren't really doing much with their capacity of mind.

This mind, Hermes tells Tat, exists in all of nature, and activates all matter: it is the ratio we call "the laws of nature." In animals, it governs their desires. In matter, it governs its activity. In humans, though, it does more: it actively pushes against our desires. It allows us to exert discipline, order, and (in the best possible sense of the word) self-denial. There is a drive for wholeness and health within our souls, and that is the ratio, the Mind described in this discourse of Hermes Trismegistus. It's also our *genos*, the thing we have in common with the gods themselves.

The gods were given a gift by the One: they were given immortality. They are the *athanatoi*, the undying. We, on the other hand, die. But we

155 Corpus Hermeticum XII:1, my translation.

were given two gifts which Hermes calls greater than immortality: the first is our share of the Mind, which the gods also get, and the second is the Word, which in Greek is *logos*, covering not only the faculty of speech but also that of reason and rationality. Hermes says that the word, which animals do not have (they have only "voices," an important distinction), is "the likeness and mind of God."[156] Our faculty for symbolic thought allows us to see the connections between things, and thus their essential oneness.

And yet, how can we—great meaty tubes filled with feces, essentially—be divine in our essence, our species? It's a strange thing to think of humanity, with its violence and weaknesses and hatreds, being divine. Even writing this, I keep wanting to hedge—"divine *in some sense*" I want to type. But it wouldn't be true to hedge: we are divine.

Mind is like a light that shines through a stained-glass window. Are we the window or the rays of light that shine through it? Are we the hairless apes who invented war and can destroy the planet, the monsters responsible for holocaust and genocide, slavery and rape? Or are we the pure beams of Mind that shine through that window, colored by our natures but nevertheless partaking of the light? That's the miracle and divinity of humans, because while we are bound by fate in every other particular, in this we get to choose. That's what makes us divine: we can create and we can destroy. Our choice.

Those other material things we recognize as synthemata of the gods are also dual in nature. Take Dionysos, a powerful and holy god, savior of humankind. His synthema is wine, which can free us of inhibitions to such a degree that we may destroy ourselves. Or take Hephaestos, god of craft, whose synthema is fire: we simultaneously embrace and fight it, because it can give us life by warming us in hostile climates and making our food edible as well as take our lives by burning our flesh. Or take Zeus, god of law and the sky, one of whose synthemata are storms: they give life to the earth, absolutely, and without them we would be a parched and dead wasteland. But they can also take life. Or Poseidon, the god of the sea, whose currents

156 Corpus Hermeticum XII:14. My translation.

hide bounties, yet sends tidal waves to destroy cities. Or Apollo, healer and poet and musician and bringer of foul plague…

Everything that we must handle with care, everything with the power to give life, also has the power to destroy and is the body of a god. Our little ape bodies, our meat toruses are synthemata of our own souls, and they too have the power to create and destroy.

Recognizing our *genos* is accepting responsibility. Spend a few nights of debauchery with a willing partner, fine. But know that you're using your creative power for that, and do it in full will and without illusions. Don't lie to yourself: you are choosing pleasure. That's not evil, despite what the authors of the *Hermetica*, the good ol' Neoplatonists, and even some of the Stoics, and the priests of Egypt—my goodness, I am outnumbered here!—argue. The Epicureans at least offer us this fillip: we can choose pleasure, as long as we know that all pleasure is equal. Sex is delightful, but it is exactly as delightful as studying Greek, playing the piano, and eating some sushi. Or would be, if you could recognize it.

So pleasure is a choice we might make, and we might also make the choice to take our pleasure at the expense of others. This isn't always violent or criminal, mind you. We sometimes take our pleasure with lies in our heart, knowing darn well we will not call the next day, no matter what. That's a choice we can make, and it can be a destructive one.

The point is, knowing that we are mortal gods is knowing that we have the power to destroy ourselves as well as the power to create. And that power is up to us, and what we create is our choice. And that creation is our *axia*, our value, the second thing that Plotinus tells us we need to remember.

I've said before that the purpose of life is to join the gods in the great work of creation. What we create becomes the action of our soul and an extension of our body. Our works are our children. Like children, they reflect their origin and carry it forward into the world. The question is, what is worthy of creation?

There's a concept in Thelema, the religion started by Aleister Crowley, of the true will. The true will is that which you were "put on earth to do," but that makes it sound rather cheesy. Really, it's that thing for which you are best suited, that problem that will most readily yield to your hand. It might be to be an engineer, as the hero in his *Diary of a Drug Fiend* turns out to be, or it might be to fly airplanes, learn to cook delicious five-course meals, or become a dominatrix. There's no way of telling what your true will is until you begin the work of magic, he suggests, although people do naturally enough stumble into it. When you set your hand to your true will, the path becomes clear—but of course what that really means is that you have little problem climbing over the rocks. When you do something hard and enjoy it *because* it is hard, that's probably part of your true will.

We can trace this idea backward in time, finding an unlikely kindred soul in Gerard Manley Hopkins, the late nineteenth-century British poet. Hopkins probably would not have thought well of a man who called himself "the Great Beast," nor would Crowley have liked Hopkins, an Anglican priest. But Hopkins writes, in his poem "As Kingfishers Catch Fire, Dragonflies Draw Flame," these lines:

> Each mortal thing does one thing and the same:
> Deals out that being indoors each one dwells;
> Selves—goes itself; *myself* it speaks and spells,
> Crying *Whát I do is me: for that I came.*[157]

Everything, Hopkins suggests, is constantly telling us its name, and that name is what it does. What we do is our name, our true name. This name is our true will, the reason we came. And that is our *axia*, our worth or value.

But the important thing to keep in mind is that we cannot judge another person's true will. They may have a true will that we regard as suspect, immoral, or unusual. But there are two features of a true will, an *axia*, that we

---

157 Gerard Manley Hopkins. "As Kingfishers Catch Fire, Dragonflies Draw Flame" Accessed 16 May 2013, http://www.bartleby.com/122/13.html

can rely on to judge our own. First, every true will is good. There is no true will that will step on another's true will, because we are all manifestations of the One and therefore all enacting the same will. While we might experience a fragmented soul, the One is not fragmented by definition, and as multifarious as the universe seems to us, it is unified. Second, and a corollary of the first principle, a true will is creative and active. It is not destructive. It is not watching TV and eating chips on the couch.[158] Sure, we can choose that pleasure from time to time as a way to recharge and relax, but when we're doing that we're not chasing our value. Just as the One is unified and cannot therefore will anything contrary to its own will, so is it active and creative.

As we act and create, knowing we are synthemata of the gods and divine in essence ourselves, we don't act separate from the world. On the contrary, we are part of the system of the world, and the wise theurgist will understand this. In popular culture, this understanding has manifested as environmentalism, which unfortunately has sometimes become glib and unthinking. Some of the things people do in the name of environmentalism are actually harming the earth. What a lot of naive environmentalist advocates—not all or even most of them, by any means—fail to recognize is that we will have an effect on the environment. We are forces. We will do something to the world, and we cannot pass through it like insubstantial phantasms. That is not a reason to give up and stop caring about environmentalism. On the contrary, rather than trying to avoid making an impact or surrendering and letting humanity lay waste to the earth, we need to understand how we can affect it positively.

As fond as Pagans are of such causes, the physical environment is not the whole point. We are part of the web of existence in other ways, too, that are less subtle and physical. The chain of cause and effect is really a web, a complex interconnection of symbols and significations. We have a unique place, as far as we know, in that web. We're the brightest light of mind in the universe (that we've seen so far), and the most capable of manipulating

158 Then again, that could be a creative act of its own, if done in concert with one's true will. It's very hard to judge.

symbols and understanding how they relate. This makes us capable of art, religion, science, and magic: the four ways of knowing that Ramsey Dukes lays out in his extremely important *S.S.O.T.B.M.E.*[159] Each of these is a way of understanding symbols and manipulating them. And we can bend any one of them in service of another, because they have symbols in common.

Theurgy is the use of magic to accomplish the aims of religion. Instead of dogma, we have praxis. We bring to bear the entire toolbox of magic: talismans, tools, offerings, and so on. To it, we add the toolbox of religion: prayer, devotion, contemplation. We end up, then, with a combination that can send us upward at great speed if we're willing to make the trip. Similar combinations can be made in other ways: the symbolic methods of religion can bend to service the aims of magic, and the symbols of religion to serve the aims of art (Beethoven springs to mind). The symbols of religion can serve science, even if they seem to be at odds right now—think of the medieval Muslims, who preserved a lot of scientific knowledge in the name of a religious reverence for learning.

I've written elsewhere that I'm suspicious that science can ever prove magic; I still believe that's a wrong tree to be barking up, because science doesn't have the tools to investigate magic any more than it has the tools to investigate religion. However, it can inform magic just as it can inform religion and vice versa, no doubt. Magic may have things to teach science if we could have a dialogue. As a magician and a theurgist and a sometimes scientist, I rather doubt that'll ever be possible. But let's hope.

The point is, all of these ways of knowing and moving symbols are unified in that they deal with symbols and with ideas that dwell within the Nous. We are nexuses of symbols, spanning all the worlds of nous and psyche and hyle. With our feet in matter and our heads in the mind of god, we're kind

159 Ramsey Dukes. *S.S.O.T.B.M.E.: An Essay on Magic.* (Netherlands: The Mouse that Spins, 2001). (Seriously, you must read it. If you have read it and didn't think it was that important, you probably should read it again.)

of remarkable creatures... as long as we don't forget too long and destroy the world in the meantime.

So that's our "race and worth," but now I want to turn my attention to a secondary, but important question that we need to deal with if we're going to be effective theurgists, and that is this: Are you crazy?

Efstathios Kollas, a Greek Orthodox priest, referred to reconstructionists of the ancient religion as following "monstrous, dark delusions."[160] I'm not a reconstructionist, but I'm pretty sure that *he* wouldn't make the distinction between me with my wildly eclectic attitude toward the divine and your typical Greek reconstructionist. On the contrary, I imagine he'd find a nice broad brush to paint us with, and he'd paint us both with the color of crazy.

Now, notice that he didn't just call them "doomed" or "sinners," which would have been an earlier age's reaction to such a heresy. There is of course a religious element to his "delusion," in that to be deluded is to be influenced by Satan against the truth, but the term also invokes the stigma of mental illness. To deny what he regards as the truth is to be deluded. He's not the only one who thinks that way. Richard Dawkins wrote a book called *The God Delusion*, which is intelligent, brilliantly and entertainingly written, and so filled with logical fallacies that you could use it as a rhetoric 101 textbook.[161] Right now I don't want to address the fallacies but instead his choice of words, which strike me as more interesting. What about a religious experience is a delusion?

A delusion is, unless my faint memories of my abnormal psychology classes in college escape me, a persistent and false belief about the world that does not yield to evidence to the contrary. At first blush, that looks a lot like faith, doesn't it? Perhaps these two men, on opposite sides of a chasm of their own digging, are shouting at the same echo. Pardon my convoluted metaphor, but I'm struck by the similarities in their rhetoric here: a religious

---

160 Malcolm Brabant. "Ancient Greek Gods' New Believers." BBC-News. 21 January 2007. Accessed 15 May 2013, http://news.bbc.co.uk/2/hi/europe/6285397.stm

161 Richard Dawkins. *The God Delusion.* (New York: Houghton Mifflin, 2008).

man and a determined, vocal atheist are both using a similar metaphor to describe believers. The religious use of the word "delusion" differs from the scientific meaning, but both uses share the same underlying preconception: any deviation from a particular view of reality isn't just a disagreement or even a mistake—it is a delusion.

A delusion isn't a mental illness in itself, but it's the symptom of mental illness; if found in a constellation with other symptoms, it could be a sign of sickness. And I've run into people (mostly on the Internet but sometimes in person) whom I suspect might benefit from a good psychologist and a script for some chlorpromazine. I could tell some stories, as could anyone else who has spent any time around occultists, but that's not the point. The point is: What's the difference between a person who thinks they are the reincarnation of a fictional character who is telling them scary things about the enemies out to get them, and a guy who prays to Hermes and then goes for a walk in hopes of a kledon? A lot of people, among them the Efstathios Kollas and Richard Dawkins, would probably say "no difference at all."

Obviously, I'd like there to be a difference. That difference could be studying ancient languages, researching in scholarly sources rather than on TV, dressing in jackets with leather patches on the elbows... but it might as well be in what we had for lunch for all the real meaning those things have. One answer is to say "who cares?" and let people think you're nuts. Ultimately that's where we end up, and we all know it. We either accept ourselves, quirks and minority ontologies and peculiar "hobbies" and all, or we loathe ourselves, and this is a path that does not line up well with self-loathing.

I would contend that that is the key to the answer to the question, "Are you nuts?" A person dedicated to the power of reason, as a theurgist must be, has to answer: Maybe, but there are crazy people who cannot function and need help, and there are those that are on the fringes who become stronger and better and happier because of their so-called "delusions." There's an important concept in the classical world, one that every single Wiccan perpetually espouses whether he or she knows it or not. It's a Greek word of five letters (well, six, actually, but one is a diphthong which is treated as a single letter): *ὑγίεια*. Rendered as *hygieia* in the Latin alphabet, this word means "health" or "wholeness," and the Pythagoreans took it as their watchword and greeting. They placed its letters around the pentagram, and regarded the five-pointed star as the symbol of health.

One of the reasons Pythagoreans placed the word "hygieia" around the pentagram was that the pentagram represents several geometrical harmonies. We can find the golden section in it as well as other interesting interlocking relationships. It is like a chord played perfectly in tune in visual form, and thus a perfect metaphor for the kind of spiritual health the word "hygieia" describes.

As we struggle up the path, we have to keep our balance. We do this by checking it periodically, and measuring ourselves not against the standards of others—after all, who knows how sane those folks are behind locked doors?—but against the standard of balance. The question we must ask ourselves is simple, actually, and quite direct:

Am I a happier, more open, and more effective person? Or am I closed off, ineffectual, hobbled? If you cannot function as a person in society, it's not a sign of spiritual advancement; it's a sign of illness. Marcus Aurelius appeals to the social nature of humans to know whether what we are doing is right or wrong: "Neither can I be angry with my brother or fall foul of him; for he and I were born to work together, like a man's two hands, feet, or eyelids, or like the upper and lower rows of his teeth."[162] Indeed, without social interaction, we cannot know who we are. That doesn't mean we can't be shy, introverted, or withdrawn—but if we cannot even deal with people or use our religion as an excuse to avoid others, that's a sign that we are not well. I contend that healthy spirituality opens one up, banishes fear, and frees us of shackles. A successful theurgist should be a very effective person both in his or her mundane

162 Marcus Aurelius. *Meditations*. Trans. Maxwell Staniforth. (New York: Penguin, 2005), 11.

life and in his or her spiritual life, because of the spiritual harmony arising from true hygieia.

It's ironic, perhaps, that people trot out terminology from psychology to dismiss minority religions. After all, what is psychology originally but "the study of the soul"? And who knows the soul better than the theurgist, who has reminded his or her soul of its origin and worth? Actually, the science of psychology does have teachings that are useful for us, among them the definition of mental illness. Merely being odd or strange isn't a mental illness. By definition, a mental illness makes your life harder. Does believing in the gods make it harder or easier to have a successful life? I contend that it makes it easier for very many people, even granted that some might use it as a way to hide from life. The majority of people who believe in gods—including gods like Jesus Christ—believe in them because they make life better.

But some do use magic as a crutch or, worse, a hobble. They bind their feet with magic or at least with its appearance. Examples are not hard to find, but one public example will serve for all the rest, and that's the example of something that happened to the fantasy author Mercedes Lackey, who has published an open letter on her webpage concerning a series of books that she wrote about an occult detective called Diana Tregarde. I can't speak knowledgeably about these books, but apparently there are a group of people who think the novels are real. They have built conspiracy theories about the books and threatened the author who—by all accounts, though I haven't met her—is a very nice person.

Is it because these people believe in magic that they went nuts? Not at all. Any religion can succumb to insanity or no religion at all, and we can convince ourselves of any number of harmful delusions. Lackey's even a bit sympathetic, writing, "When your life is in the crapper, you can't get a job that doesn't involve a paper hat and a nametag, and you think that if you dropped off the planet no one would miss you for weeks, it's comforting to believe that all your misfortunes can be blamed on an Evil Occult Force."[163] And if you scratch even the most curmudgeonly of occultists, you'll find that we've probably got some ridiculous and embarrassing moments in our pasts. In fact, if you question a mature Christian, a mature Jew, a mature Buddhist, a mature atheist, you might well find that they have beliefs or attitudes or actions in the past they're no longer proud of. That's growth.

And magic, especially theurgy, is about growth. It's about growing up, even if we're already grownups. I can't promise you a "job that doesn't involve a paper hat" or an easy life. Magic may help with such things, especially if you're good at it and can unify your will. But it may not. Sometimes magic doesn't work. Sometimes we fail. Even the gods are subject to necessity. What I can promise you if you pursue theurgy and philosophy is that you will achieve, perhaps not all the time, but at least from time to time, what the Greek philosophers call *ho agathos bios*, the good life.

In English, the phrase "the good life" implies a life of material success: drinking champagne, eating caviar, and sailing about on a yacht named after your mistress or poolboy. But to the philosophers of ancient Greece, a good life was a life of contemplation. They saw that the pleasure of challenge, devotion, and contemplation of the One had advantages over the pleasures of material things. Material things decay, fail, and betray us—it's necessity. But the forms we contemplate and the gods we make offering to are *athanatoi*, undying. They are worthy of our attention not because we're commanded to attend to them. I think the fact that they haven't destroyed the world in the last one thousand years is evidence that they're really not starving for worshipers. No, they're worthy of our attention because it is pleasant to attend to them and it helps us grow.

If your religion or magical practice does not help you grow into your idea of a better person, then you need to reassess the decisions you have made about it. There are a group of people who picket funerals of soldiers because

163 Mercedes Lackey. "The Last Straw." *The World of Mercedes Lackey*. Accessed 15 May 2013, http://www.mercedeslackey.com/features_laststraw.html

they believe it's part of their religion to protest homosexuality (the connection between military funerals and homosexuality escapes me, but so it goes). Look at the damage their religion has done to them: they have chosen a stunted, vicious, stupid god to worship, and they bask masochistically in the loathing of most of the general population. There must be pleasure there too, but I have to think that my pleasure is greater than theirs since I can love even those who disagree with me, learn from those who believe differently from me, and find an occasion for learning and growth in every experience.

Devout Muslims pray five times a day to Mecca, turning in the direction that they call the qiblah, the direction Mecca lies in from their current location. Jason Louv writes in one of his stirring essays on magic, "Love is the qiblah of evolution and of divinity."[164] Even though he is a contemporary writer and not one of those long-dead philosophers I'm so fond of, I can't think of a better motto for the theurgist: Love is our qiblah. After all, among some mystery religions, Eros was the first god, and it was he who drew together the universe in mutual affection.

Sometimes people make the claim that ancient religions offered no personal connection to their deities, because the concept of "divine love" is lacking. This is erroneous. When Aristotle writes "it would be strange if one were to say that he loved Zeus," he does not mean that one cannot love God.[165] He is talking about reciprocation. It's not absurd to say that Zeus loves us, but it might be a bit strange to say that we love him back. Love is an action: what action can we take to help Zeus become healthier, better, happier? He is maximally happy; he's a god. When we make him offerings, which we do out of love and *charis* (grace), we do not do it to improve his lot. It's not Zeus we love: it's the Good in ourselves. By loving the gods, we learn to love that part of us that is divine, which is Plotinus' ultimate point:

---

164 Jason Louv. "Spooky Tricks" in *Generation Hex,* ed. Jason Louv. (New York: Disinformation, 2006), 116.

165 W. D. Ross, trans. *Aristotle: Magna Moralia.* (Oxford: Clarendon, 1915). Accessed 16 May 2013. http://archive.org/stream/magnamoralia00arisuoft/magnamoralia00arisuoft_djvu.txt

we can become well, healthy, and complete when we understand that we are divine and therefore worthy of pure love. And that means taking care of ourselves and aiming to make ourselves healthier, better, happier.

So that's how I'll end the book. Love is the highest god. When we raise our hands in prayer, we raise them to love. Our offerings are always offerings of love. And being One, love of one part of the universe is love of the whole. We may be single and like it that way. We may have no family to speak of or few friends—but love of anything is love of everything. Love of a garden, of a table of irregular verbs, of the soft blue color of fresh morning snow, of ourselves, it's all love of the entire universe in its perfect unity. Getting there, that's the work of henosis. It's the whisper that tells us there's something outside of our cave. There's a light out there, and what we love so much are just shadows of something so much more lovable. That's the theurgy, the work of the gods: to love.

Epilogue

Philanike: So you had something you wanted to tell me? Want a cookie first?

Euthymios: Who says no to cookies? Milk?

Ph: Always. Now, what's your news?

Eu: I was at work yesterday and reading the diagnostic for this Honda, and suddenly I realized something.

Ph: What's that?

Eu: The numbers on the computer are synthemata of the logos, of the underlying ratio of the universe.

Ph: You don't say?

Eu: And so's this cookie. My shirt. The table. The air I'm breathing. The lungs I'm breathing it with. It's all the same symbol of the same underlying rationality.

Ph: The same? So there's one?

Eu: Yeah, but it's so "one" that it's also many. To say it's one is to say it can't be many, but my shirt isn't this cookie. Wouldn't want to confuse them! But at the same time, my shirt and this cookie have to coexist in a single, unified universe along with the gods, the Honda, you, and everything and everyone else.

Ph: Well, we could have the shirt without the cookie.

Eu: The shirt is cotton. It grows because the sun shines—Helios, I suppose. The cookie is made from butter, that comes from cows that eat grass, and that also relies on the sun.

Ph: So there's a sun. That's what unifies everything? Helios?

Eu: That's a handy shorthand, but no, there's more. Helios—the sun, I mean—only shines because of certain fundamental physical constants, and they don't have to be the way they are. One tiny variation in any of a number of constants, and the sun wouldn't shine. It'd collapse or explode. Neither are good for cookies or shirts.

Ph: Well, of course, that's the teleological argument for the existence of god, and it's flawed in that we exist in a perfect universe for life. For all we know there were countless garbage universes where there was no life. We observe a universe ideally suited for life, but of course we do: we're alive.

Eu: I'm not making that argument. Obviously we can only observe the universe because it's a universe in which observing beings can exist. But it's still marvelous. The cookie, the shirt, my body, this house, you, everything—if there were not these laws of the universe, they wouldn't be. So they all depend on this one thing: the logos of the universe.

Ph: So you've experienced the oneness of everything. What does it change?

Eu: Nothing. Everything. I don't know. All three, I suppose, at the same time. After all, they're one, aren't they?

Ph: You going to quit your job, go barefoot into the wild?

Eu: I don't have to. My job is devotion now. Everything is a prayer, and everything is a god.

Ph: That sounds airy and not very practical.

Eu: My boss is a jerk.

Ph: Oh, how quickly we fall from henosis.

Eu: No. It's okay that he's a jerk. He's a jerk because this cookie is delicious, because this shirt is cotton, because the sun shines.

Ph: So you'll just let him be a jerk?

Eu: I'd rather he wasn't. And if he wants to be nicer, I'll help him.

Ph: So you'll make him a project?

Eu: No. The sun doesn't make growing grass for cows to eat a project. It happens because the sun radiates.

Ph: So you'll radiate. That sounds like an excuse to be lazy.

Eu: You won't trip me up anymore, Philanike, because I can see the root of things. I'm questioning myself all the time now, and digging down to truth myself. The sun isn't lazy. It's active. Here's what I'll do: I'll be pleasant, focused on my job—after all, why be distracted? The distractions are the same thing as the job!—and maybe, just maybe, he'll respond to that. And if he doesn't, well, he's a jerk, the sun shines, cookies are delicious.

Ph: I have to warn you. Tomorrow you may forget all of this. It'll be a high you remember as a high but not exactly why you were there. It'll turn into trite platitudes in your head. "All is one!" "Love is the answer!" You'll get annoyed at car problems, a bad back, a rainy day.

Eu: Sure. You've got to climb back down once you climb up, but the climb up is easier the second time.

Ph: And the third, and the fourth, and the fifth. It's not "I got it! Aha!" It's "I got some of it! For a moment." And that's the way it is, so that's okay.

Eu: It's a kind of being, not a sudden becoming. And it's okay to be annoyed with car problems or to be human, because that's part of what we are. We have to be what we are.

Ph: Listen to you, a downright philosopher. You know what "Plato" means?

Eu: It means something?

Ph: His real name was Aristocles, "Noble glory," but Plato was his nickname. Roughly, very roughly translated, it means "fatso."

Eu: Then give me another cookie. I'm emulating ol' Aristocles.

Ph: Better to emulate yourself.

Eu: Already working on it. I was just kidding about trying to be like Plato.

Ph: Oh good.

Eu: But I wasn't joking about the cookie.

Appendix—
Pronunciation of Greek Words of Power

The Ancient Greek language was spoken for a very long time over a very large area, so to say that there is a "right" pronunciation of Ancient Greek is a bit misleading. There are certainly bad ones (i.e., pronunciations that make it impossible to learn or read the language), and there are some accepted for scholarly purposes but are not historically accurate. And there are reconstructions for particular dialects. But probably the most historically authentic pronunciation of Ancient Greek, particularly Ancient Greek of Late Antiquity, is "badly." After all, by the era of Koine or common Greek, it was the dialect of diverse people who used it as a trade language and a lingua franca, as well as for scholarly sharing of information. That means a lot of the people who spoke and wrote the language did so as a second (or third, or fourth) language. By the arrival of Christianity in Rome, a very large percentage of those speaking Greek were doing so with a "foreign" accent.

So take heart. Screwing it up is historically accurate.

Here's a fast, dirty, and very much unscholarly approach to pronouncing enough Greek to get through some barbarous words of invocation with confidence. You can't utter the words "pronounce" and "Greek" without picking a fight, so let me immediately say that I just downright concede. Yes, this isn't reconstructed Koine. No, I don't think Erasmus pronounced Greek the way the ancient Greeks did. No, Ancient Greek was not pronounced like Modern Greek. (No, it wasn't. No. It has changed. Seriously. Really. If you insist, fine, pronounce it however you want. No skin off my nose. But really, it has changed.) I'm just not interested in any of the fights about it, except maybe that last one (really, seriously, it has changed—all languages do). Anyway, here's how I pronounce the words of power.

All the letters are pronounced as in English except these:

A: like *ah* in "father." Alpha can be long or short. There's no way to know which it was in words of power, though, since it's never marked with a macron. So I pronounce it long in open syllables and short in closed ones, on the theory that barbarous words of invocation may have sometimes been Semitic in origin and that feels kind of Semiticky to me. If that's a word.

E: short *eh* as in "let."

Ē: long *ay* as in "say."

I: like *ee* in "feet." It has the same long/short distinction as alpha, and similarly, isn't marked. Wing it. Call it good. Just be confident.

O: short *oh* in "caught," if you happen to speak my dialect of English.

Ō: long *oh* as in "boat."

U: put your lips together as if saying "ew" but then say "ee" instead. This has the same unmarked long/short distinction as alpha and iota, but you've got enough stuff to worry about. If you know French, it's like the French u.

OU: like *oo* in "boot."

OI: like *oy* in "boy."

ŌI: the i is silent.

EI: like *ai* in "bait" with that little "ee" sound at the end a little more pronounced.

ĒI: the I is silent (if you forget these silent i's, it's not a disaster. They were pronounced at one time, just not at the point most of this stuff was written). If you're a native English speaker, you will probably end up pronouncing this a lot like EI and Ē. Try not to let that little "ee" sound at the end come out, but don't obsess about it. So you have an accent! So what?

AI: the i may or may not be silent depending on whether the alpha is long, but since you can't know for sure if it is or not, just say *ay* as in "sky."

UI: like "buoy."

TH: pronounce it like the *th* in "both."

PH: like the *ph* in "telephone."

CH: like the *ch* in "loch." If you can't do this sound, make a k sound and then drop your tongue enough to let some air hiss through. Lots of people will argue with these last three, saying they should be "windy" or aspirated t, p, and k. It is incredibly hard for native English speakers to distinguish between aspirated and unaspirated stops. It's easier for us to turn them into fricatives, which is what happened to them anyway at some point late in the development of Greek.

X: like the *x* in "box," ***not*** like "xylophone." Even at the beginning of a word.

PS: both the P and the S are pronounced in all locations, unlike in English. So *PSUCHĒ*, meaning "soul" is pronounced like "p-su-khey," not "sai-kee."

Ancient Greek also had an elaborate system of intonation and accentuation you must learn if you're going to learn to read it, but *not* if you're just wanting to pronounce some words of power. Accents in Greek are not entirely predictable, so most Greek texts mark the accents on each word. These particular accents aren't marked on the barbarous words, however, and since we usually have no idea what the words might have meant, we usually have no idea where the accent might have gone. I myself treat barbarous words as if they all have recessive accent, meaning that the stress falls as far as possible from the final syllable, but no farther than the antepenultimate syllable if the penultimate syllable has a long vowel; similarly, the accent falls on the penultimate if the ultimate syllable has a long vowel, and the... you know what? Put it on the second to last syllable. That's just as likely to be right as anything we might guess.

It's worth putting a little time into thinking about how you want to pronounce these words, or any words in magic from any foreign language. But don't get hung up on it. And for the love of all that's holy, if someone in a ritual is speaking Greek or Latin or Hebrew, don't comment on their pronunciation. It doesn't sound cultured and discerning when people criticize the pronunciation of dead languages; it just sounds annoying. Anyone who can wrap their tongue around any word at any time in any foreign language is doing pretty darned good, accent or not. I've heard some downright amazingly skilled practitioners brutalize Hebrew, for example. While it might not have been fun to hear them do such violence to the guttural consonants, their magic still worked.

If, however, you become a man or woman after my own heart and decide, "I want to learn to read these ancient languages myself," then it does help to learn one or two of the reconstructed pronunciations and give them a try. In my experience, it won't make your magic any better, but it is kind of cool to try to re-create as carefully as possible what Plato might have sounded like to contemporary Athenians.

Bibliography

Agrippa. *Three Books of Occult Philosophy.* Edited by Donald Tyson. Woodbury, MN: Llewellyn, 2007.

Augustine. *Confessions 8.12.* Edward Bouverie Pusey, trans. Accessed 1 November 2013, http://www9.georgetown.edu/faculty/jod/augustine/Pusey/book08

Aurelius, Marcus. *Meditations.* Translated by Maxwell Staniforth. New York: Penguin, 2005.

Baines, John, Leonard H. Lesko, and David P. Silverman. *Religion in Ancient Egypt: Gods, Myths, and Personal Practice,* ed. Byron E. Shafer. Ithaca, NY: Cornell University Press, 1991.

Ball, Allan Perley, trans. Seneca the Younger, *Apocolocyntosis.* West Sussex, Columbia Univ. Press, 1902. Accessed 14 May 2013, http://en.wikisource.org/wiki/Apocolocyntosis

Betz, Hans Dieter. *The Greek Magical Papyri in Translation: Including the Demotic Spells.* Chicago: University of Chicago Press, 1992.

Brabant, Malcolm. "Ancient Greek Gods' New Believers." BBC News. 21 January 2007. Accessed 9 January 2014, http://news.bbc.co.uk/2/hi/europe/6285397.stm

Bruno, Giordano. *Cause, Principle and Unity: And Essays on Magic.* Translated by Richard J. Blackwell. Cambridge, UK: Cambridge University Press, 1998.

Burkert, Walter. *Greek Religion.* Cambridge, MA: Harvard University Press, 1985.

Butler, Samuel, trans. *The Odyssey of Homer.* Accessed 14 May 2013, http://classics.mit.edu/Homer/odyssey.mb.txt

Caputo, G. B. "Strange-face-in-the-mirror illusion," *Perception* 39.7 (2010): 1007–1008.

Clarke, Emma C., John M. Dillon, and Jackson P. Hershbell, trans. *Iamblichus: On the Mysteries.* Atlanta, GA: Society for Biblical Literature, 2003.

Copenhaver, Brian, trans. *Hermetica: The Greek Corpus Hermeticum and the Latin Asclepius in a New English Translation with Notes and Introduction.* Cambridge, UK: Cambridge University Press, 1992.

Crowley, Aleister. *Magick in Theory and Practice.* Accessed 15 May 2013, http://www.sacred-texts.com/oto/aba/aba.htm

———. *Magick Without Tears.* Scottsdale, AZ: New Falcon, 1991.

Dawkins, Richard. *The God Delusion.* New York: Houghton Mifflin, 2008.

Dervenis, Kostas. *Oracle Bones Divination: The Greek I Ching.* Rochester, VT: Destiny Books, 2014.

Dr. Seuss. *Oh, the Places You'll Go!* New York: Random House, 1990.

Dukes, Ramsey. *S.S.O.T.B.M.E.: An Essay on Magic.* Netherlands: The Mouse that Spins, 2001.

Edwards, Mark, trans. *Neoplatonic Saints: The Lives of Plotinus and Proclus by their Students.* Liverpool, UK: Liverpool University Press, 2000.

Evelyn-White, Hugh G., trans. *Hesiod: Works and Days.* Accessed 16 May 2013, http://www.sacred-texts.com/cla/hesiod/works.htm

———. *The Theogony of Hesiod.* Accessed 14 May 2013, http://www.sacred-texts.com/cla/hesiod/theogony.htm

Falconer, W. A., trans. *De Divinatione by Cicero. Loeb Classical Library, vol XX.* (Cambridge, MA: Harvard University Press, 1923). Accessed 13 May 2013, http://penelope.uchicago.edu/Thayer/E/Roman/Texts/Cicero/de_Divinatione/

Flowers, Stephen Edred. *Hermetic Magic: The Postmodern Magical Papyrus of Abaris.* York Beach, ME: Weiser, 1995.

Fontenrose, Joseph. *The Delphic Oracle.* Berkeley, CA: University of California Press, 1978.

———. *Didyma: Apollo's Oracle, Cult, and Companions.* Berkeley, CA: University of California Press, 1988.

Fortune, Dion. *The Goat-Foot God.* York Beach, ME: Weiser, 1999. Originally published in 1936.

Frankl, Victor. *Man's Search for Meaning.* Boston: Beacon, 1957.

Graf, Fritz. *Magic in the Ancient World.* Cambridge, MA: Harvard University Press, 1997.

———. "Rolling the Dice for an Answer," in Sarah Iles Johnston and Peter T. Struck, eds., *Mantike: Studies in Ancient Divination.* (Leiden, NL: Brill, 2005).

Greer, John Michael. *A World Full of Gods.* Tucson: ADF Publishing, 2005.

Guthrie, Kenneth Sylvan, ed. *The Pythagorean Sourcebook and Library.* Grand Rapids, MI: Phanes, 1988.

Guthrie, W. K. C. *Orpheus and Greek Religion.* Princeton, NJ: Princeton University Press, 1993.

Hansen, William, ed. *Anthology of Ancient Greek Popular Literature.* Bloomington, IN: Indiana University Press, 1998.

Havell, H. L., trans. *Longinus: On the Sublime.* London: Macmillon, 1890. IX.2 Accessed 15 May 2013, http://www.gutenberg.org/files/17957/17957–h/17957–h.htm

Higbee, Kenneth. *Your Memory: How it Works and How to Improve It.* Boston: Da Capo Press, 2001.

Hooper, W. D., and H. B. Ash, trans. *Cato: De Agricultura.* Loeb Classical Library Vol. . 139. Accessed 15 May 2013, http://penelope.uchicago.edu/Thayer/E/Roman/Texts/Cato/De_Agricultura/I*.html

Hopkins, Gerard Manley. "As Kingfishers Catch Fire, Dragonflies Draw Flame." Accessed 16 May 2013, http://www.bartleby.com/122/13.html

Johnston, Sarah Iles. *Hekate Soteira.* Atlanta, GA: Scholars Press, 1990.

Jones, Horace Leonard, trans. *The Geography of Strabo.* Loeb Classical Library Vol. VIII. Accessed 14 May 2013, http://penelope.uchicago.edu/Thayer/E/Roman/Texts/Strabo/17A3*.html

Jowett, Benjamin, trans. *The Apology by Plato.* Accessed 15 May 2013, http://www.gutenberg.org/files/1656/1656–h/1656–h.htm#link2H_4_0002

———. *Phaedrus by Plato.* Accessed 10 May 2013, http://classics.mit.edu/Plato/phaedrus.html

Jowett, Benjamin, trans. *The Symposium by Plato.* Accessed 15 May 2013. http://classics.mit.edu/Plato/symposium.html

Lackey, Mercedes. "The Last Straw." *The World of Mercedes Lackey.* Accessed 15 May 2013, http://www.mercedeslackey.com/features_laststraw.html

Louv, Jason. "Spooky Tricks" in *Generation Hex,* ed. Jason Louv. New York: Disinformation, 2006. 101–117.

Luck, Georg. *Arcana Mundi: Magic and the Occult in the Greek and Roman Worlds.* Baltimore: John Hopkins University Press, 1985.

Lycrouinos, Damon Zacharias. "Conjuring Magical Assistants in the Greek Magical Papyri" in *Occult Traditions,* ed. Damon Zacharias Lycourinos. Melbourne, Australia: Numen, 2012.

MacKenna, Stephen, and B. S. Page, trans. *The Six Enneads by Plotinus.* London: P. L. Warner, 1930. Accessed 10 January 2014, http://www.sacred-texts.com/cla/plotenn/enn416.htm

Majercik, Ruth. *The Chaldean Oracles: Text, Translation and Commentary.* Leiden, NL: Brill, 1989.

Maslow, Abraham. *Motivation and Personality.* New York: Harper, 1954.

Mathers, S. Liddell MacGregor, trans. *The Key of Solomon the King.* York Beach, ME: Samuel Weiser, 1974.

Mauss, Marcel. *The Gift: The Form and Reason for Exchange in Archaic Societies.* New York: W. W. Norton, 2000.

Meyer, Marvin W. *The Ancient Mysteries: A Sourcebook of Sacred Texts.* Philadelphia: University of Pennsylvania Press, 1987.

Miller, Jason. *The Sorcerer's Secrets: Strategies in Practical Magic.* Franklin Lakes, NJ: New Page, 2009.

Murray, Gilbert. *The Five Stages of Greek Religion.* Boston: Beacon Press, 1955. Accessed 10 May 2013, http://www.gutenberg.org/files/30250/30250-h/30250-h.htm#Page_218

Nock, A. D., and A.-J. Festugière, trans. *Corpus Hermeticum.* Paris: Collection des Universités de France, 1945.

O'Brien, Elmer, trans. *The Essential Plotinus.* Indianapolis: Hackett, 1975.

Ogden, Daniel. *Magic, Witchcraft, and Ghosts in the Greek and Roman Worlds: A Sourcebook.* Oxford, UK: Oxford University Press, 2002.

Peterson, Joseph H., trans. *Arbatel: Concerning the Magic of the Ancients.* Lake Worth, FL: Nicolas-Hays, 2009.

Pinch, Geraldine. *Egyptian Mythology: A Guide to the Gods, Goddesses, and Traditions of Ancient Egypt.* Oxford, UK: Oxford University Press, 2002.

———. *Magic in Ancient Egypt.* Austin: University of Texas Press, 2010.

Plotinus. *The Ethical Treatises, being the Treatises of the First Ennead, with Porphry's Life of Plotinus, and the Preller-Ritter Extracts forming a Conspectus of the Plotinian System, translated from Greek by Stephen Mackenna.* Boston: Charles T. Branford, 1918. Accessed 10 January 2014, http://oll.libertyfund.org/title/1272/6766

Porphyry. *On Abstinence from Animal Food.* Thomas Taylor, trans. Accessed 6 June 2014, http://www.tertullian.org/fathers/index.htm#Porphyry_Abstinence

Remes, Pauliina. *Neoplatonism.* Berkeley, CA: University of California Press, 2008.

Rives, James B. *Religion in the Roman Empire.* Maldon, MA: Blackwell, 2007.

Robertson, Donald. *The Philosophy of Cognitive-Behavioural Therapy: Stoic Philosophy as Rational and Cognitive Psychotherapy.* London: Karnac, 2010.

Ross, W. D., trans. *Aristotle: Magna Moralia.* Oxford: Clarendon, 1915. Accessed 16 May 2013, http://archive.org/stream/magnamoralia00arisuoft/magnamoralia00arisuoft_djvu.txt

Rouse, W. H. D., trans. *Great Dialogues of Plato.* New York: Penguin, 2008.

Sargent, Thelma, trans. *The Homeric Hymns: A Verse Translation.* New York: W. W. Norton, 1975.

Shaw, Gregory. *Theurgy and the Soul: The Neoplatonism of Iamblichus.* University Park, PA: University of Pennsylvania Press, 1995.

Sophistes, Apollonius. "A Greek Alphabet Oracle." Accessed 14 May 2013, http://web.eecs.utk.edu/~mclennan/BA/GAO.html

"Theoi Greek Mythology." Accessed 14 May 2013, http://www.theoi.com/greek-mythology/agricultural-gods.html

Uždavinys, Algis. *Philosophy and Theurgy in Late Antiquity.* San Rafael, CA: Sophia Perennis, 2010.

Von Worms, Abraham. *The Book of Abramelin.* Steven Guth, trans. Lake Worth, FL: Nicolas-Hays, 2006.

Warrior, Valerie M. *Roman Religion: A Sourcebook.* Newburyport, MA: Focus, 2002.

Wilkinson, Richard H. *The Complete Gods and Goddesses of Ancient Egypt.* Cairo: The American University in Cairo Press, 2003.

Index